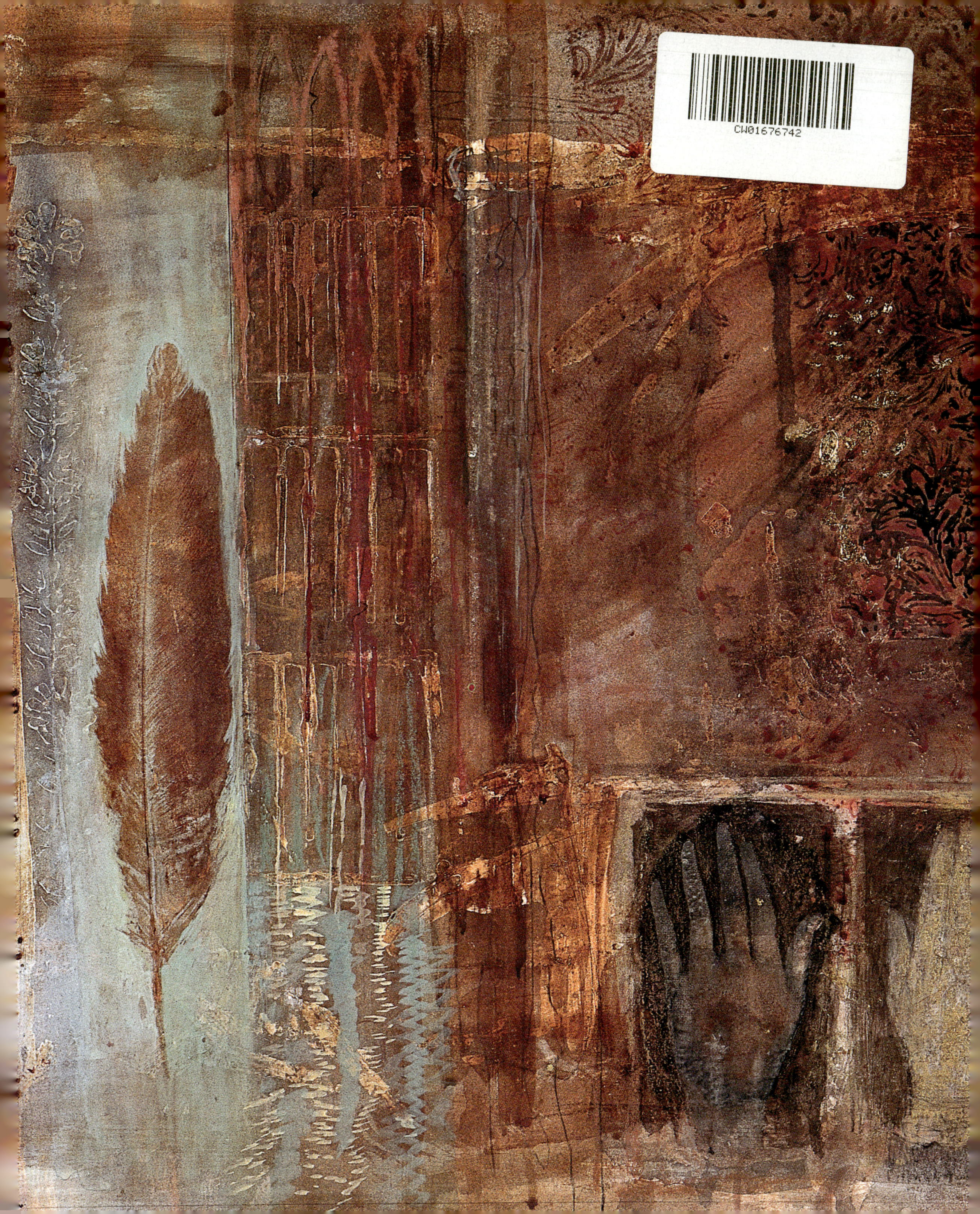

# VICTORIA CROWE

Painted Insights

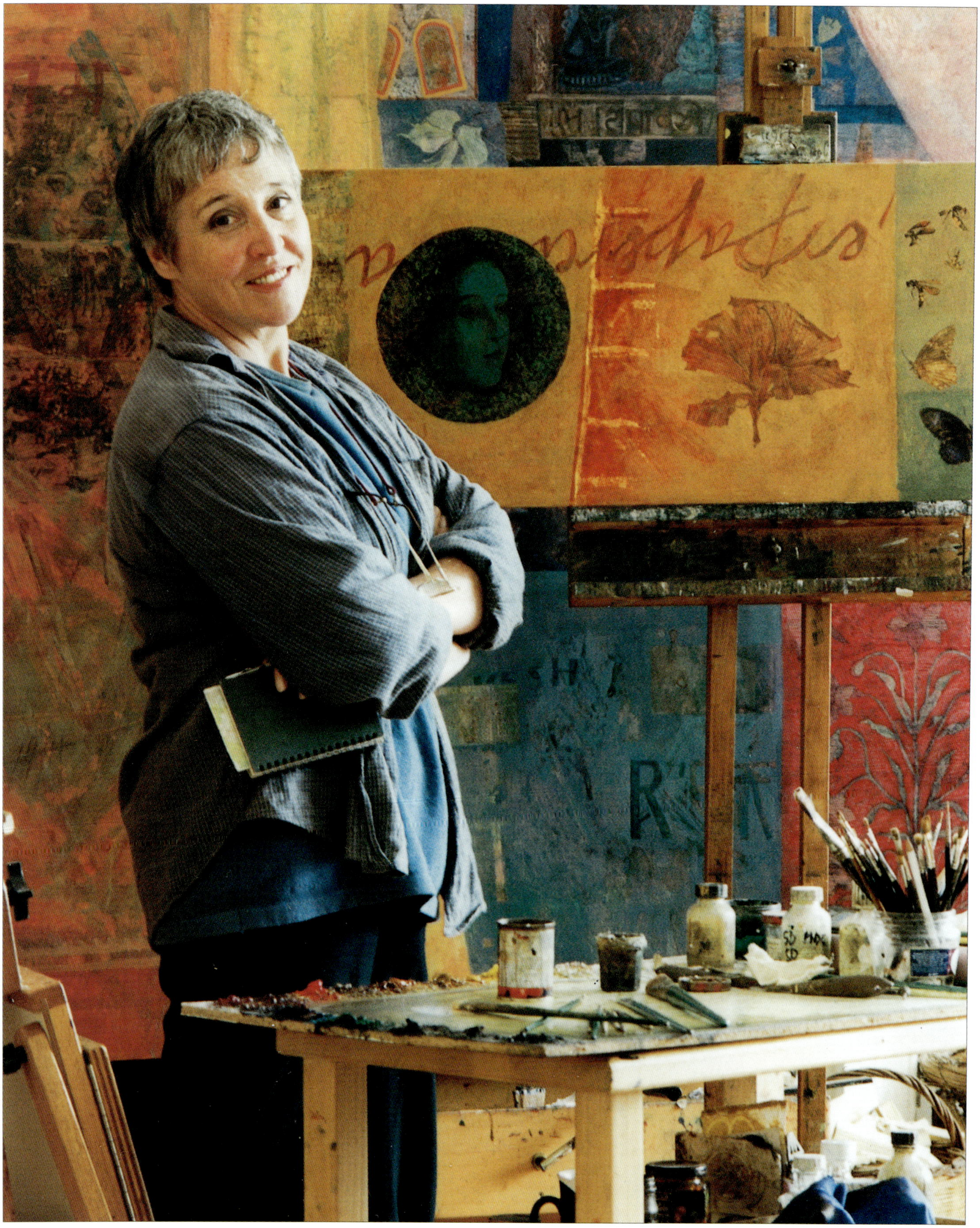

# VICTORIA CROWE

## Painted Insights

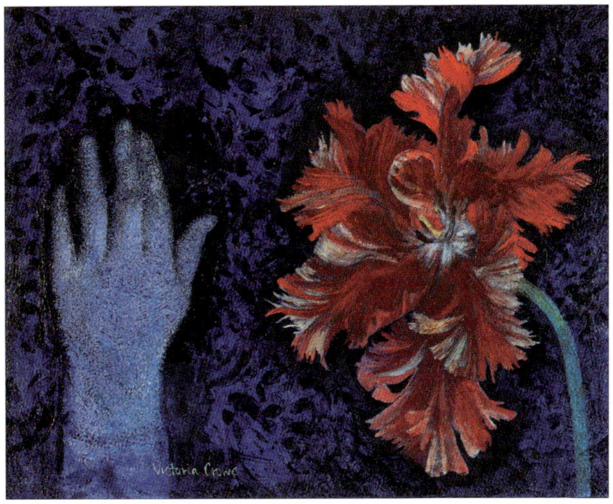


Victoria Crowe

Supported by
BANK OF SCOTLAND

ANTIQUE COLLECTORS' CLUB

ISBN 1 85149 337 9



British Library Cataloguing-in-Publication Data
A catalogue record for this book is available from the British Library

This book
is dedicated to ...
The Family

Frontispiece: Victoria Crowe in her studio. Photograph © Michael Walton

Printed in England
by the Antique Collectors' Club Ltd., Woodbridge, Suffolk

# CONTENTS

# ACKNOWLEDGEMENTS

This book was the brainchild of Anne Thomson and Sarah McDonald-Brown of the Thackeray Gallery, London, together with Diana Steel of the Antique Collectors' Club of Woodbridge, Suffolk. Without their unswerving support and enthusiasm for the project, it would not have seen the light of day.

We should like to thank the following: Primrose Elliott, the editor, and Andrew Winton, the designer of the book; Dr Colin J. Bailey for an insightful introduction and for his invaluable help at every stage; all the galleries, in particular the Thackeray Gallery, London, The Scottish Gallery, Edinburgh, the Bruton Gallery, Leeds, The National Galleries of Scotland, the National Portrait Gallery, London, and Frederiksborg, Denmark; all collectors involved for their continued interest and allowing access to their works; and the Bank of Scotland for their financial support.

Thanks are also due to the following for permission to quote from their work: Mary Taubman, Derek Hyatt, Dr Duncan Thomson, Mary Sara and Clare Henry. Their work is their copyright. Kathleen Raine's work is quoted by permission of the author and Golganooza Press from *The Collected Poems of Kathleen Raine,* copyright Golganooza Press 2000. Photographs of work are by Antonia Reeve, John Dewar, Sarah Quick and staff of the galleries listed above.

In a venture of this kind there are deadlines and constraints, with some works more easily to hand than others. This has inevitably influenced what it has been possible to include, so, for any omissions or oversights, please accept our sincere apologies.

Michael Walton
Victoria Crowe

# PREFACE

This book does not set out to be a *catalogue raisonné* – how could it? The artist is still relatively young. Rather, it provides an introduction to Victoria Crowe's work at a particular point in time – now – when the artist is at the height of her powers, with much achieved already, but with still more to accomplish.

The book starts with a perceptive and illuminating essay by Colin Bailey accompanied by reproductions of the artist's most recent paintings. It then follows a roughly chronological path through the life and work of the artist concluding with images that relate closely to the recent paintings. Thus it forms a cyclical link, emphasising a theme, that runs as a constant thread through the work itself. In this book the journey is told in the artist's own highly individual words, punctuated by the voices and out-takes from critics writing about her artistic development.

Victoria Crowe has been fortunate in having, since before leaving art school, a group of informed and loyal supporters who have encouraged her by collecting her work, in many cases for over thirty years. It is rare for a collector to have *one* painting by Crowe. As time has gone by this group of supporters has grown and spread north and south of the border and internationally. Her art has both a specialised and general appeal and is in many public and private collections. The recent exhibition *A Shepherd's Life* at the Scottish National Portrait Gallery attracted over 33,000 visitors and was enthusiastically reviewed in papers as diverse as *Scotland on Sunday* to the *Wall Street Journal*. We have, therefore, in Victoria Crowe, an artist who has always supported herself by the work of her own hand and mind. For an artist who has never bowed to current fashion or overworked a successful formula, this says much. For Crowe it is the *next* challenge which is the important one, not the one just accomplished. Her concerns are more to do with deeper and older values, yet they are not backward looking. In her work one is as likely to come across a reference to DNA sampling as a reference to early Italian painting, a commission for a neuroscience department as often as for an Oxford college.

So what is a Victoria Crowe painting about? Readers may find themselves asking such a question as the works are highly individual and defy easy categorisation – one painting may incorporate elements of realism, myth and pure abstract values. However, Time, Light and Memory may be as close as one comes by way of an answer. Crowe shares with us openly the significant events, influences in her life and work to date. One is offered a glimpse into the subjective and transforming mind of the artist, a view through her eyes into our own more mundane world and one comes away revitalised, awakened and with a shared sense of mystery and wonder. Crowe makes much of the inevitable struggle to realise and accomplish the goal, the work of art; this she faces with integrity and discipline. The image is hard won, yet the results are often, to our eyes, light and joyous. They speak for themselves, as coming from an unswerving certainty that, however hard the path may at times be, ultimately *all will be well,* if life and work are tackled with honesty and love.

Michael Walton

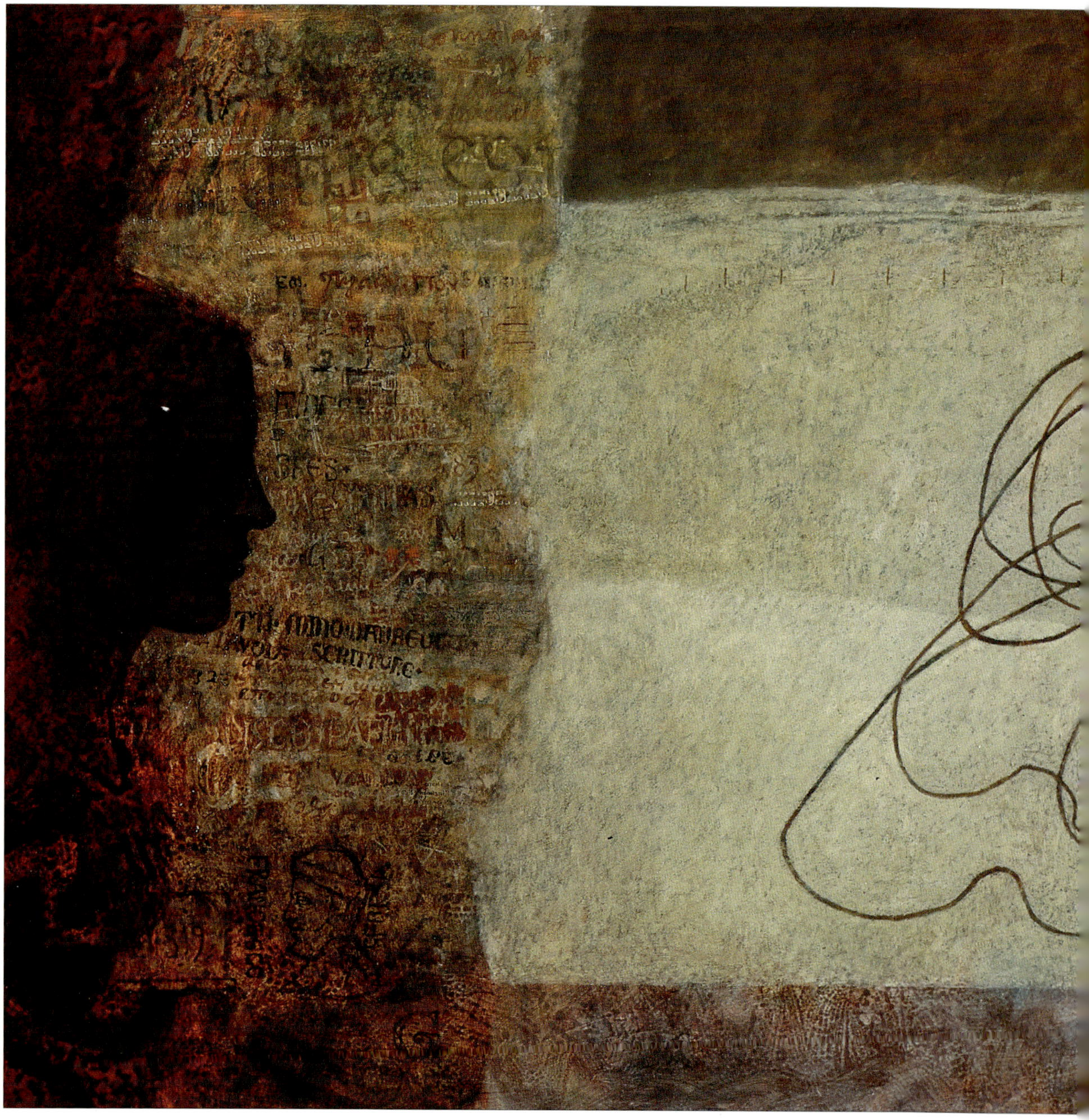

# INTRODUCTION

MESSAGES AND CONNECTIONS
1999. Oil on board. 24in. x 48in.
Fleming-Wyfold Art Foundation

Elsewhere in this book Victoria Crowe recounts how Robin Philipson, Head of the School of Drawing and Painting at Edinburgh College of Art (and later President of the Royal Scottish Academy), invited her in 1968 to join his staff. Her appointment in Edinburgh at the age of twenty-three marked the beginning of a distinguished career as a caring and dedicated teacher and, more pertinently, as one of the most original and thought-provoking figures in contemporary British art. Her election as a Member of the Royal Scottish Society of Painters in Watercolour in 1982 and her election as an Associate of the Royal Scottish Academy and the Royal Watercolour Society, in 1987 and 1991 respectively, reflect the esteem in which she is held by her fellow

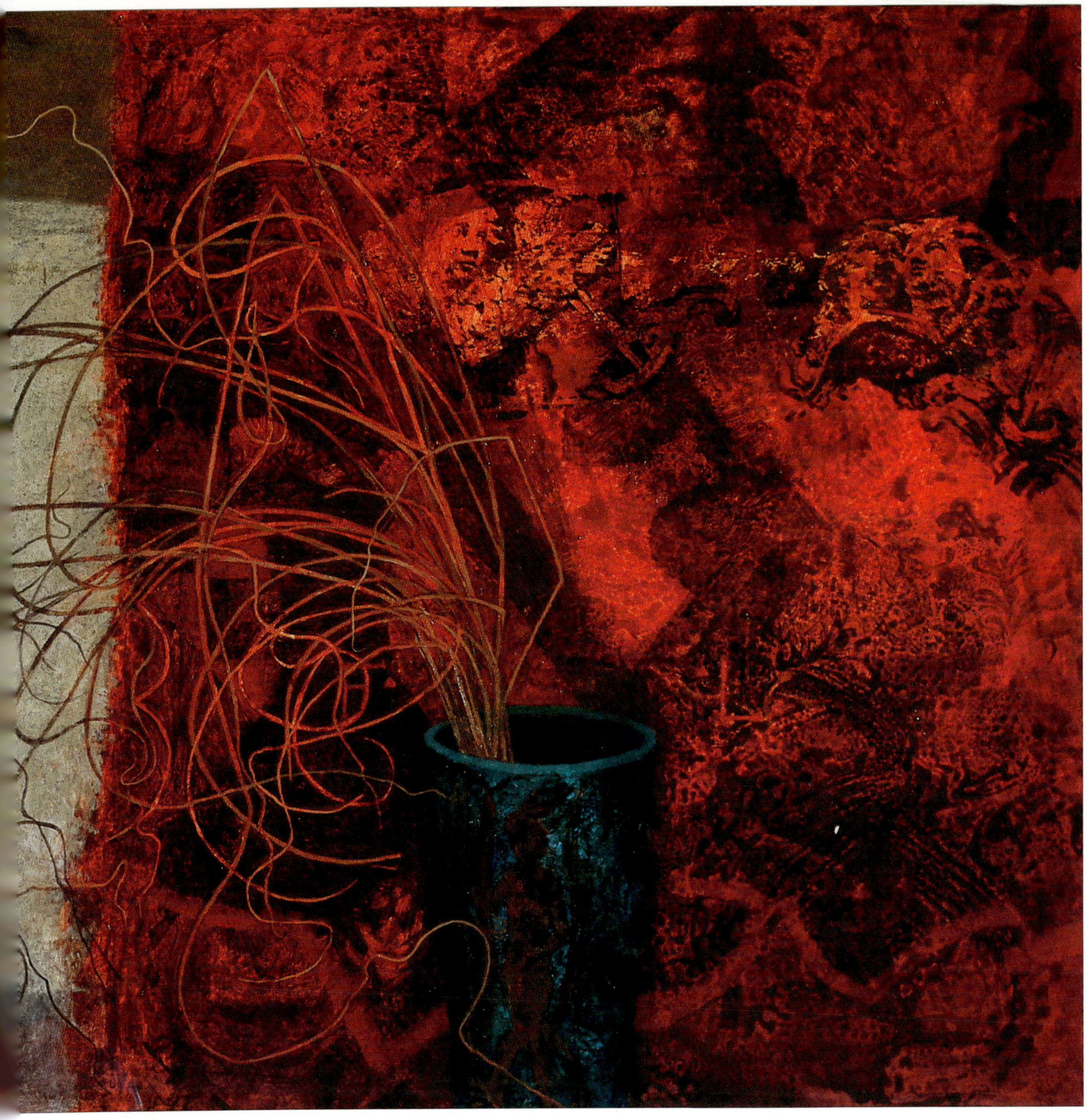

painters. She has been the worthy recipient of numerous bursaries and scholarships, including an award from the Sir William Gillies Bequest for travel and study in Italy, and has works in many private collections in Britain and abroad and in public collections that include the National Portrait Gallery in London, the Scottish National Gallery of Modern Art, the Scottish National Portrait Gallery, the Royal College of Art and the Contemporary Art Society.

She has participated in countless group exhibitions and has had solo exhibitions almost annually since 1969, culminating recently in what is a rare honour for a living artist, a one-person show at the Scottish National Portrait Gallery. The exhibition, *A*

*Shepherd's Life: Paintings of Jenny Armstrong,* celebrated the life of her friend and neighbour, the eponymous Borders shepherd, in a series of paintings and drawings covering a period of some eighteen years.

Never intended originally to be brought together in the form of an exhibition, Victoria Crowe's works commemorating the heroism in the 'ordinary' life of Jenny Armstrong reveal at once her continuous and unwavering pursuit of certain themes in her art and typify the wide variety of her subject matter, which consists mainly of what are conventionally called landscapes, portraits, still lifes and interiors. Much of her work, however, defies such precise categorisation, and the terms 'still life' and 'interior', for example, are inadequate in conveying an idea of the rich layers of meaning and the often intensely personal resonances with which her pictures are imbued. For all their variety (one is reminded by turns of Brueghel, Monet, Friedrich and Wyeth), the

INTO AN OLDER LAND
2000. Oil on linen. 40in. x 50in.

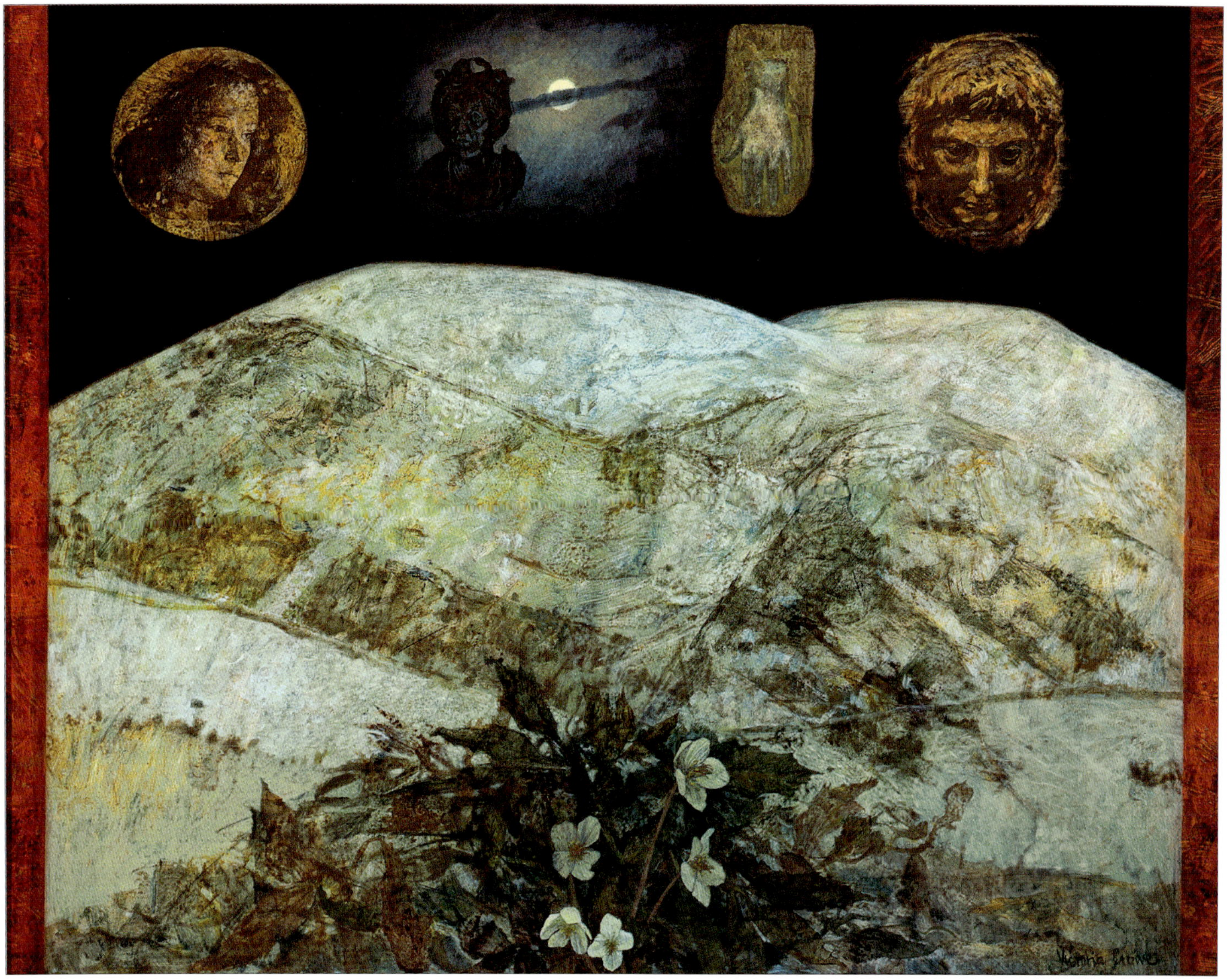

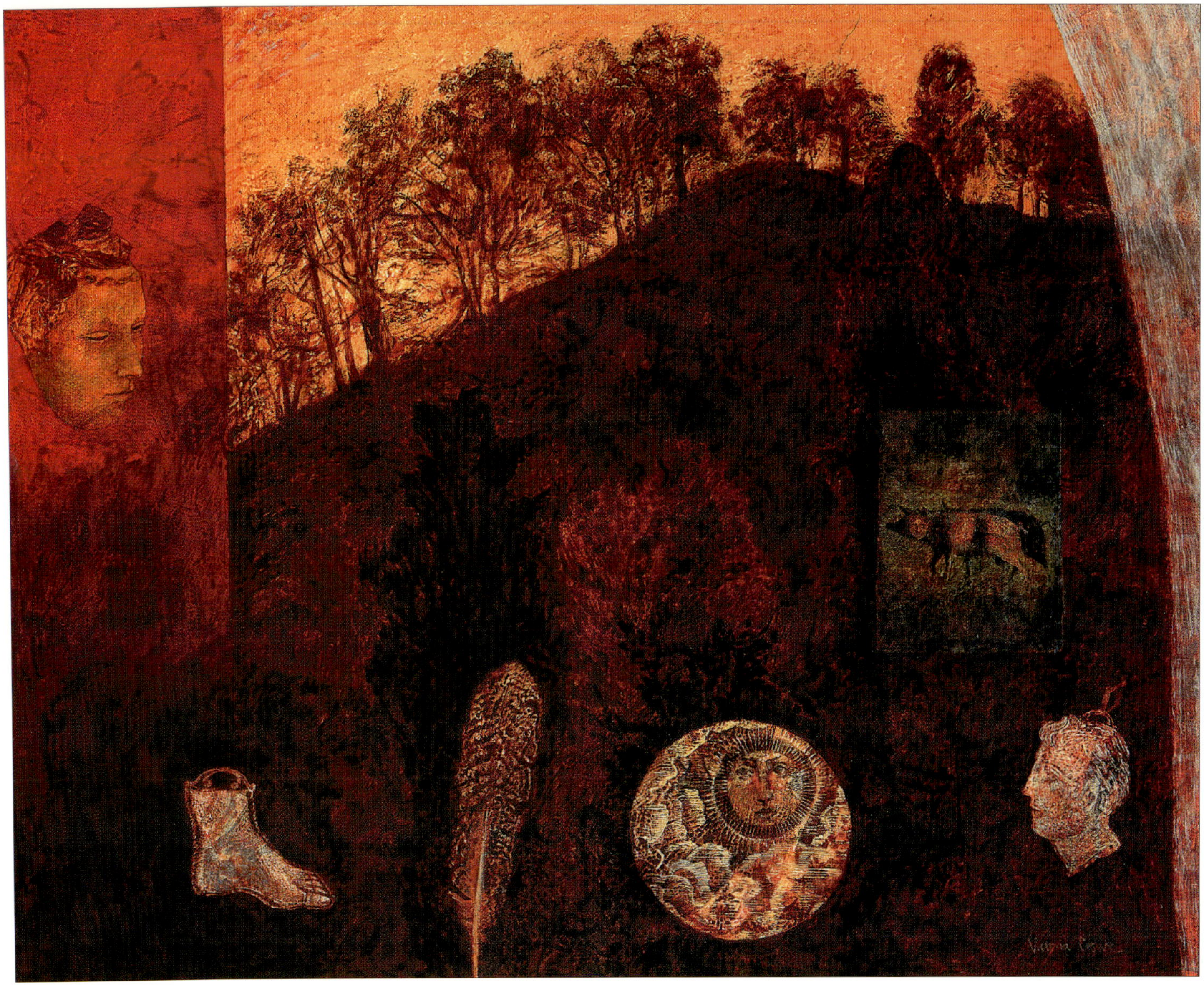

REMEMBERED LAND
1999. Oil on linen. 39½in x 46¾in.

paintings depicting Jenny Armstrong's life and surroundings share with Victoria Crowe's other work a number of common concerns which touch upon our own humanity. In one way or another her works are an investigation of the human condition; often they are Proustian; invariably they are enriched with imagery that derives from the great post-Medieval Western tradition admixed with a kind of personal mythology based on objects and experiences that are the exclusive domain of the artist herself. The outcome is a pictorial continuum in which certain basic themes recur in different guises confronting the same age-old preoccupations with life and mortality that have been the preserve of artists as diverse as Masaccio and Holbein in the early fifteenth and sixteenth century to Gilbert and George or Andy Goldsworthy in our own.

In the lives of many great artists (Poussin and Goya come immediately to mind), there are events or experiences so momentous that the very essence of their work is changed irrevocably thereafter. In the case of Victoria Crowe, two experiences above all others have determined the course her art has taken in the last decade. The first of these was her visit to Tuscany and Umbria in 1992 on sabbatical leave from the

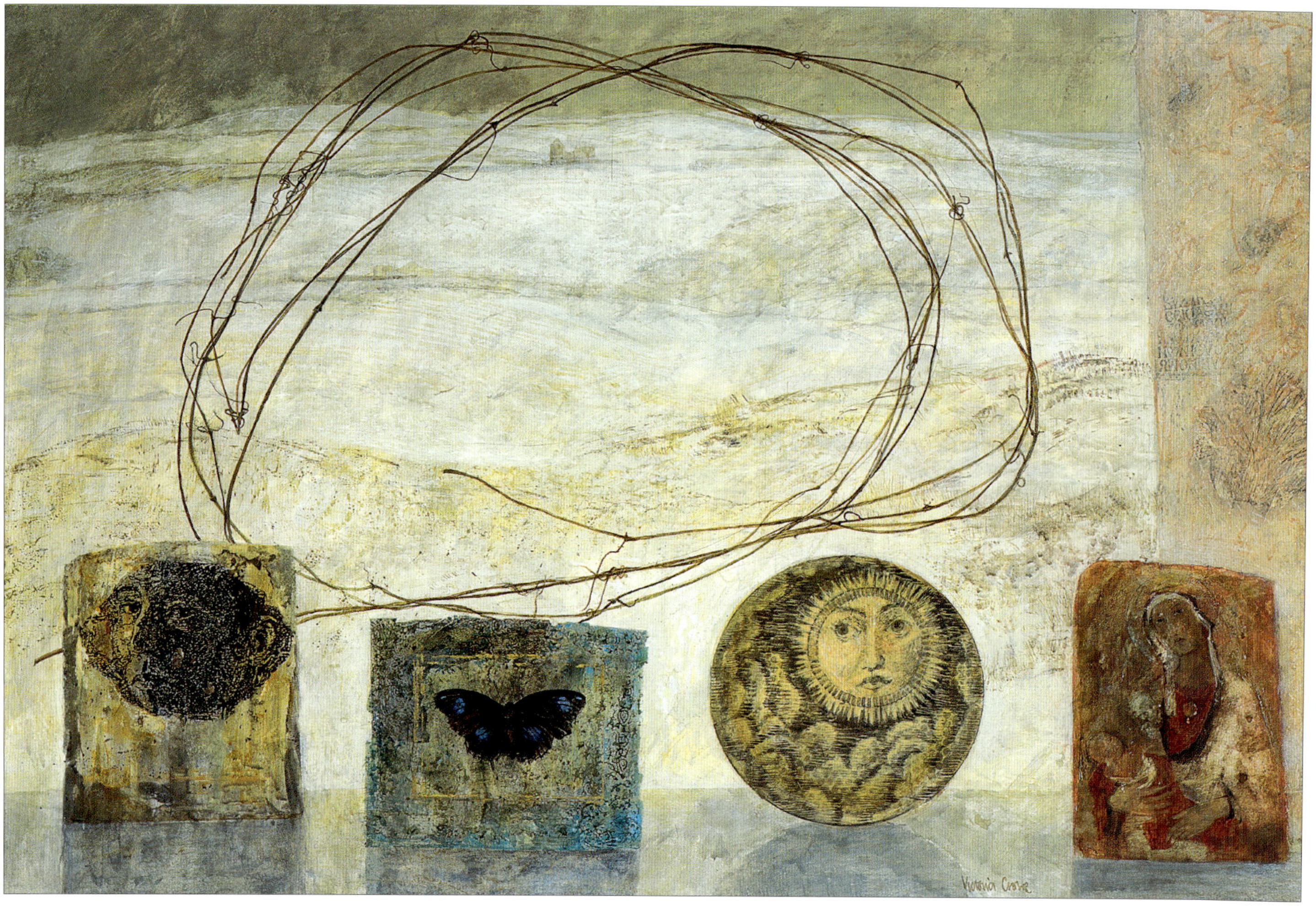

LANDSCAPE WITH POWERFUL OBJECTS.
2000. Watercolour. 27in. x 39in.

College. The impact upon her of the light and the landscape of Italy and her all-absorbing fascination with Italian trecento to cinquecento art (Giotto, Uccello, Ghirlandaio, Signorelli and Piero della Francesca especially) are immediately apparent in certain formal aspects of her subsequent compositions, the intensified brilliance of her colours, the introduction of symbols and motifs culled from Renaissance paintings and frescoes (in particular the Angel of the Annunciation) and the occasional reference to the Tuscan or Umbrian countryside. The second event was the death of her son. Paintings in which previously Victoria Crowe had dealt at one remove with issues of transience, mortality and decay at once became lifelines, vehicles for coping with the most vital issues in her personal life and that of her family. As she herself acknowledges, this was the juncture in her life when Victoria Crowe realised why she was an artist. Her passionate commitment to her painting enabled her to cope with the ensuing traumas and cathartically to transmute harrowing experiences into images that in a uniquely personal way would honour memory and celebrate life while dealing with the issue of mortality in a way to which all compassionate human beings can relate.

Whereas many artists are reluctant to speak publicly about their work, or find it difficult to do so, Victoria Crowe talks succinctly, lucidly and with consummate ease about her paintings in a way that elucidates the works themselves and simultaneously provides an insight into her working methods and her thought processes. In this, she is

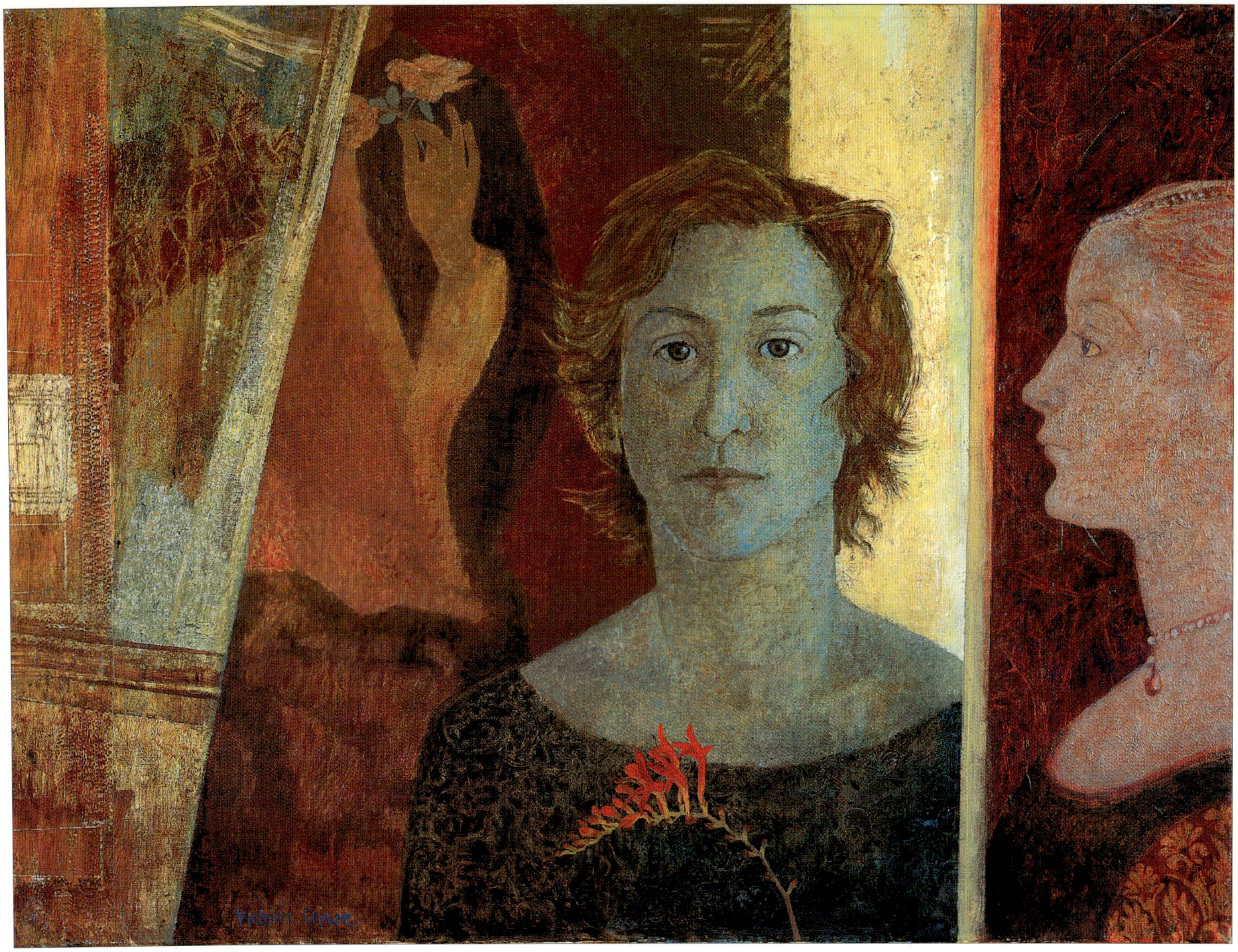

**PORTRAIT OF A YOUNG WOMAN, MILAN**
2000. Oil on canvas. 20in. x 26in.

the equal of Delacroix or Hockney. She could, therefore, have written this introduction herself, but there would undoubtedly have been omissions occasioned by her innate modesty, and there are sometimes in an artist's oeuvre subconscious references whose origins and *raison d'être* are not always explicable or fully comprehended by their author. The curtain, used in the seventeenth century by the Dutch to indicate a secondary meaning in a picture, or the butterfly, employed since the Renaissance as a symbol of the soul, are motifs to be found in the work of Victoria Crowe, wholly consistent with the meaning she wishes to convey, which none the less were incorporated paradoxically without always comprehending why they came unbidden into her mind. Perhaps this has to do with the fact that, when she is painting, her concentration is focused less on individual objects than on what might be termed the abstract elements. Though the images she creates contain easily recognisable forms, to her 'they are always a bit of red against a bit of white, or a scumbled bit of turquoise'. Through her friendship with Winifred Rushforth and the Dream Groups she attended, Victoria Crowe is more prepared than perhaps most artists to acknowledge the role of the unconscious mind in helping formulate images more by intuition than by any intellectual or emotional process. The dreaming mind, after all, freely associates signs

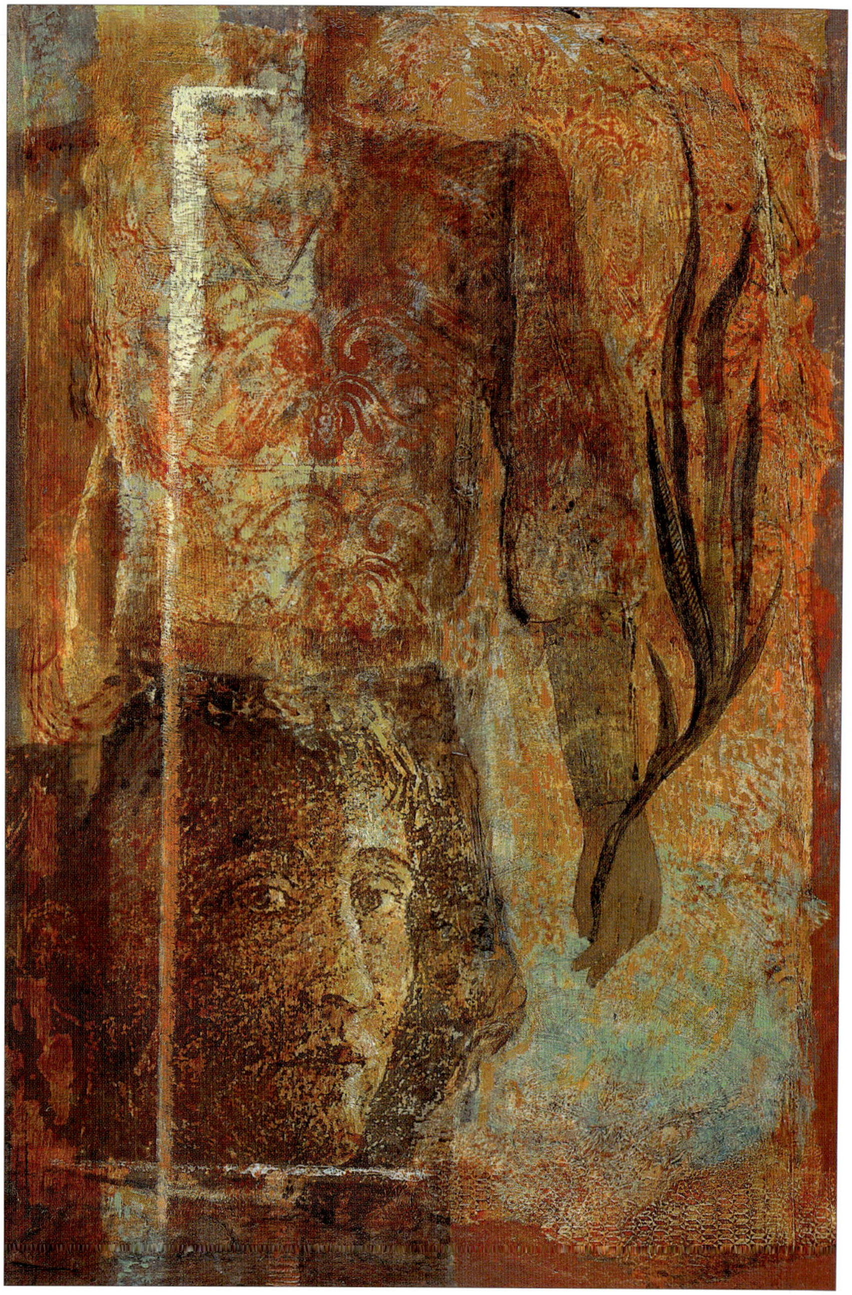

BRERA DIPTYCH, LEFT-HAND PANEL
2000. Oil on board. 20in. x 13in.

and symbols in a manner disorienting to the rational mind. It is possibly for this reason that the power of each of her pictures is invariably greater than the sum of its parts.

Almost from the very outset of her career, Victoria Crowe has produced pictures that are *sui generis* – immediately recognisable as her own and impossible to confuse with those of any other artist. They owe their unique quality to a variety of factors ranging from the dream-like or visionary juxtaposition of images on different, often dislocated planes; the ethereal representation of normally clear and tangible forms; to a technique which derives its authority from an absolute mastery of the oil and watercolour media conjoined with the occasional use of prints or the judicious application of gold leaf. Behind all this lie acute and meticulous powers of observation (frequently of things that others would ignore or simply overlook), a fundamental respect for the importance and value of drawing, a highly retentive visual memory and

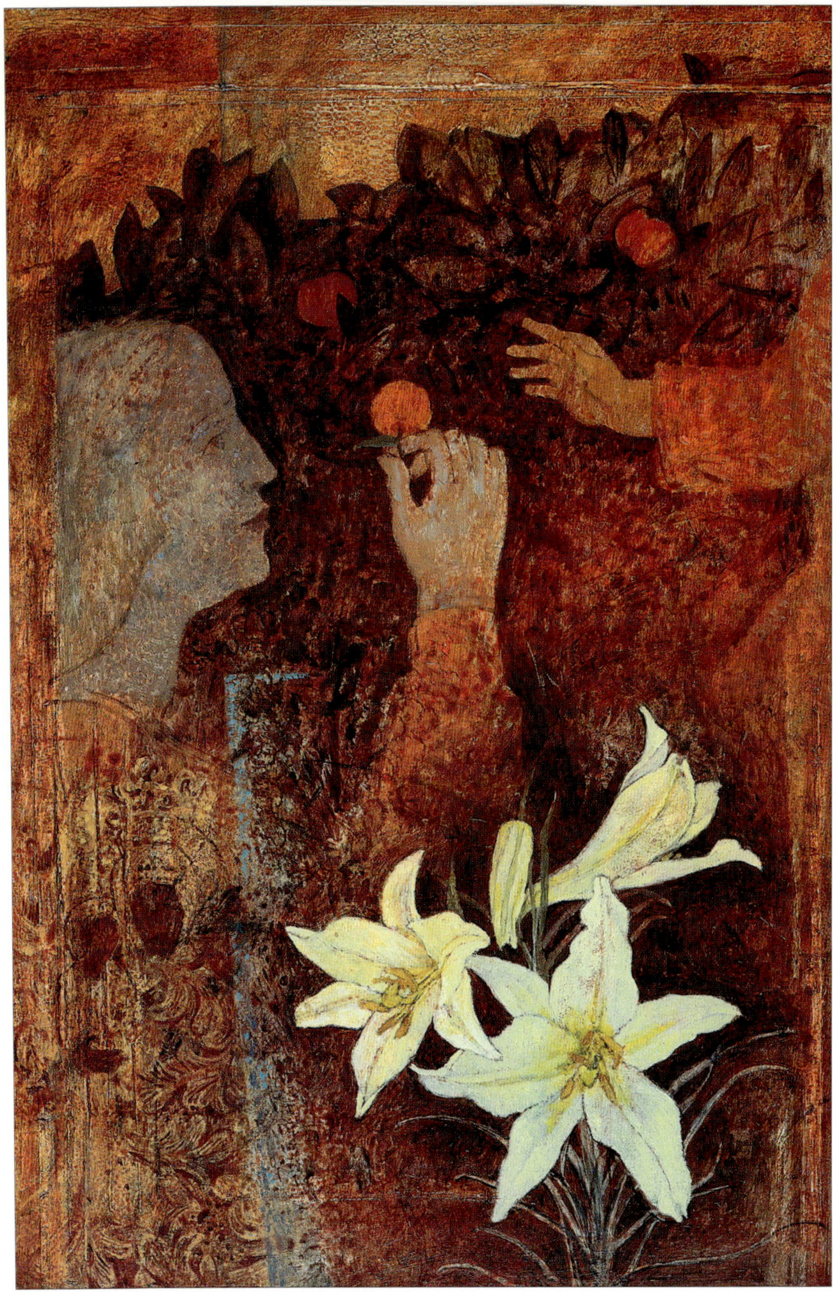

BRERA DIPTYCH, RIGHT-HAND PANEL
2000. Oil on board. 20in. x 13in.

the patience to synthesize the accumulated data before proceeding to paint. As *aides-mémoire* Victoria Crowe makes extensive use of her many sketchbooks, all containing exquisite drawings made *in situ* of subjects that have caught her attention: a crumbling wall, a Roman inscription, some detail of a fresco, a poster advertising Perugino. Photographs have little part to play in researching source material, other than indicating very general starting points. Antipathy to the objective reality a photograph may provide, in respect to her own creativity, can most readily be understood in the light of works such as *Landscape Icon, Travelling by Moonlight* or the recent *Brera Diptych,* which are multi-dimensional and non-illusionistic.

In *Brera Diptych,* which contains in mirror image one of the three frequently recurring self-portraits of the artist in the left-hand panel, we have a picture that eloquently expresses much that is typical of Victoria Crowe's work. First, there is the self-portrait itself, as solemn as one of Gauguin's Tahitian women, gazing out at the spectator much in the same way as Benozzo Gozzoli stares at us from the wall in the Palazzo Medici-Riccardi or Botticelli from among the bystanders in his Uffizi *Adoration*. The diptych, like so many of her paintings, testifies in other ways to her love of Italian Renaissance art. The diptych form transfers us to another time, another place, and in the backgrounds, dimly discerned, are a martyr saint with his palm and figures picking fruits, both based on paintings in the Brera. In contrast, the foreground lilies on the right are depicted with such verisimilitude that, like the flowers in the Portinari Altarpiece by Hugo van der Goes, our senses are confounded by their apparent reality. The variegated surfaces shimmer in red and gold and intensify the painting's spatial and temporal ambiguities. *Gateway – Milan,* conceived as a kind of triptych, likewise juxtaposes and superimposes images redolent of the present and the past, whose formal and thematic interrelationships demand our concentration. The gateway of the title was recorded by Victoria Crowe as she walked with her daughter towards the Brera. The left of the arch is adorned with portraits of those long dead; on the right, in the painting, are hands and mouths and tracings of DNA. Centrally, in place of the Milan traffic, the artist has substituted Renaissance fruit pickers and a lily (grown in her own home) so palpable that it puts to shame those ubiquitous specimens of the Annunciation, those mere symbols of the Virgin's purity.

Flowers of many types – lilies, jonquils, crocosmia, stephanotis, helleborus niger – feature, often prominently, in Victoria Crowe's still lifes, interiors and landscapes, as also do withered seeds and grasses and the occasional dried acanthus and Solomon's seal. In *Night Stephanotis*, the plant is presented to us twice: growing vigorously in its pot on the windowsill, its waxen greens and whites magically silhouetted against the pitch-black moonlit sky; and, on the right, more stylized, another view of itself, as though reflected in a fiery golden mirror. To the left, a curtain billows gently in the night air. In *Into an Older Land* a bushy Christmas rose, set against a bleak snow-covered hill, appears to speak defiantly of life, when all around seems dead, and surreal sculpted heads hang at some indeterminate point between the window and the clouds. There is strength to be drawn from the knowledge that spring follows winter and that night gives way to day. We also know, however, that the distant hill will remain long after we and the Christmas rose are gone. There is a long tradition of floral symbolism in Western art and Victoria Crowe enriches her pictorial language by reference to it. The lily, so intimately associated with the archangel Gabriel, has come to signify good news, while the poppy, the violet and the cyclamen have been used as portents of death at least since the fifteenth century. In seventeenth century Dutch iconography, individual flowers still retained their special connotations, but the floral still life (a new and distinct genre) was invariably intended as a general metaphor of the transience of all earthly things, a *vanitas,* and a *memento mori*. Beautiful yet fragile, flowers are doomed from the moment they are picked; the dead grasses in *Do not Disturb the Dreaming World* and the vases of flowers in *Travelling by Moonlight* are timely reminders of the brevity of human life and its (albeit temporary) beauty, while in the seed heads lies the solace of regeneration. In

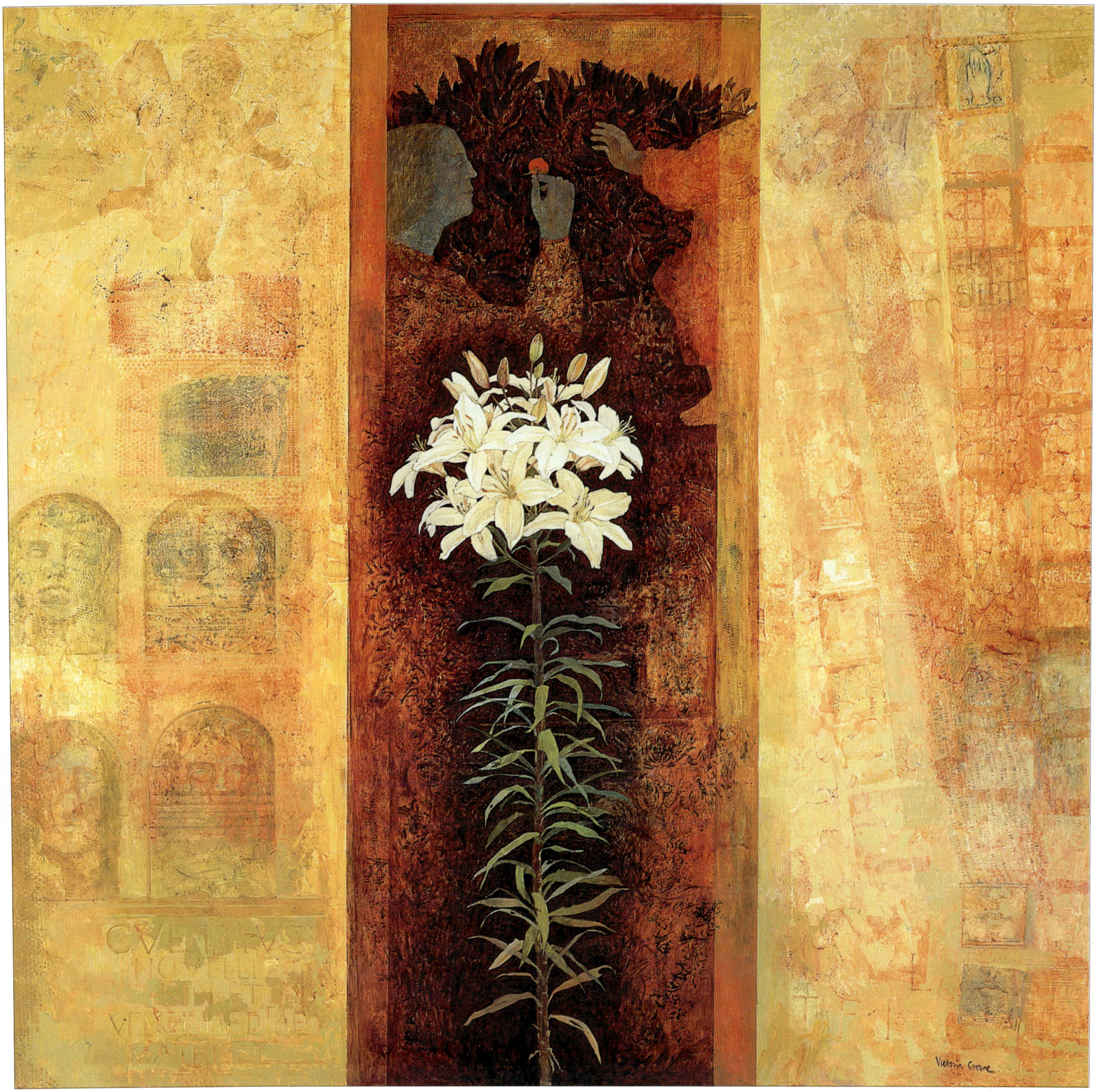

**GATEWAY – MILAN** 2001. Oil on linen. 60in. x 60in.

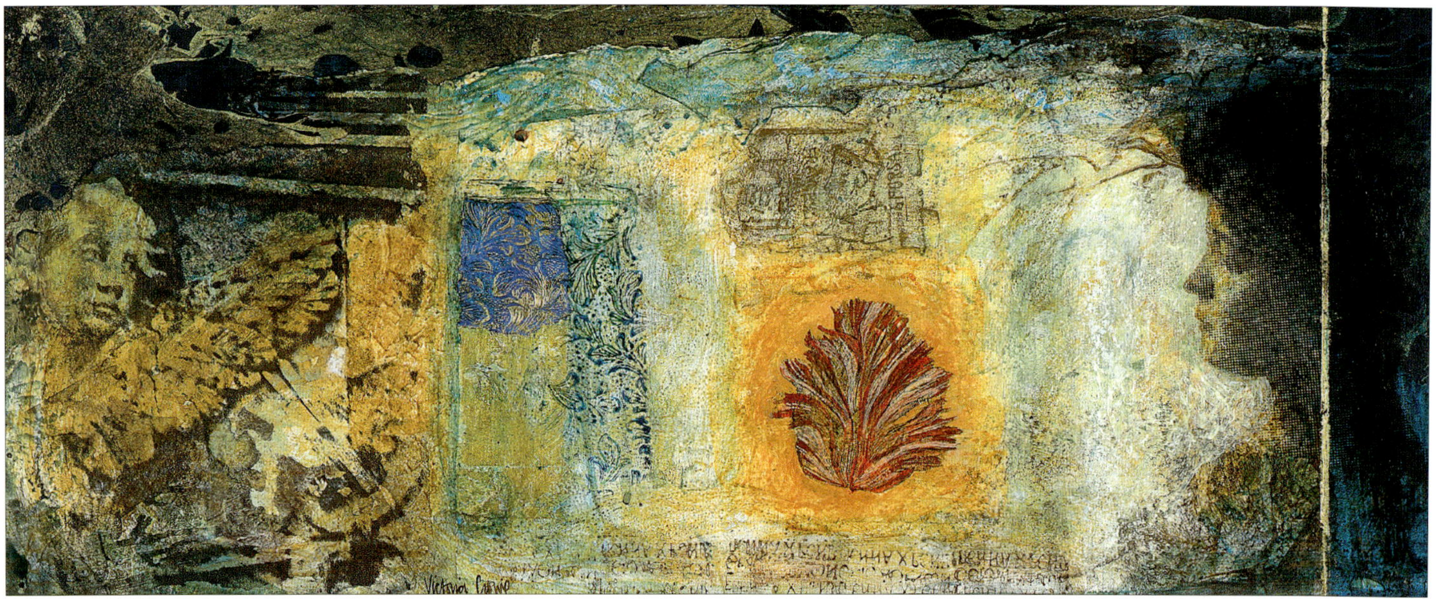

WHISPERING, VENICE
2000. Mixed media. 13½in. x 31½in.

*Travelling by Moonlight* a tiger moth found on the island of Lindisfarne alludes, like its counterpart in Pisanello's posthumous portrait of Ginevra d'Este and countless Dutch examples from Bosschaert to Huysum, to the ultimate triumph of the soul. In *Turn of the Year* the hollow cheer of the Christmas cards and the ice-locked landscape beyond the window is emphatically refuted by the jonquils bursting into life like the flowers from the corpse of Narcissus. Similar imagery occurs in *Night of the Dragonfly,* in which the tulip and the dragonfly, ancient symbols of transience and immortality, emblems of the rhythms and cycles of nature, are sharply outlined against the eternals of moonlit ocean and sky.

In addition to flowers, another recurring *vanitas* motif in Victoria Crowe's work is the mirror. Employed as a compositional device to underscore a picture's spatial ambiguity or to create pictorial tension between the interior and the outside world, the mirror functions on a number of other levels. It provides, of course, an alternative view of an object or objects represented elsewhere in the composition, and can be used to suggest another point of planar recession. Also, like the pane of glass in a window, it can reflect images of things that lie beyond the confines of conventional pictorial space. As a *vanitas* element, it serves to remind us of the inevitable passage of time, recording – imperceptibly day by day, alarmingly year by year – the ageing and atrophy of our own bodies.

Victoria Crowe's portraits, and the self-portraits she insinuates into her still lifes and interiors, have the effect of arresting time in a way that the mirror cannot. Only with Dorian Gray does the picture degrade while the sitter himself remains young. The image of the artist is *de facto* not as she now appears but rather as she thinks of herself. The images of Ben are trapped in the amber of selective memory. The naturalistic image of her daughter Gemma in *Portrait of a Young Woman, Milan* has beside it on the right a portrait of a young woman by Pollaiuolo in standard Renaissance profile. Gemma's verve and beauty, symbolized by the crimson-red crocosmia, stand in sharp contrast to the pallid marmoreal effigy alongside her. Thematically, the picture is similar to a portrait by Titian in the National Gallery entitled *La Schiavona* in which we see the sitter, lifelike, turned towards us, while below her on

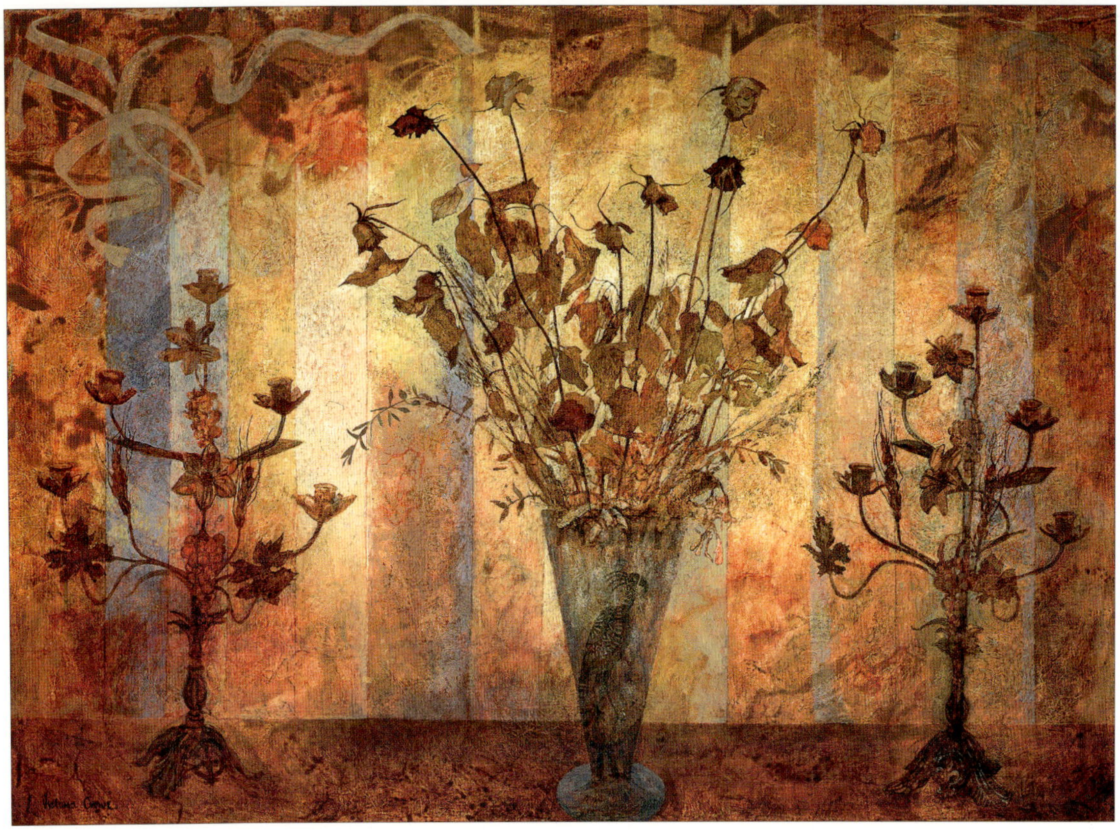

TIME SPENT, THEN AND NOW 2001. Oil on board. 36in. x 48in.

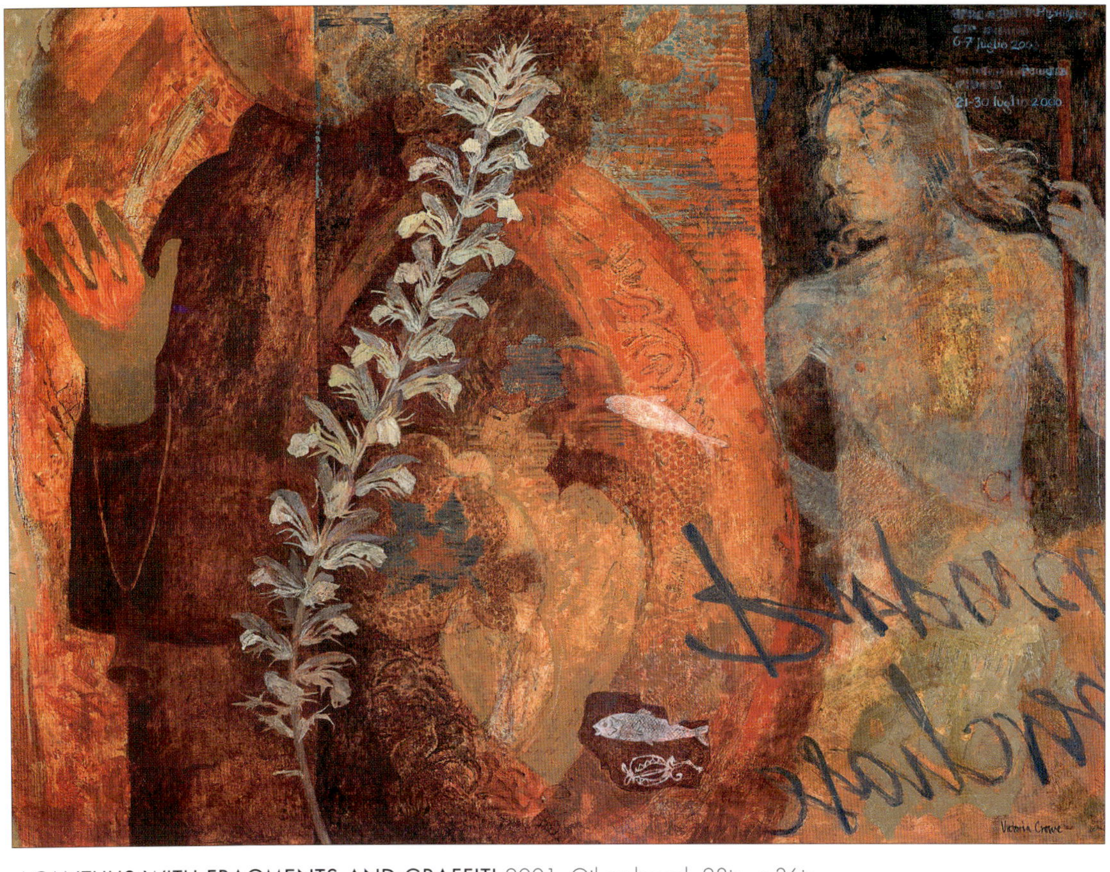

ACANTHUS WITH FRAGMENTS AND GRAFFITI 2001. Oil on board. 28in. x 36in.

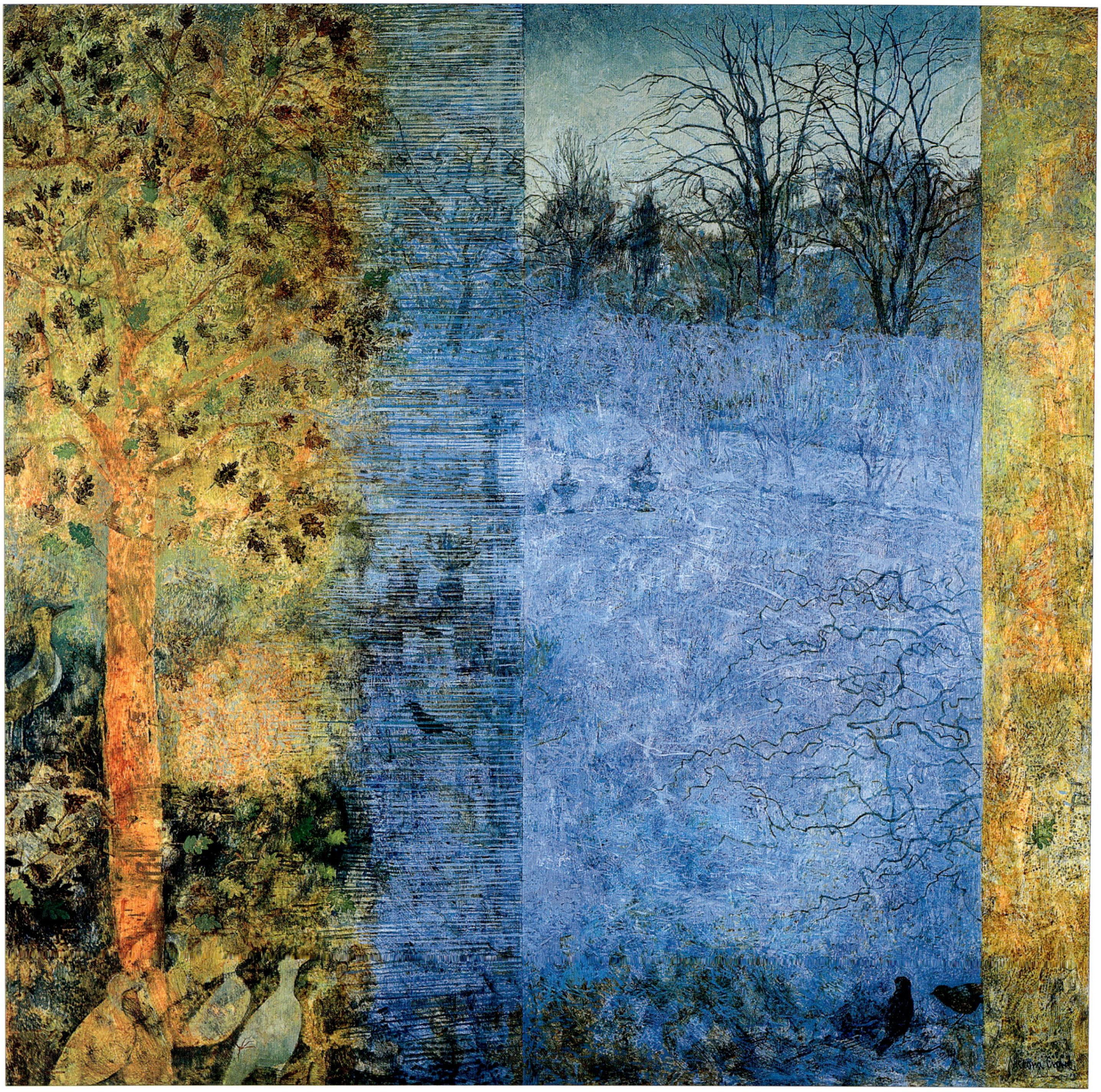

FEEDING THE BIRDS
2001. Oil on linen. 60in. x 60in.

the parapet in *trompe l'oeil* is her own profile carved in stone. Titian's message is clear: the painted image will outlive the sitter, the stone carving will outlive the painting. The image of 'La Schiavona' will endure forever, ensuring both her eternal fame as well as that of the artist: *ars longa, vita brevis*.

*Portrait of a Young Woman, Milan* contains not only the Pollaiuolo portrait but also, on the left, a partial depiction of the Virgin and Child in Milan Cathedral. Throughout her career, Victoria Crowe has incorporated in her work elements of paintings by other artists – Anubis the Jackal from an Egyptian wall painting, a half-length female figure

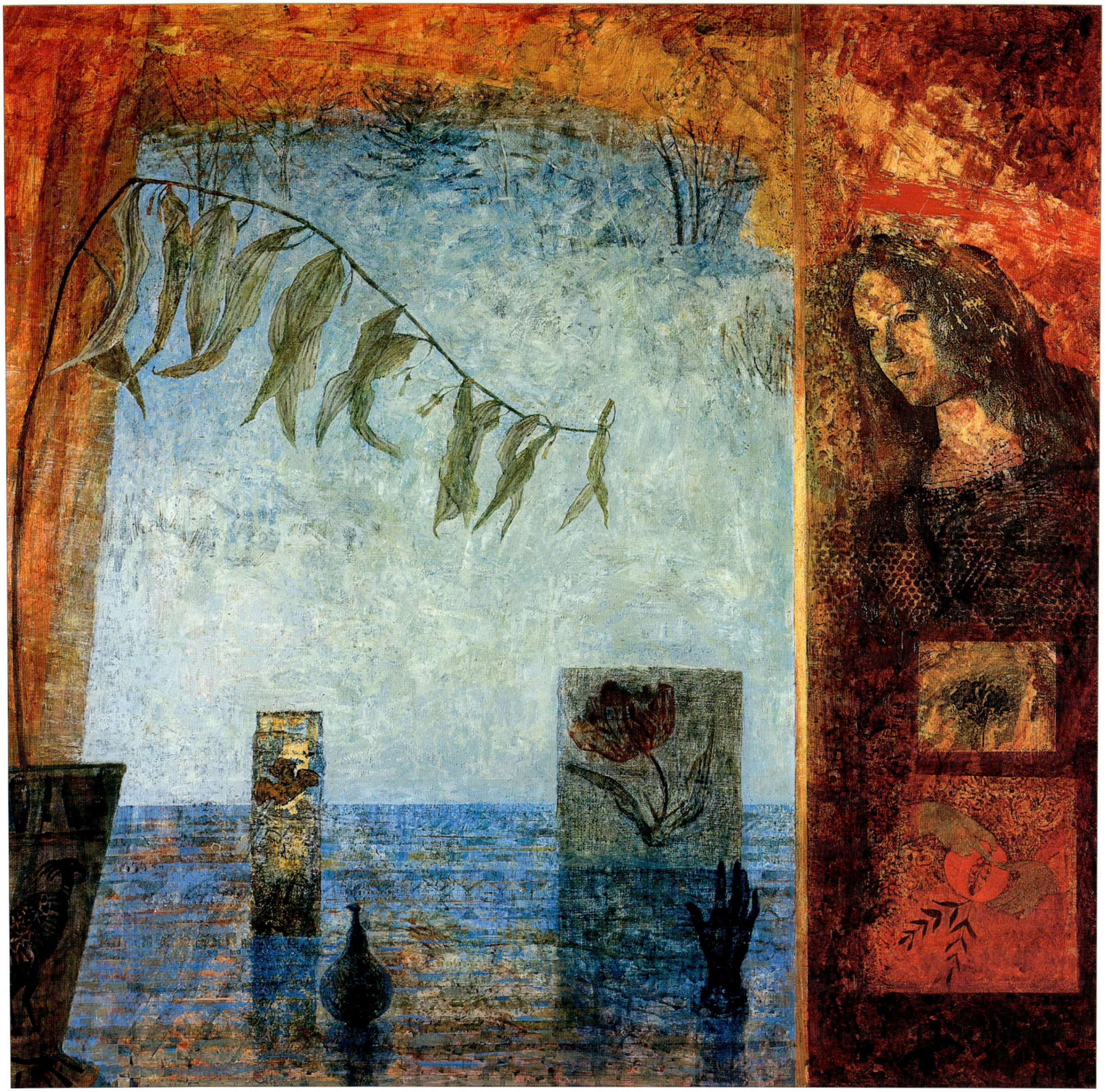

from Pompeii, a landscape by Giotto, an icon by Rublev. These out-takes are integrated into her overall compositions not as mere copies. Rather, they emphasise, question or define the personal dialogue established within the painting. In her company in Umbria last year I was privileged to see her at work, 'squirrelling away information' in her sketchbooks, standing, looking, marvelling and, finally, enervated by the intensity of it all, declining a good meal in order to be alone and assimilate what had clearly been for her profound emotional experiences. One of the most haunting images to appear in her work is the serene head of Mary Magdalen,

SILENT INTERIOR
2000. Oil on board. 36in. x 36in.

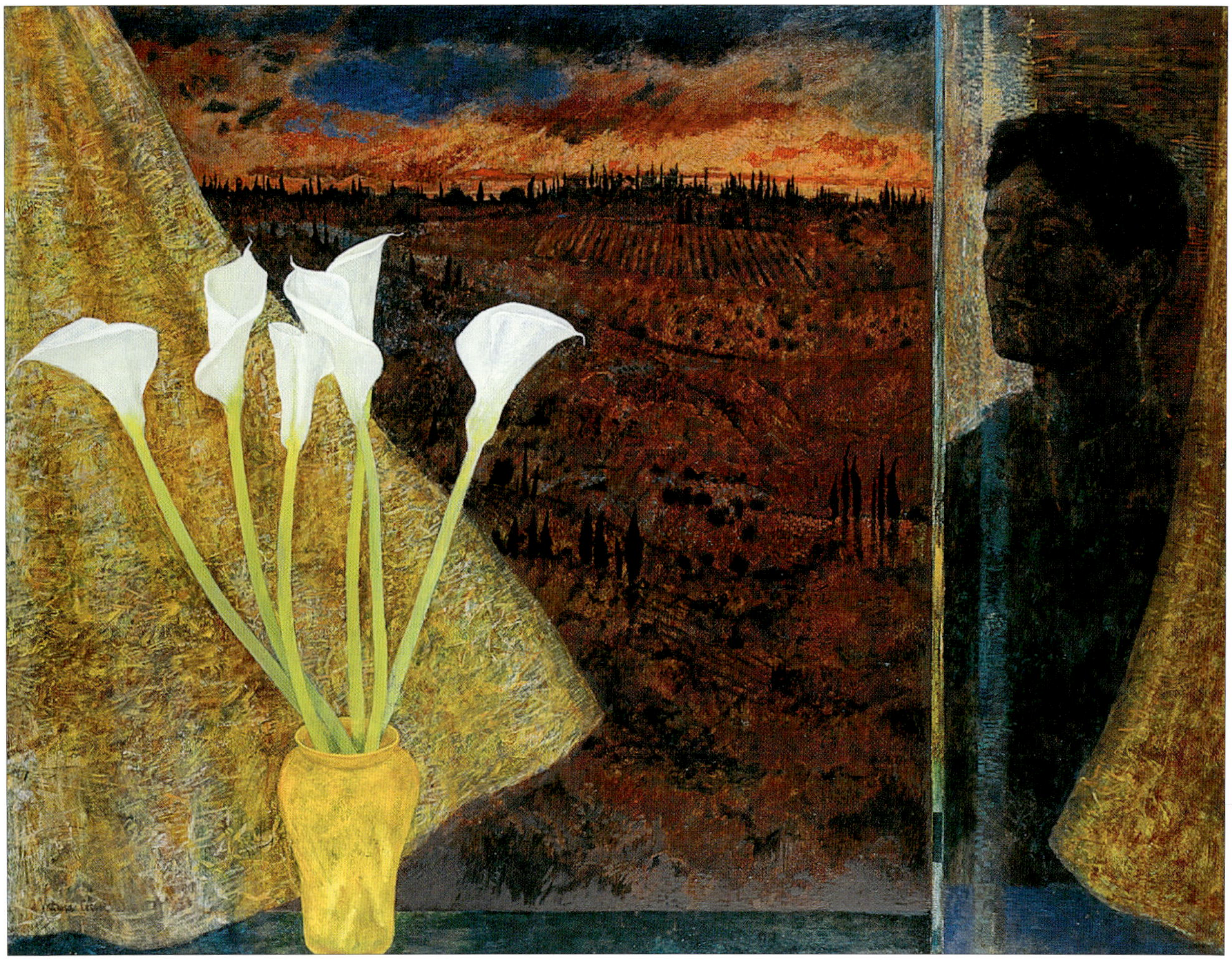

ECHOING VALLEY 1997. Oil on board. 38in. x 48in.

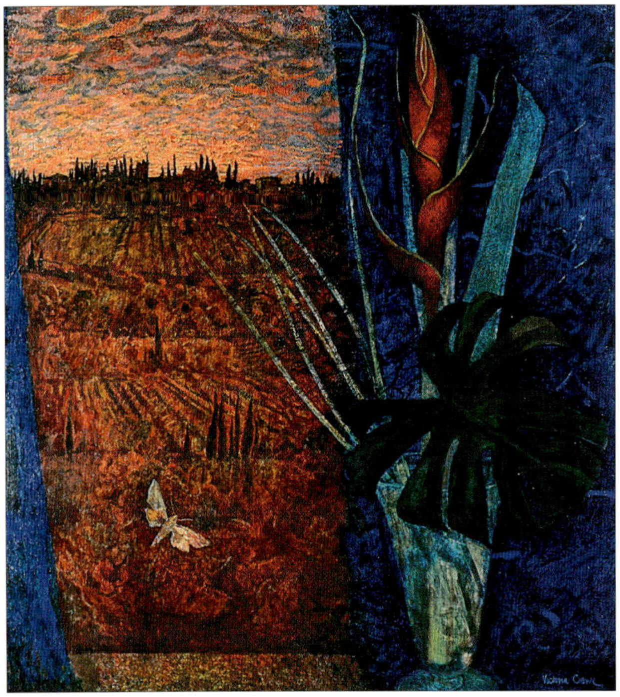

ENCHANTMENT 1997. Oil on canvas. 40in. x 36in.

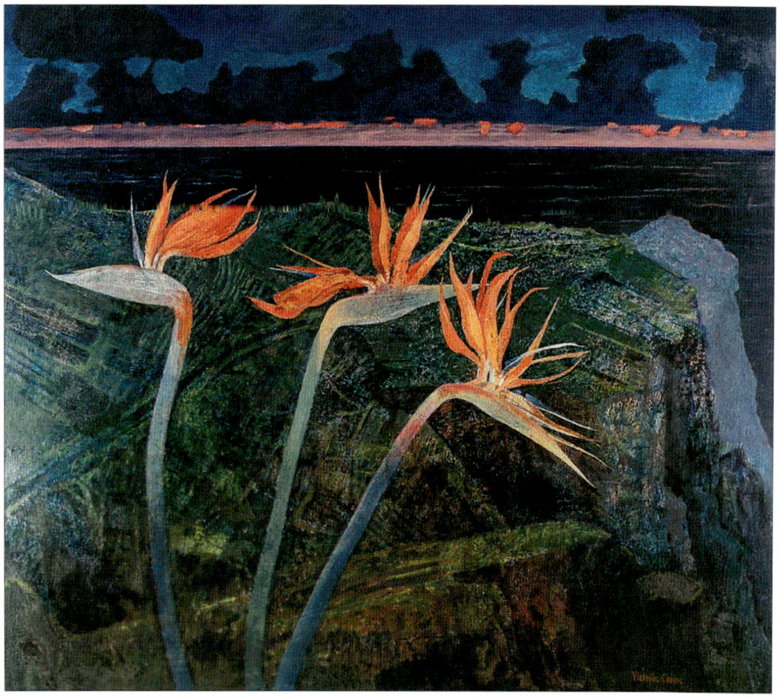

VERTIGINOUS LANDSCAPE 1997. Oil on canvas. 36in. x 40in.

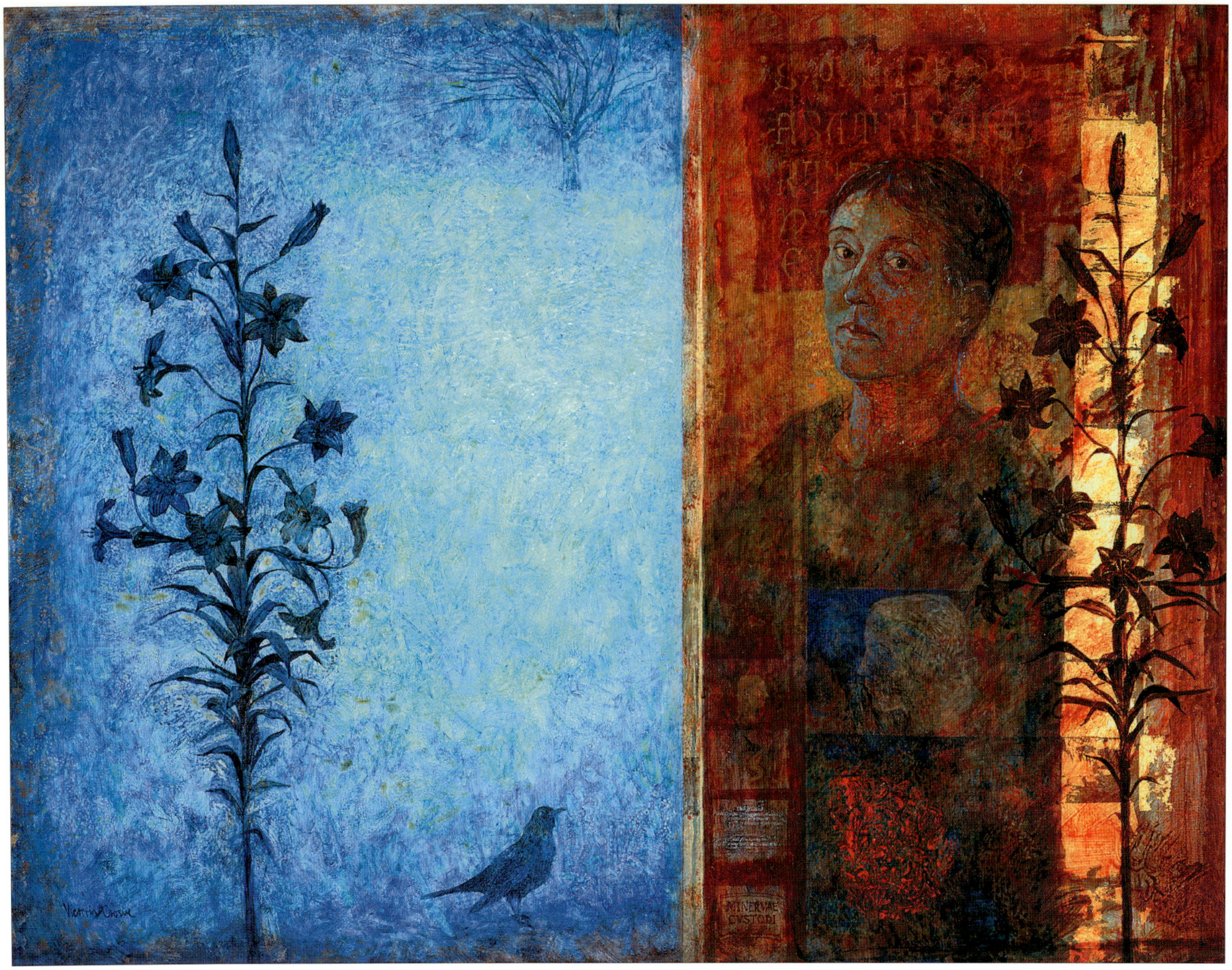

MIRROR OF THE SOUTH
2001. Oil on linen. 40in. x 50in.

derived from a painting by Giovanni Bellini in the Accademia. She appears in many guises in the series of paintings and prints echoing Venice; with hands folded on her breast, reversed, within the form of a roundel or as a single head. Likewise, Piero della Francesca's St Julian and the sublime profile of Pontormo's Gabriel from the *Annunciation* in Santa Felicità in Florence are components in many of the paintings. Among the other *dramatis personae* of Renaissance art, we encounter Leonardo's angel of the Annunciation in *Being in Italy;* a beauty from the Gonzaga Palace by Mantegna in *Italian Interior, Oblique References,* and beasts from Piero di Cosimo's *Forest Fire* in *Remembered Land.*

Piero's picture, in the Ashmolean Museum in Oxford, brings us to the topic of landscape painting. Victoria Crowe was struck by its 'great sense of mystery' and admired the way he used the landscape 'as a vehicle to explore the element of fire, evolution, civilization and myth', declaring that she wanted her landscapes 'to have a similar layering of our human concerns, dreams and hopes within the context of an enduring land'. Her responses to natural phenomena, and her appreciation of the landscape and the *genius loci* increased as a result of her trips to Madeira, Italy,

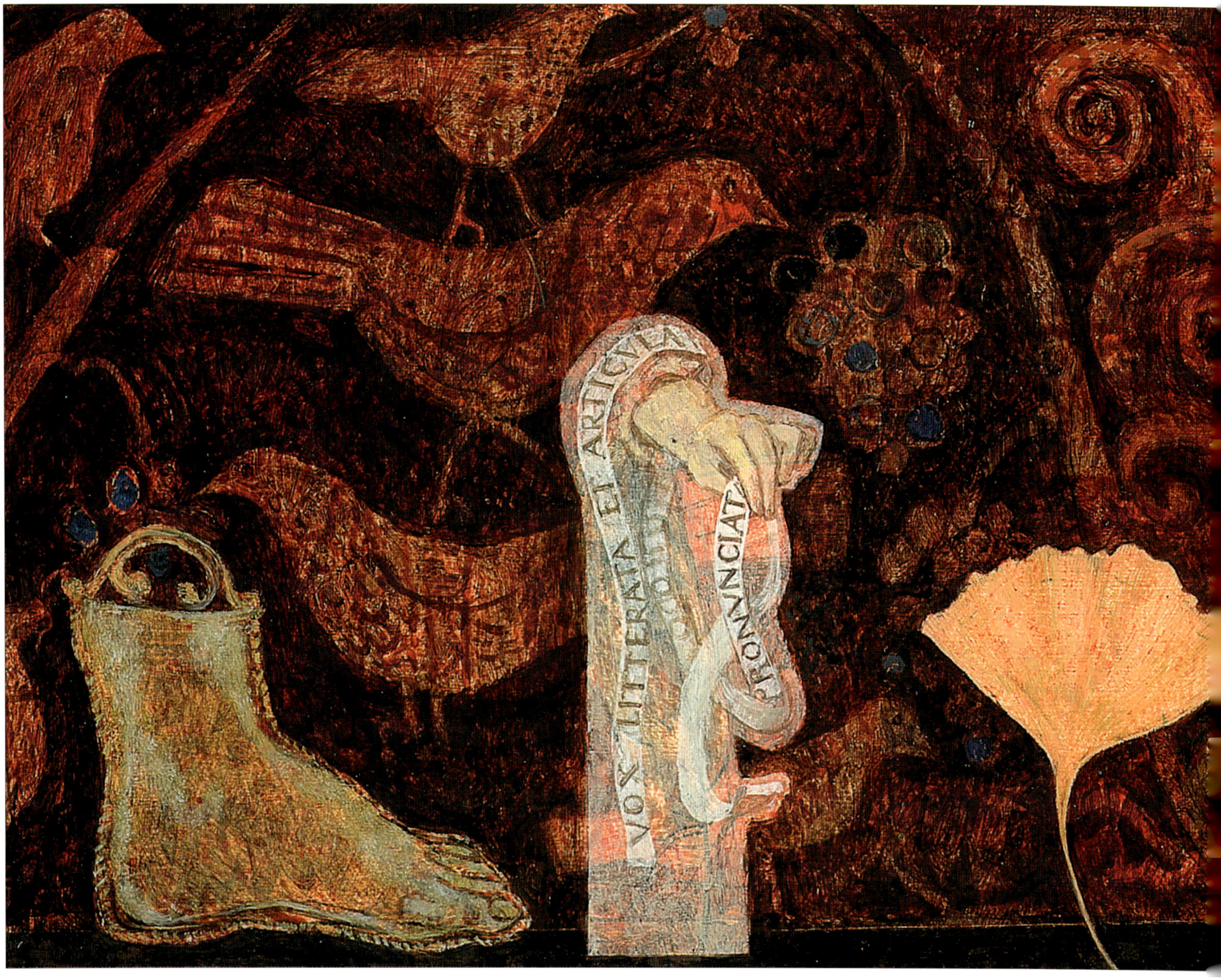


**AN AID TO MEMORY**
2000. Oil on board. 12in. x 30in.

Egypt and India. She inevitably became deeply attached to the landscape around her home at Kittleyknowe with its vast open horizons of moorlands and distant hills. It was here that she brought up her children, here that she befriended Jenny Armstrong, and here that she lived for some twenty years of her adult life. The local landscape was imprinted so indelibly on her mind that it remained as a powerful motif in her work even after she had moved to West Linton. But, just as the terms 'still life' and 'interior' are insufficient to convey the multiplicity of ideas inherent in her works, the simple word 'landscape' also needs some qualification here. Admittedly, there are more or less conventional landscapes in the painted oeuvre focusing on Jenny Armstrong but, like the later landscapes, in them too Victoria Crowe is concerned – as in her still lifes and the interiors – with the issues of past, present and future, with permanence and change, and, perhaps above all, with the close interrelationships between the landscape and the activities associated with it. In *Echoing Valley* we look out over a darkening landscape of cypress trees, olive groves and vines. The afterglow appears

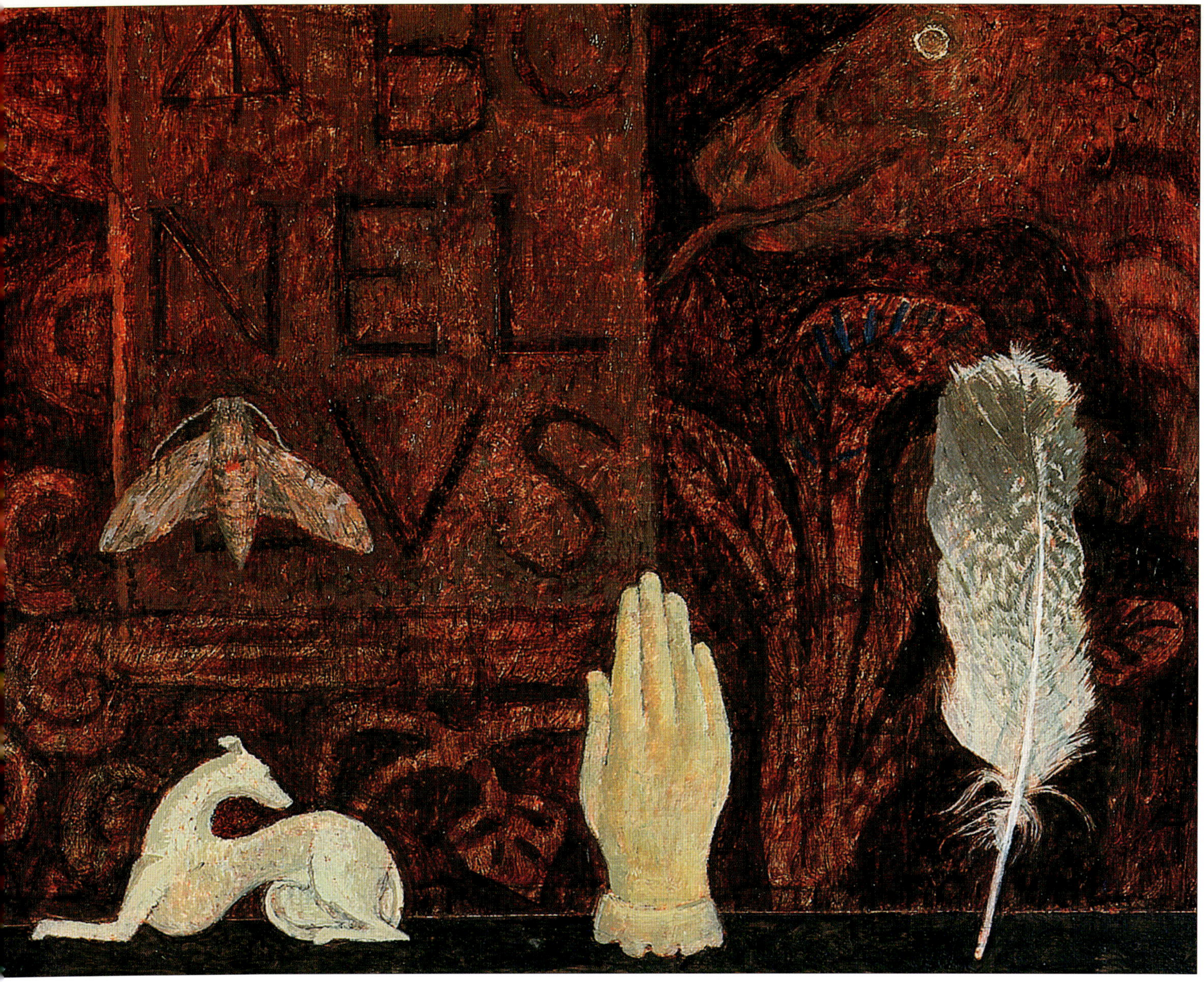

like a belt of flame across the horizon, casting more of the cypresses into stark silhouette and ending the working day with a spectacular finale. Man is now replaced in the landscape by bats and night insects, and in a similar piece entitled *Enchantment* a moth appears in the evening sky, as if to denote a shift in time. In *Vertiginous Landscape* three flame-like orange strelizia blooms, placed at the very forefront of the picture plane, tower majestically over the distant headland, their iridescent petals pointing towards the turquoise and orange sky.

In *Being in Italy* and *Painted Room with a View,* the landscape element is little more than a brief glimpse of the Tuscan countryside, as though seen through a small window from within. In *Landscape Icon* we are privy to two views of the snow-covered Borders landscape: on the left in the form of a narrow vertical band, on the right reflected in a mirror revealing another of the artist's self-portraits. *Landscape Icon* is, like others, a combination of landscape, portrait, still life and interior. *Mirror of the South* similarly juxtaposes an invitingly warm interior containing the artist's self-portrait

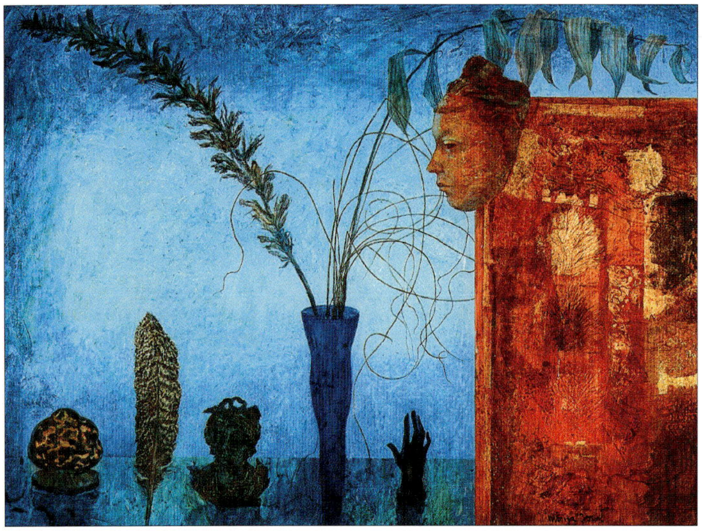

JOURNEY FROM VENICE 2000. Oil on canvas. 30in. x 40in.

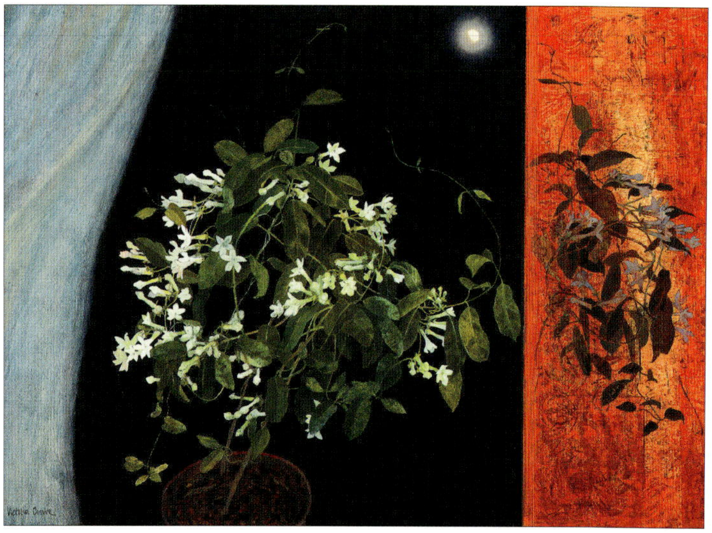

NIGHT STEPHANOTIS 2000. Oil on linen. 30in. x 40in.

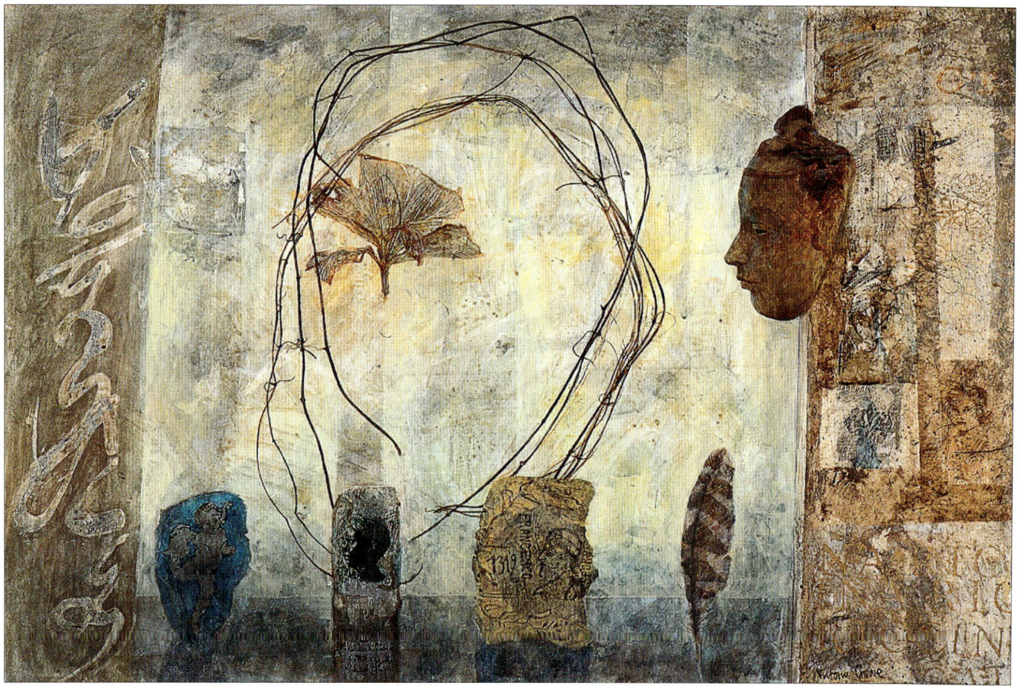

MEMORY AND LIKENESSES
2000. Watercolour, 27in. x 39¼in.
Private Collection

and a bleak winter landscape populated only by a bird and a distant leafless tree. Beneath the self-portrait are the sculptor Michael Snowden's head of Gemma, Uccello's little head of Eve, and the Latin inscription MINERVAE CUSTODI copied from a tablet in the Ducal Palace in Urbino, one of many such inscriptions in the artist's recent work. Two matching ornamental lilies purchased in Venice lend symmetry to the composition and allow the artist, as in *Night Stephanotis,* to contrast the effects of cool and hot colours on the same object, but the precise spatial relationship between the two parts of the picture remains disturbingly ambiguous. In *Landscape with Powerful Objects,* the connection between the interior and the exterior world is clearer: the wintry landscape lies immediately beyond the window, on whose sill are arranged (from left to right) another of the artist's self-portraits, a black Indian butterfly, a plate of the moon by Fornasetti (a gift from the artist's husband) and an image based on a

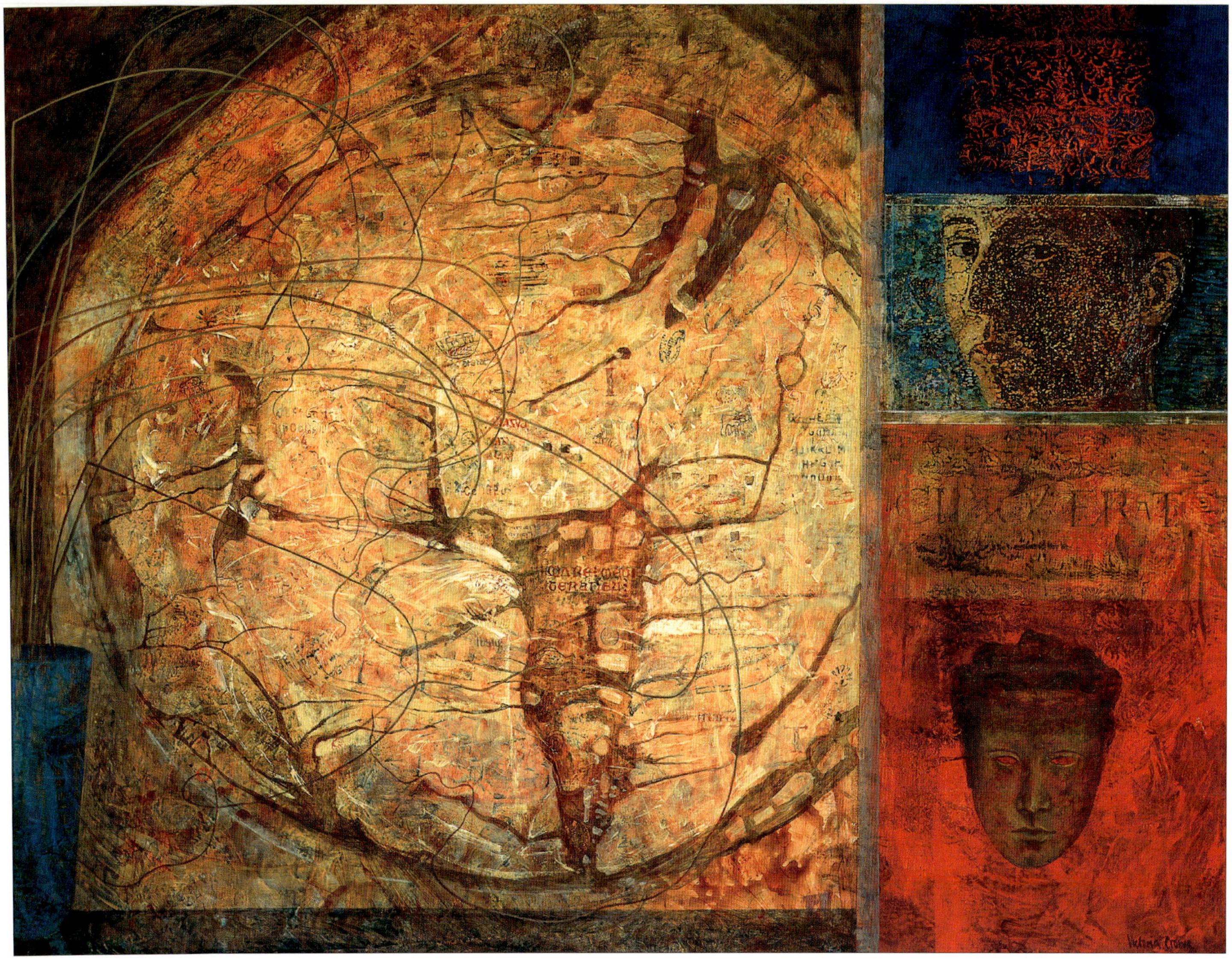

Sienese Madonna and Child. Coiled like wire behind them are the woody tendrils of a clematis.The mere enumeration of these foreground objects serves to emphasize the diversity of the images that Victoria Crowe introduces into her work. All of them, of course, have personal associations, though some, naturally, are more intensely personal than others and are part of a private rather than a universal iconography.

Victoria Crowe has a refreshing humility; she is an intelligent, articulate, warm and compassionate human being whose own experiences have been distilled in the form of images accessible, with only a little effort, to us all. None of the components of any of Victoria Crowe's pictures is arbitrary or whimsical, though what catches the artist's eye may be, and often is, very different from what others would observe. To appreciate her work to the full we must, however, be prepared to enter a parallel world, more akin to the world of dreams, in which reason and intellect play an inferior role to intuition and the unconscious. Her choice of subject may be governed by an initial intellectual curiosity or, in the case of the *mappa mundi*, the principal motif of *World View*, by feelings of humility in face of an artefact at once mysterious, mythical and naïf, the product of a civilization whose faith was so strong, whose knowledge so incomplete.

Colin J. Bailey

**WORLD VIEW**
2000. Oil on linen. 40in. x 50in.

# ORIGINS

I was born the day the Second World War ended, V.E. Day – hence Victoria Elizabeth. I think I was a solitary child, somewhat out of step with suburban Kingston, but I loved the relative remoteness of Richmond Park, which I visited regularly with my father, and the occasional holidays to distant rural Cornwall where my mother's family came from.

I've always drawn, but because of the war, with its shortages and rationing, it was often on shiny 'Bronco' toilet paper and to my mother's annoyance on walls around the house. Christmas for me had the added bonus of envelopes and the backs of cards to draw on.

I started at art college when I was sixteen, and felt, really for the first time in my life, a great sense of belonging. I liked all the debate with fellow students, visits to London's art galleries and museums and the warm crowded Life Room where the mysteries of drawing began slowly to unravel. We were lucky enough, at Kingston, to have Prunella Clough as a visiting lecturer. My tutorials with her really taught me to see and to transform, to look at the internal as well as the external world. An understanding of plastic values – tone, colour, opacity, etc. as a means of controlling tension and surface structure within the work – is, to me, very much part of her legacy.

At eighteen I went abroad for the first time – a train journey through Belgium, East and West Germany and Poland to Kruschev's Soviet Union. I became interested in Soviet street-art, in Eisenstein's films, in Malevich and Suprematism. I was very impressed by the spiritual, hieratic and abstract qualities of Russian icon painting.

Many of these concerns, alongside a growing interest in the so-called Italian

SELF-PORTRAIT WITH ICON
1967. Oil on board. 30in. x 36in.
Private Collection

DRUMMER BOY WITH WHITE HORSE
1971. Oil on board. 36in. x 48in.
Private Collection

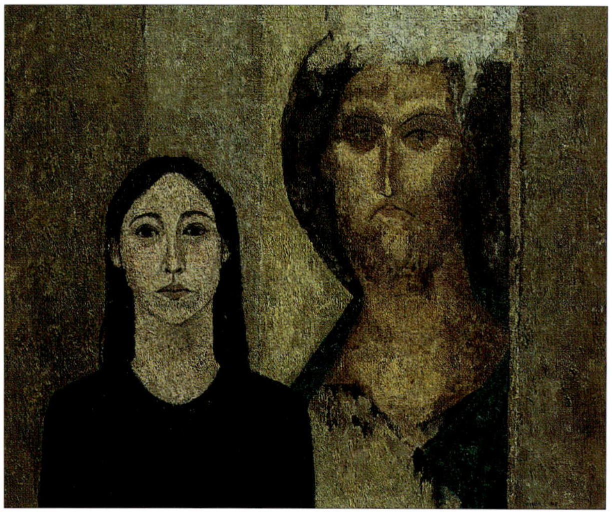

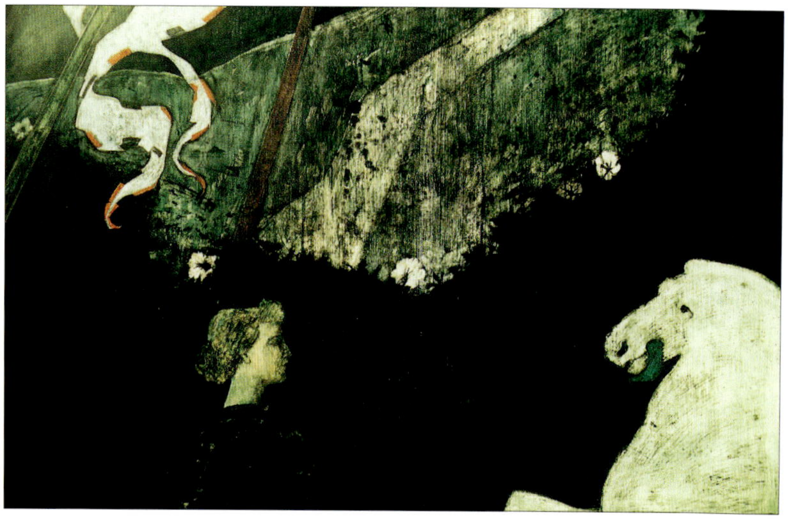

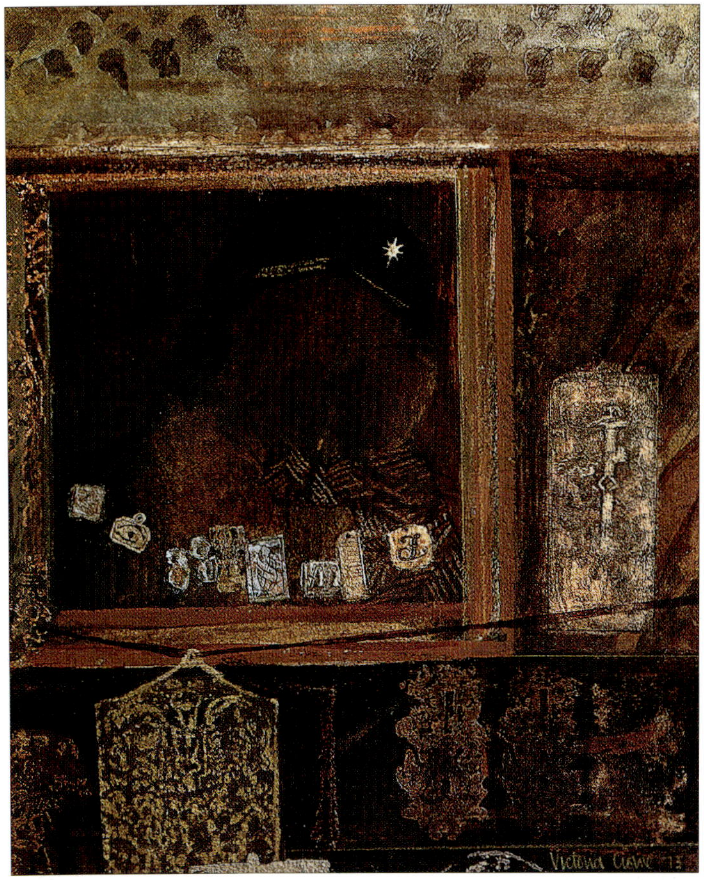

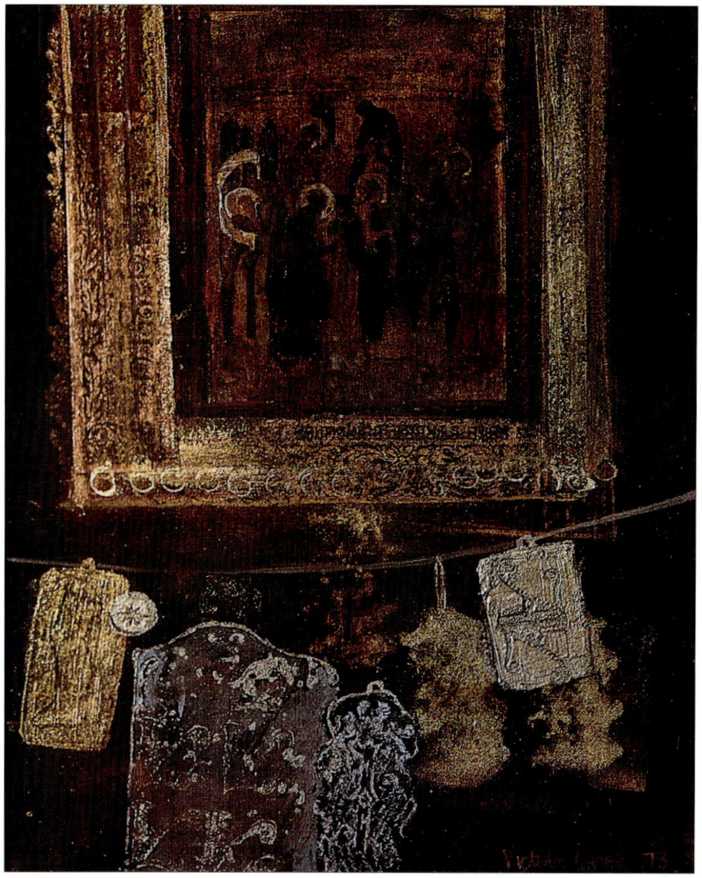

primitives, motivated my work at the RCA, where I found Leonard Rosoman and Carel Weight to be particularly influential friends and tutors. The painting school was physically part of the Victoria and Albert Museum, and we could go down an adjoining staircase, an inspirational daily trip past silver, polychromed figures and tapestries, on the way to the canteen.

At my degree show I was invited by Robin Philipson to come to Edinburgh College of Art to teach drawing and painting. By that time I was married to Michael Walton, and so we ventured north together. I was stimulated by the teaching, the painting school's excellent facilities (with purpose-built north-lit studios and fantastic views of the Castle), the city itself and, of course, the surrounding landscape. After the suburbs and London, at last a chance to live in remote and rather challenging countryside. Our move to the Borders was certainly a dramatic change of environment, and one which, over the period of the next twenty years, was to provide me with constant subject matter and inspiration.

ICONOSTASIS FRAGMENT
1973. Mixed media. 14in. x 12in.
Private Collection

ICON WITH VOTIVE OFFERINGS
1973. Mixed media. 14in. x 12in.
Private Collection

# NEW BEGINNINGS

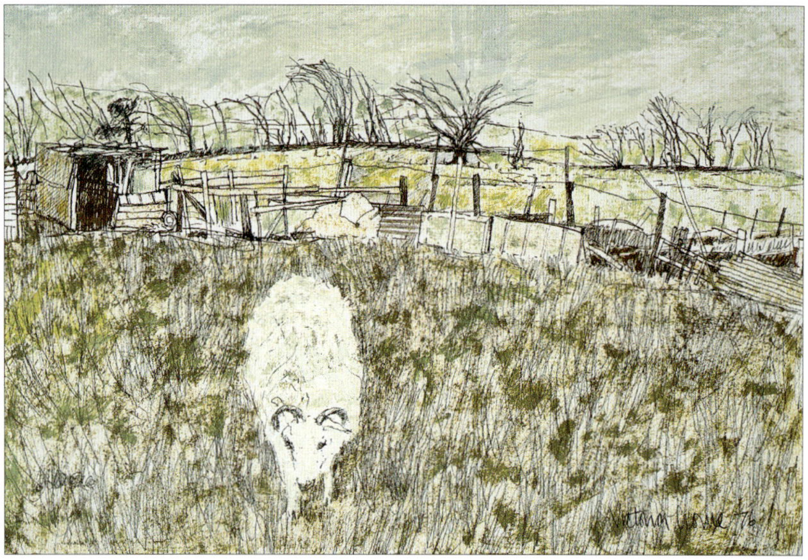

SHEEP AND FENCE
1976. Pencil, ink and oil. 7in. x 10in.
Scottish National Gallery of Modern Art, Edinburgh

*Victoria Crowe's work, spanning twenty years living at Kittleyknowe, in the Scottish Borders, painting the landscape and her neighbour Jenny Armstrong's way of life, was brought together in an exhibition at the Scottish National Portrait Gallery, Edinburgh, in Spring 2000, entitled* A Shepherd's Life.

*The aim of the Millennium year's exhibitions at the Scottish National Portrait Gallery were to celebrate the heroism of everyday life, extraordinary 'ordinary' people as indeed Jenny Armstrong was. The following piece was written by Victoria Crowe in 1989 while still living at Kittleyknowe. It conveys a cogent and intimate insight into her work at that time. The piece was first published in 1990 in* The Artist *magazine.*

In 1968 I came to teach at Edinburgh College of Art. I have lived and worked in Scotland ever since and my painting has been very much concerned with the environment around my home and studio in the Scottish borders. After three years of living in Hammersmith while I was at the RCA, and all of my previous life in suburban Surrey, the major impact of new life in Scotland was the landscape. Living 1,000ft. up on the broken moorland of the Pentland Hills, the experiences of the enormity of the sky, the ever-present wind, long winters, hills bitten into with snow and ice, the marvellous sunsets and long light of early summer days and nights were the starting points of many early paintings.

My studio gives immediately on to and into the landscape, so not only from every window is one reminded of the hills and fields, but during every walk and outing one becomes part of the elements. The mile-long walk to the village, helping with feeding the sheep and hens, walking with the children through snow and gale, frost and long soft summer evenings, sharpen and deepen one's response to the land. Living in, and

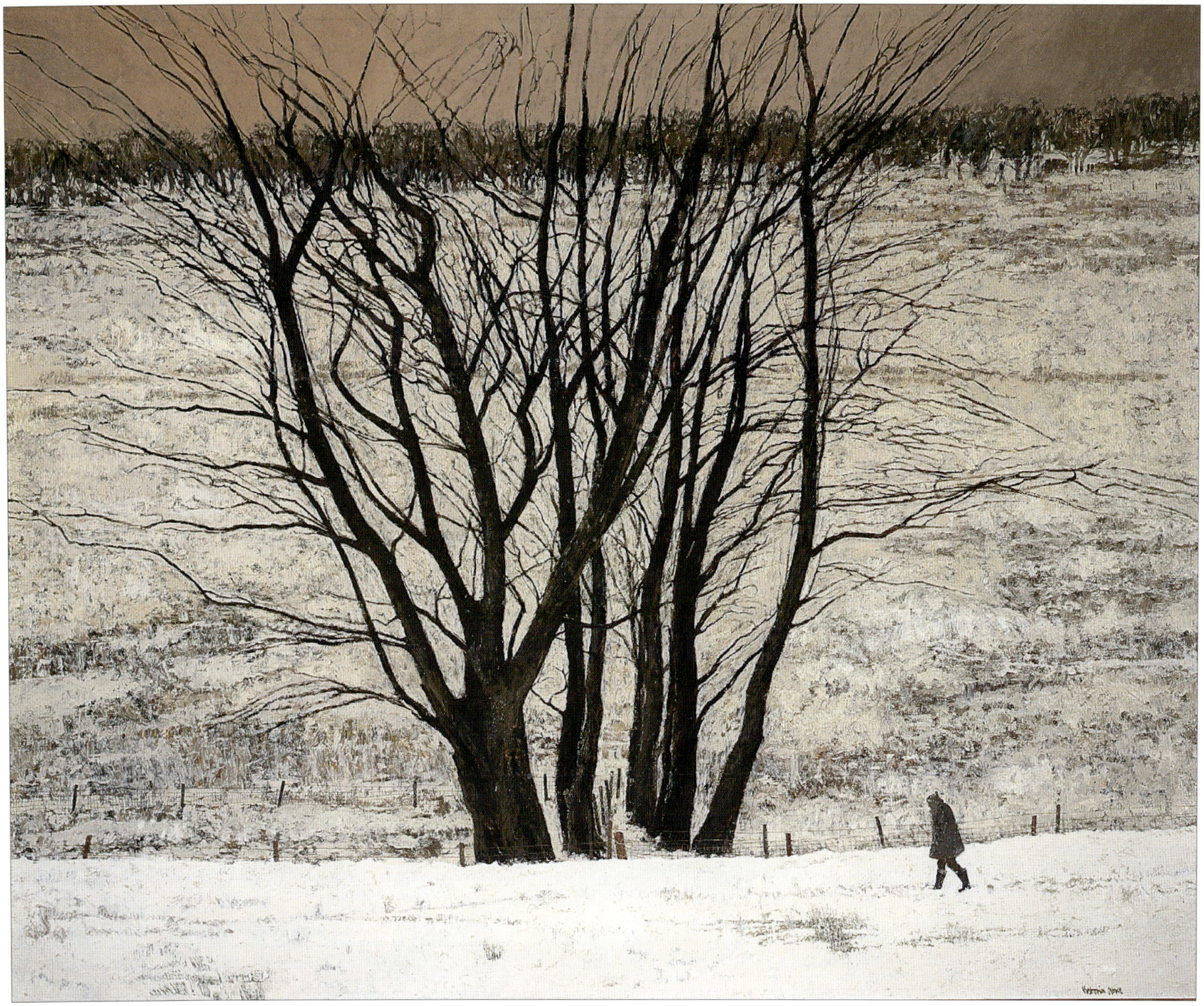

LARGE TREE GROUP
1975. Oil on board. 36in. x 40in.
Private Collection

feeling part of the landscape has meant that the subsequent painted images have been born out of a familiarising process.

I painted a whole series of snow paintings, enjoying the tracery and pattern of branches, reeds, and dead grasses against the snow. I liked the transforming nature of the snow – the common place becomes strangely different, the familiar contours of field and hill become softened and unsure. Muddy dull colours of riverbank and last year's leaves, the grey-green of tree bark and lichen become sudden unexpected patches of sonorous colour against the sweep of white and the heavy grey sky. The familiar sheep change from creamy white blobs against the green or ochre of the field into angular dark shapes against the white snow. My landscape paintings incorporated many of these observations of rural living.

I looked not only at the structure of the land, the tone and extent of the sky, the trees and the burns, but also at the straw bales and feeding troughs dotted in the fields, the patterns of ploughing and the lines of winter-feed turnips in the black and frosty

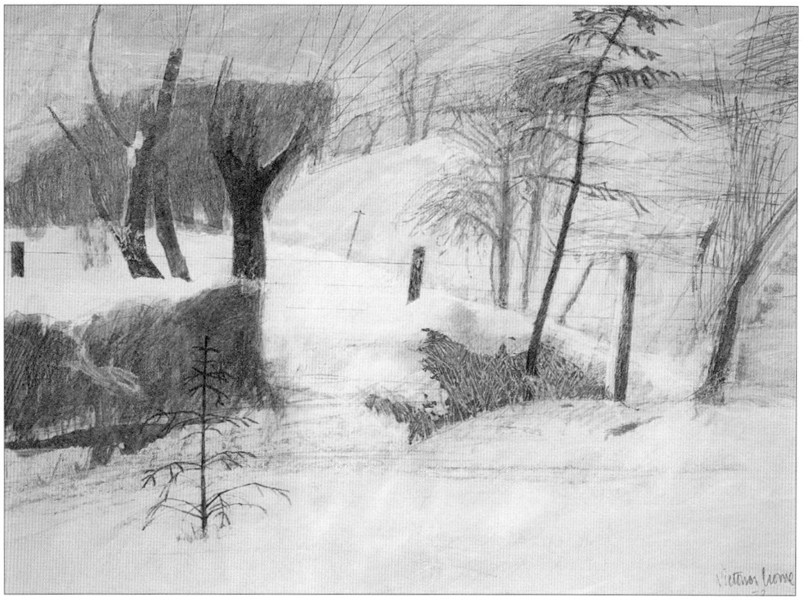

GARDEN WITH SNOW
1973. Gouache and pencil on paper.
11¾in. x 14in.
Private Collection

earth. I accompanied my neighbour, the retired shepherd Jenny Armstrong, across the moor to feed her 'far-away' hens and to gather in her own small flock from amongst the tenant farmer's sheep. Seeing the landscape through her eyes often led to a wider understanding – the tracks of weasel and fox around the distant hen-house were not just visually interesting evidence of unseen night visitors but threatening and unwelcome marks from intruders. Sandy hollows, scars of long past quarrying, and the dip in the field along by the dry stone dyke, which were to me visual punctuations and embellishments to the painted landscape, were, for Jenny, exactly the places to go to in a blizzard when looking for lost sheep. Several of the paintings from that time were about the minutiae of observed detail, within the framework of a landscape setting.

I painted about the hen-house and the tied-up fences and gates with the animals behind them. The paintings of trees and fields in the snow began to include footsteps, tracks, animals and birds. I drew and painted Jenny feeding the sheep, carrying bales of hay, walking with the two dogs and collecting fuel. I watched her shutting various pet hens and cockerels into idiosyncratic houses made from richly textured rusting corrugated iron, swollen wooden planks revealing several flaking layers of paint, and wrinkled bitumen-coated felt. Such surfaces, the tonal formality of frost and snow in landscape and the sudden observed detail, made relevant through knowledge or experience of its purpose, fuelled my work for many winters.

The corollary of this, of course, were the long soft summer evenings – a kind of protracted twilight when my attention was caught again by the shifting light silhouetting the trees around the house. The first snow paintings of the back garden began a series of paintings in different seasons about the sheltering line of trees which separated our garden from the windswept moorland. Through these trees one is looking due west and so inevitably the golden light of setting sun and the after-glow – even more captivating from my point of view – became part of that series.

I have always enjoyed the mood of the Barbizon landscape painters and of the Swedish Post-Impressionists – painters of forest and lake, sky and reflection. I enjoy Klimt's horizon-less birchwoods and orchards, full of close observation, but also full of

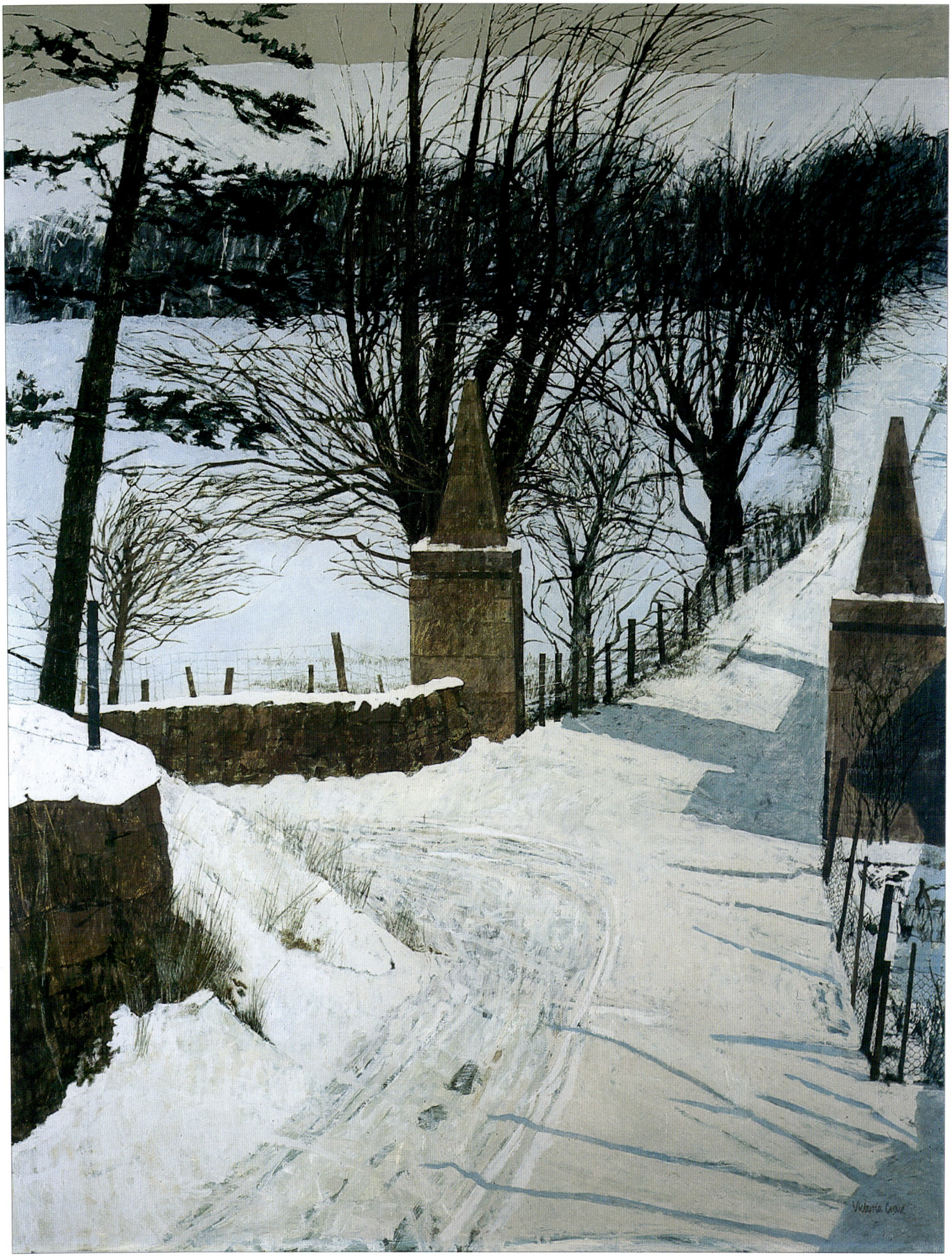

**WINTER AT KITTLEYBRIG** 1974. Oil on board. 48in. x 36in. Private Collection

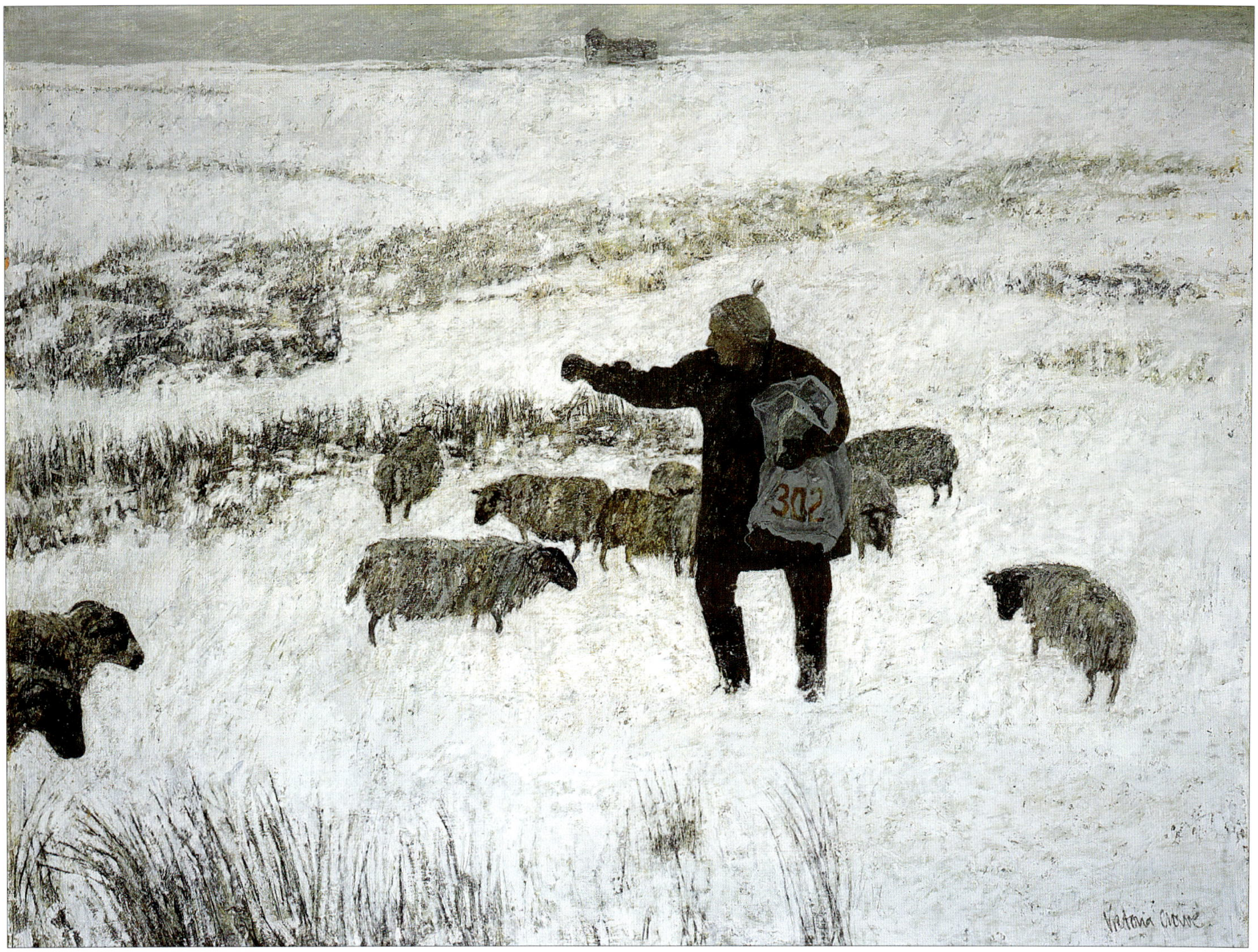

SHEEP, SHEPHERDESS AND HARBOUR CRAIG
1975. Oil on board. 31in. x 39in.
Private Collection

mystery, symbolism and spirit of place. This 'spirit of place' is, I think, very important for me. I've lived in the same place for so long now, and recorded my surroundings so frequently, that I feel I have become more receptive to broader aspects of the landscape – not in terms of content, but in terms of intensity of image and a response to nuances of mood. When Jenny became housebound and progressively more infirm, she retired from active herding and kept only a few 'pet' sheep. She began spending more time indoors and so the paintings 'came in' too.

The landscape was referred to in these works mainly by showing glimpses through windows or doorways and by mirror-reflections of the outside world. Curiously, in many of these interiors, the one landscape image became more telling and intense by virtue of its isolation and unexpected juxtaposition with household objects.

The content of the work gradually changed, becoming more about the interior of her two-roomed cottage. Jenny appeared in these paintings moving through the room, sitting by the fire, or silhouetted against a window looking out on to a snowy landscape.

The room itself was used for a variety of purposes. The iron range fuelled by gathered sticks, logs and coal provided heat, hot water and rather primitive cooking

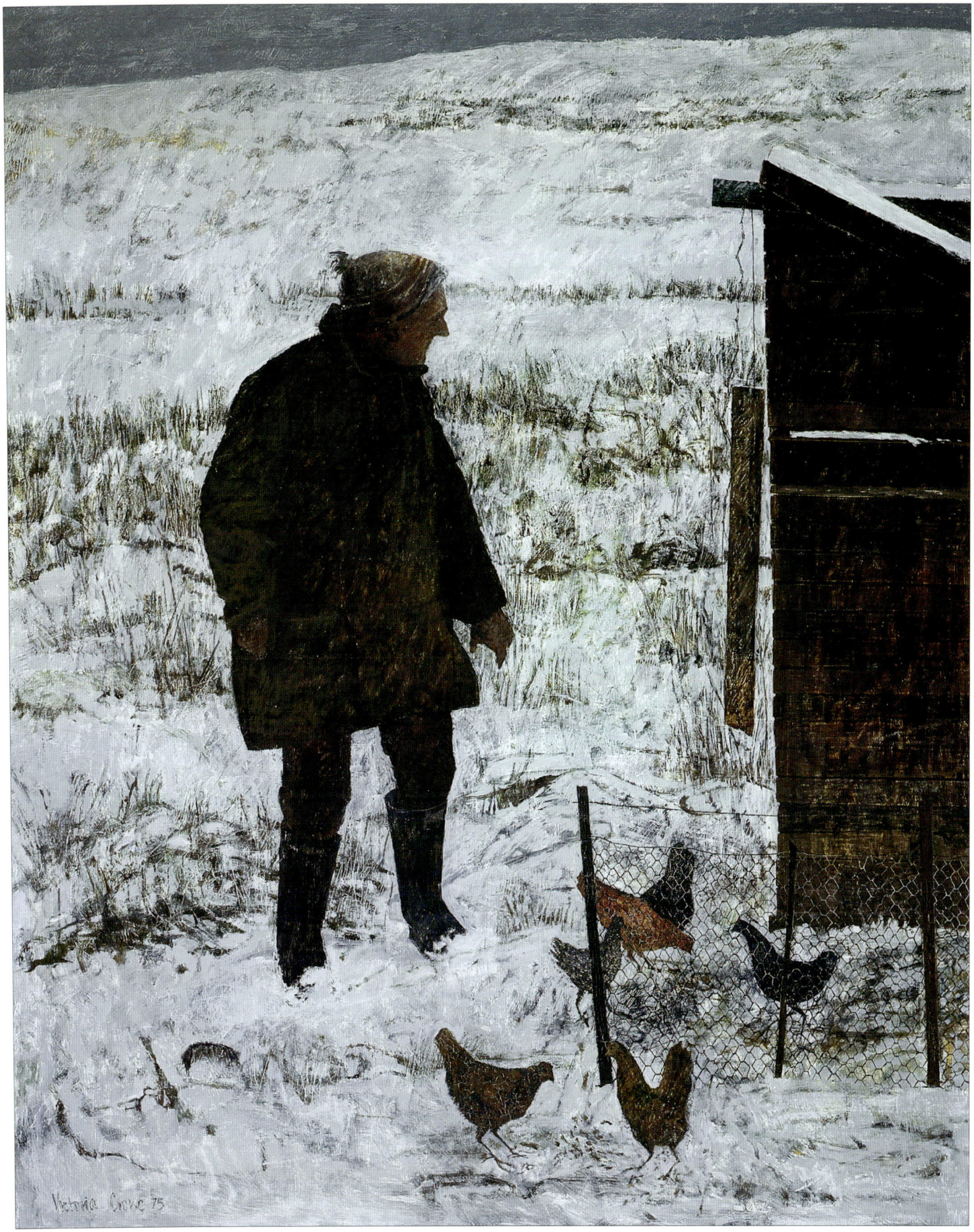

JENNY AND THE FARAWAY HENS 1975. Oil on board. 36in. x 28in. Collection H.M. the Queen and H.R.H. The Duke of Edinburgh

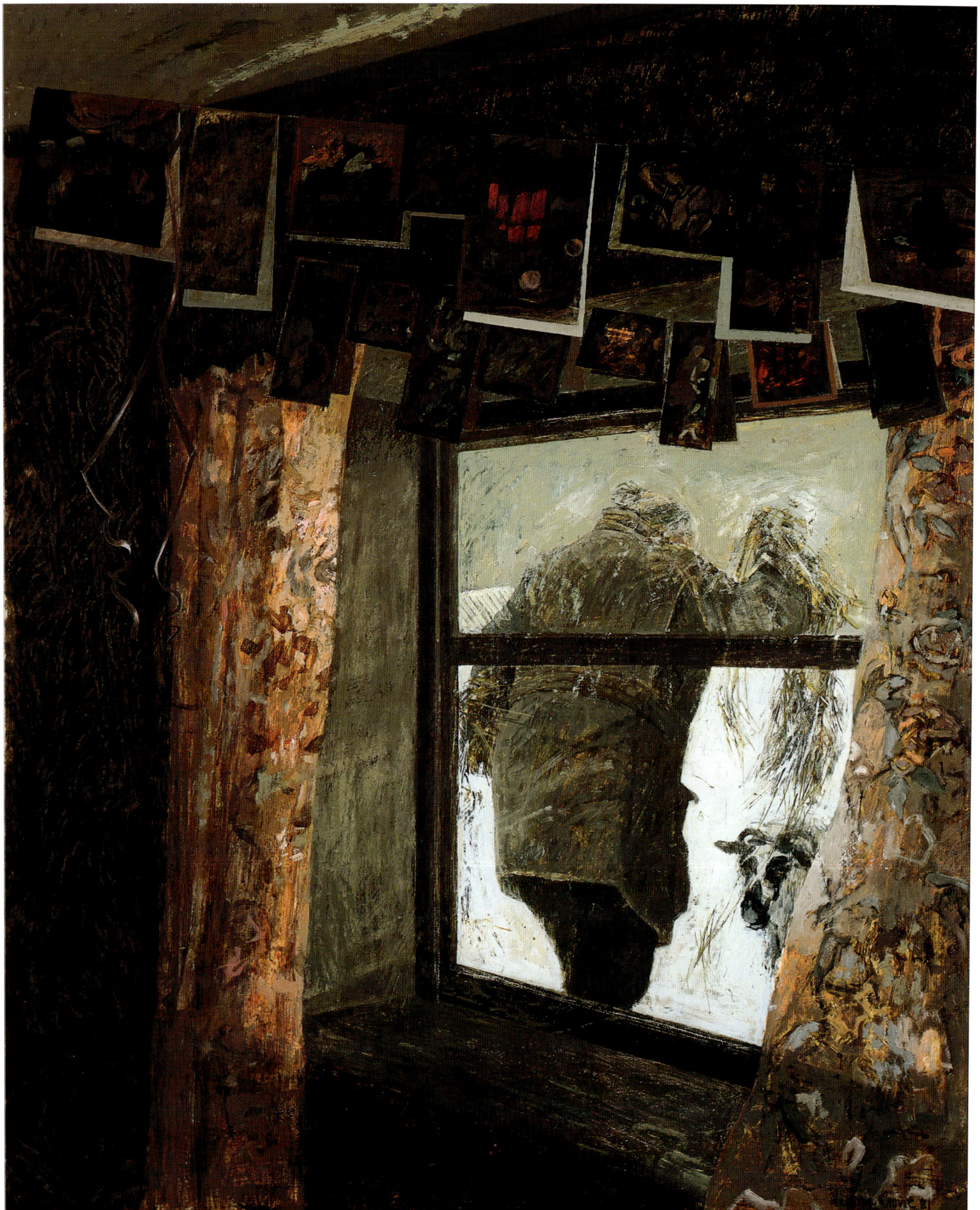

**DECEMBER 25TH** 1981. Oil on board. 36in. x 28in. Private Collection

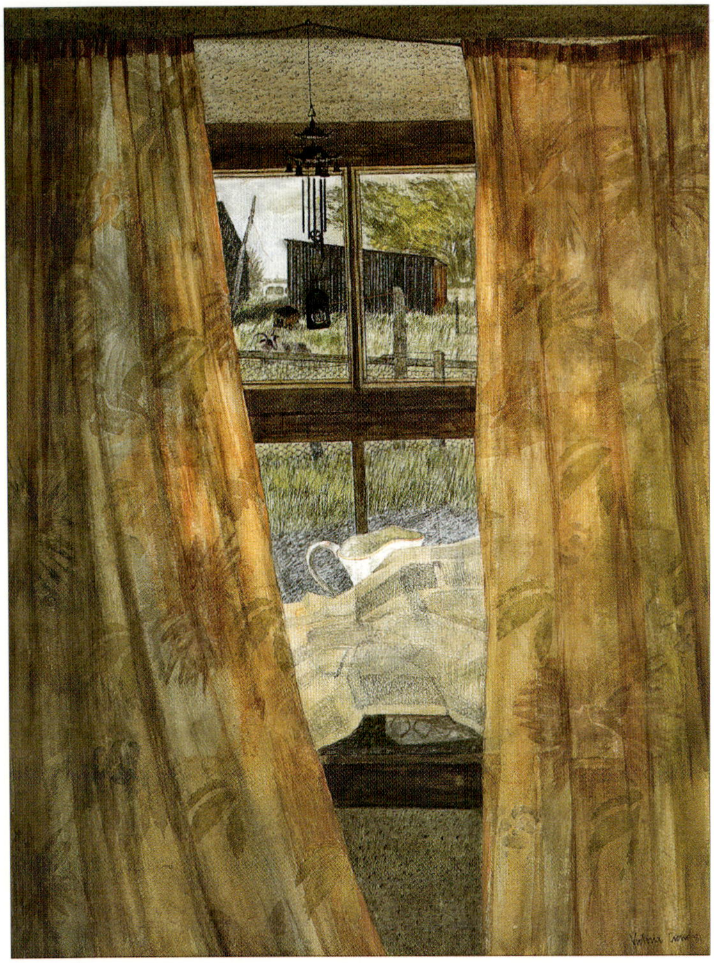

facilities by way of a slow oven and movable, hinged trivets which held pot or kettle over the flames. The range also provided essential dry, warm storage for 'kindlers', a drying place for washing and a lamb nursing area. Every available surface in the room – window sill, piano top – (and keyboard), mantelshelf and tables were covered with a lifetime's hoarding of interesting and useful items. An amazing juxtaposition of photographs of a dead friend, a Bonnie Scotland tartan calendar, a plastic tub of hairpins, baler twine (salvaged to mend fences), 'Coty' air-spun powder – a concession to femininity along with the 1950s bottle of Brilliantine – sheep shears, three clocks – all telling different times and each sometimes right – and electric boot warmers.

This room was my inspiration for years, its contents and possibilities revealing themselves slowly as Jenny and I sat and talked. During these conversations, Jenny would tell me of her childhood in 'Fairlie Hope', an isolated hill farm, her early life as a shepherd with a large herd working in the Pentlands and the move, with her mother, to Monks Cottage some fifty years ago. As she talked, I drew, and in the dim, fire-lit interior I grew to know and identify the faces in the photographs, the cold, shifting snow-light through the thin curtains, the unexpected sunlight on the stained wallpaper, and to enjoy the visual potential of the accumulated bric-à-brac of her life.

By the early 1980s Jenny had become ill and eventually spent over a year in hospital recovering from a double amputation. Despite all advice and with her own particular brand of courage and determination she returned home in a wheelchair to

LANDSCAPE THROUGH DRAWN CURTAINS
1982. Watercolour and ink on paper.
29½in. x 21½in.
Private Collection

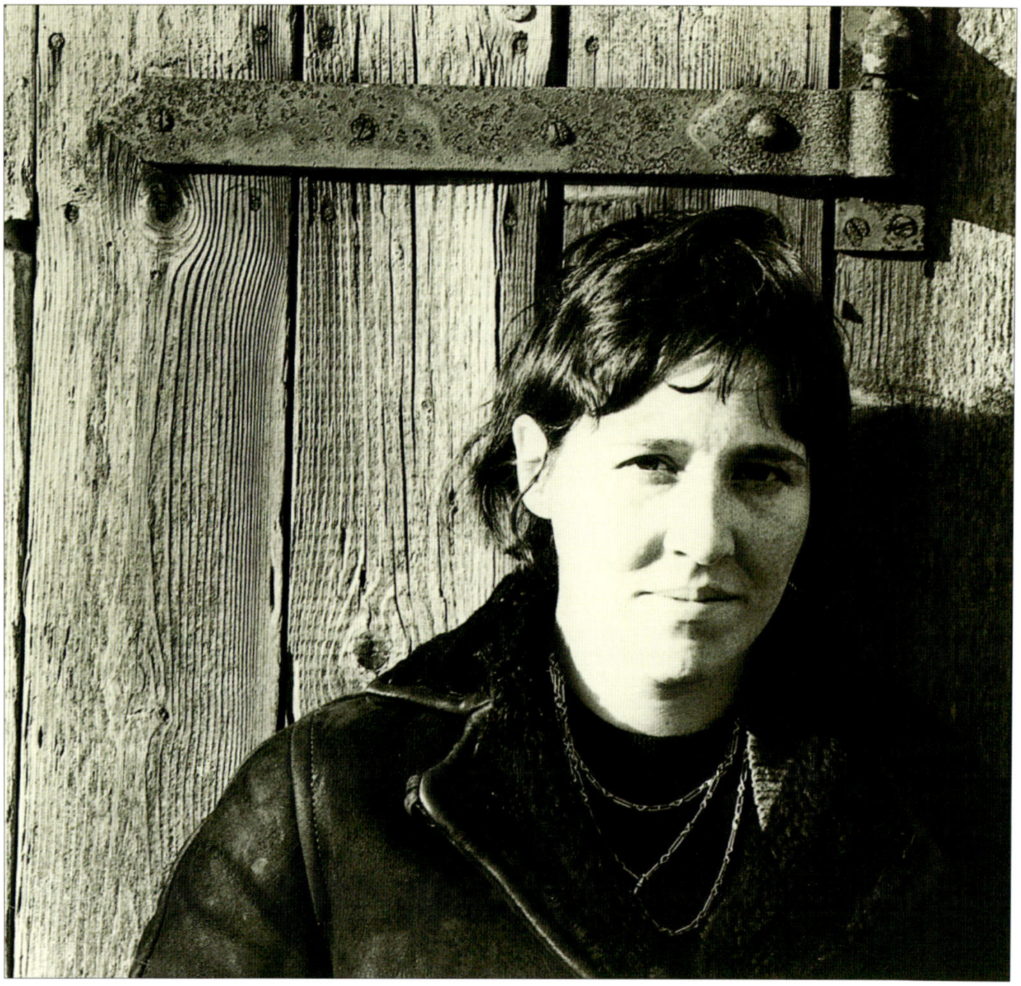

VICTORIA CROWE AT KITTLEYKNOWE
1970.
Photograph © Michael Walton

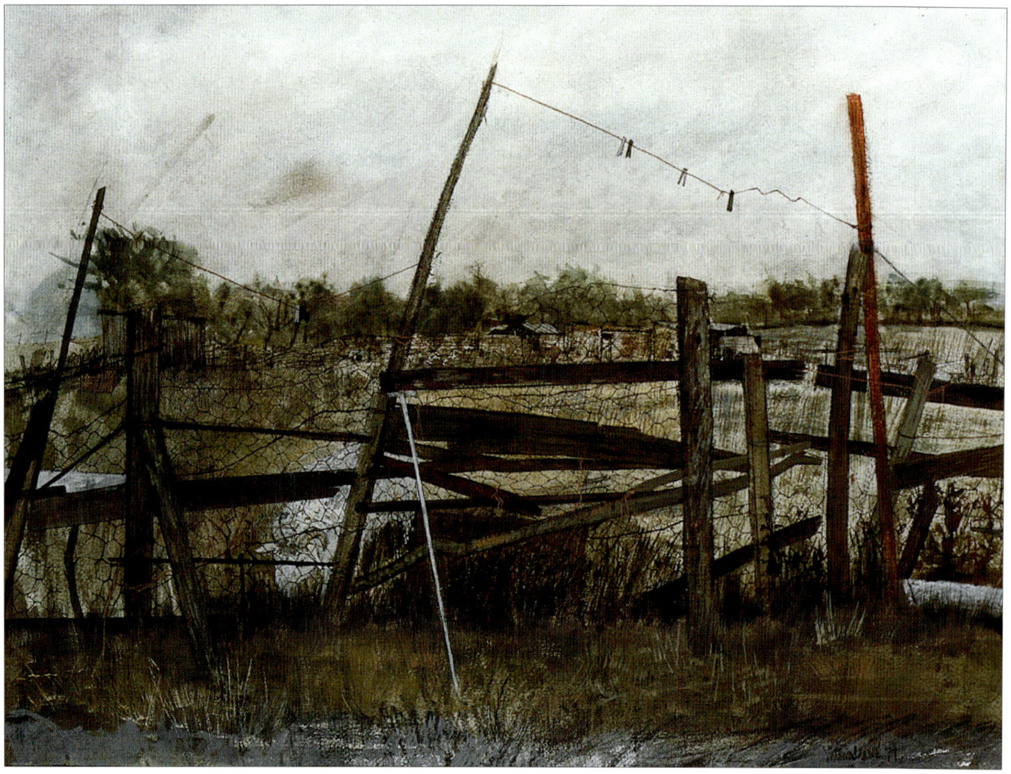

A FENCE TO KEEP THE RAM IN
1977. Watercolour with ink on paper.
23in. x 30in.
Stirling Smith Art Gallery and Museum

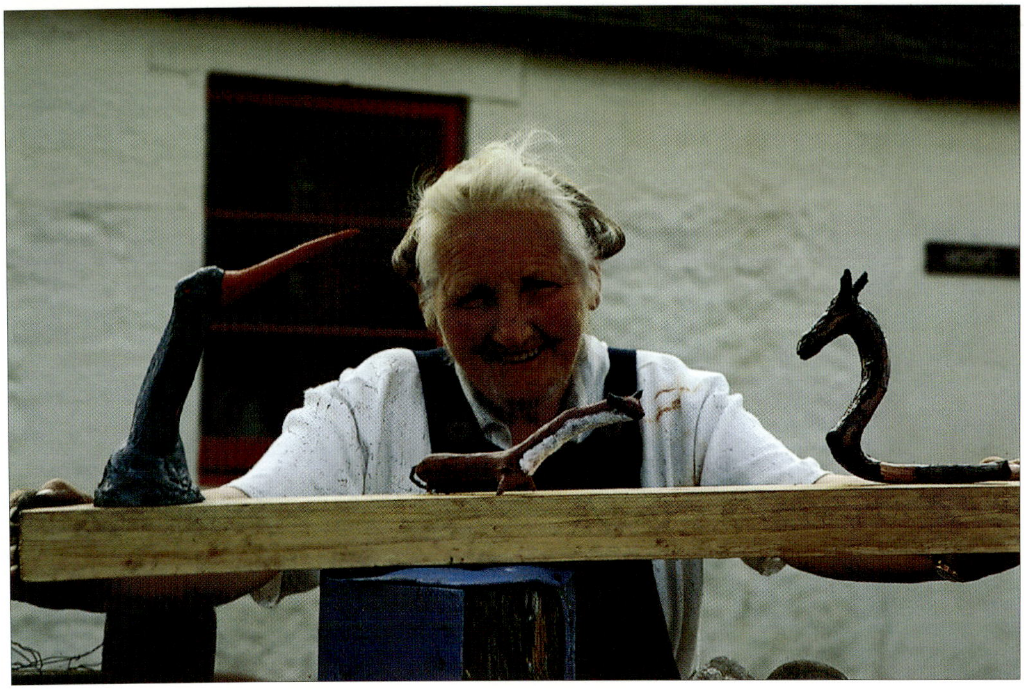

JENNY AND HER CARVINGS
November 1972.
Photograph © Michael Walton

the room with its range for cooking and heating, and which now had to function as a bedroom too. She had had to give up the remaining sheep and even her border collie as it would have been impossible to keep the place clean enough for her to stay. However, she did have a new companion – a budgie – to keep her company in the changed and difficult circumstances. These changes were noted in sketch-books, and by now the paintings of that room had become a kind of visual diary which continued until her death about eighteen months later.

When Jenny was alive I never photographed in Monks Cottage – it was too dark and one would have had to use a tripod – also it would have seemed to Jenny an intrusion into her privacy in a way that drawing never was. After she died I took a series of black and white photographs to record the room as it was, for my own reference. The results were terribly depressing and bore no relationship to the sense of place that I had been painting for so long. I suppose they are useful as an objective record – if, for example, I needed to check the pattern on a jug or the shape of the wheelchair's handle – but I have never been able to work with them in any creative sense.

Because of the nature of the images at Monks Cottage, on the one hand complexity of form, pattern and texture and on the other the broad tonal and atmospheric aspects of the room, lit by sun, firelight or the glow of snow, I used a mixture of media to convey these concerns. Source material comes from memory, observation and countless drawings and sketches made there.

The oil paintings of the room have been most particularly about the mood and atmosphere of the place. In these paintings the detailed observation of the initial drawings and watercolours gives way to a much broader statement and has primarily been a response to the differing light sources. I have painted about how the light in that room, whether from within or without, silhouetted, encompassed, emphasised, obscured, threw into shadow, enfolded, animated or revealed the objects, surfaces and inhabitants of that room.

# TRANSITION

For several years after Jenny Armstrong's death, Kittleyknowe seemed to be in a state of flux. As an artist I was still digesting the ideas generated by the series of landscape and interior paintings. I continued to paint about that interior – I had drawn it so often I could recall it easily. I had a freedom, now that it no longer existed in reality, to select from all the images of that room, to make the juxtapositions more telling and to let the sunlight fall wherever I wanted it to. I had some of Jenny's objects

**THEN AND NOW**
1989. Watercolour. 14½in. x 37in.
Private Collection

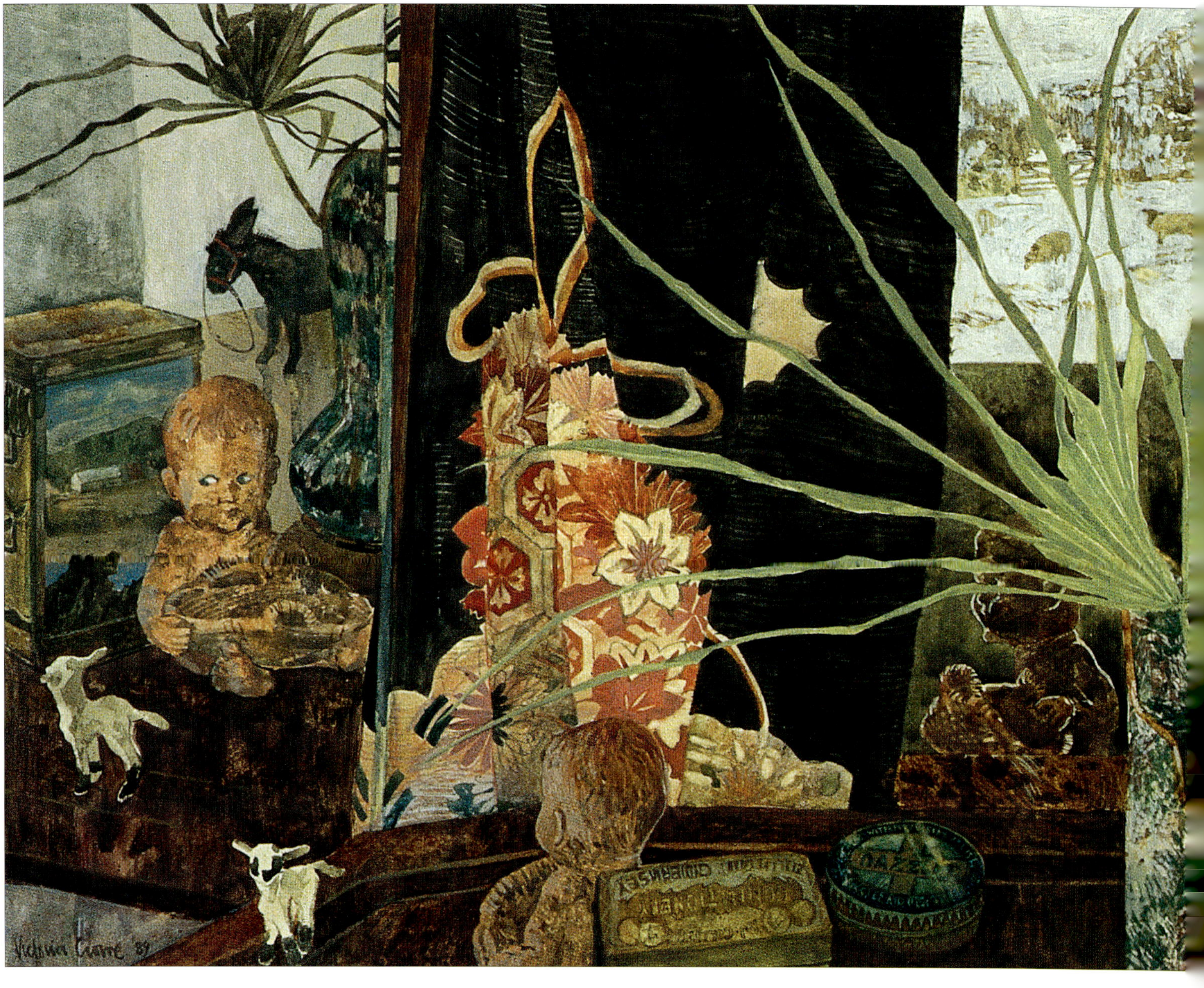

as mementoes – plaster swallows, a nodding dog, plastic tulips and photographs – and I incorporated several of these into groups set up in my own studio. I was using earlier images together with those of my present life; I became more concerned with notions of time past and passing and changes within and without seen against the constancy of the land and the predictability of the season. And what changes there were! One very bad winter we were the only inhabitants at Kittleyknowe; the old

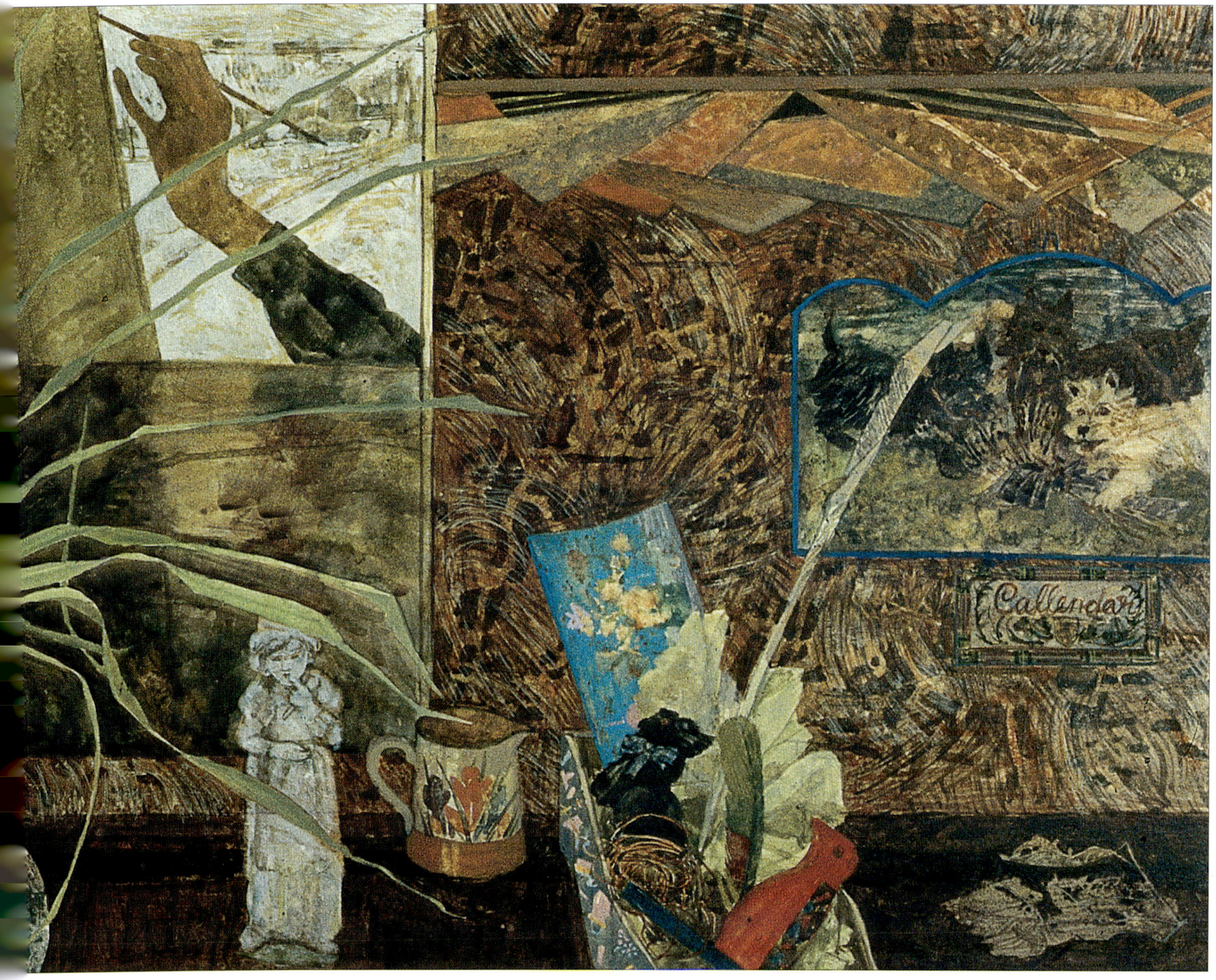

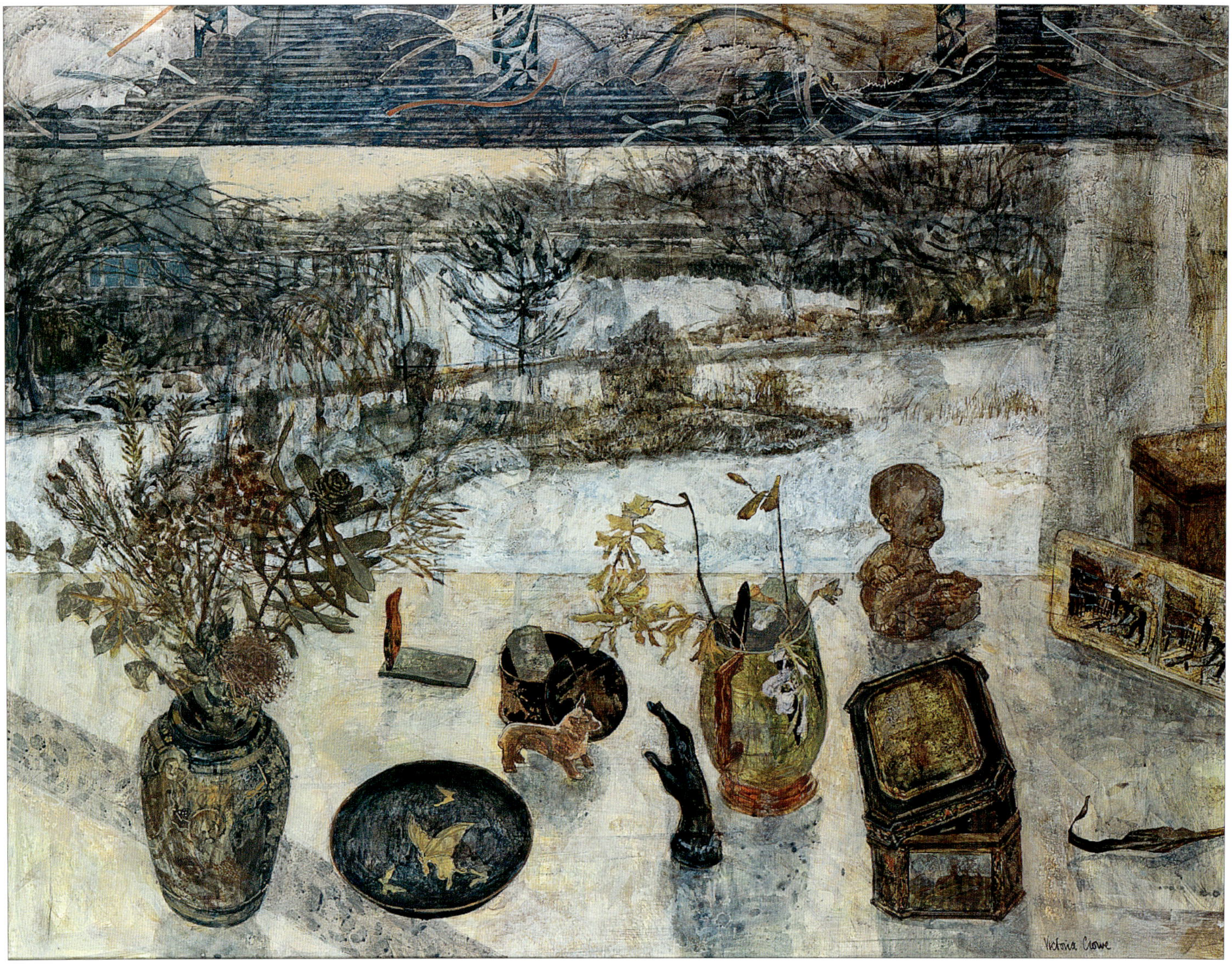


CLEARING SNOW
1993 Watercolour 32in. x 40in.
Private Collection

people had moved from the gate cottage, Jenny's place was being extended and modernised into a family home and the ruinous farm steading, occupied for some forty years by the reclusive and eccentric Tom, was set to become executive housing with 'en-suite master bedrooms' and 'landscaped' gardens. By Harbour Craig, among the bog-cotton and reedy grasses near Jenny's 'far-away hens' shed, and after all the peat had been stripped out, an open cast coal mine became operational. We realised it was time to move on. The idyllic place of our children's childhood and the inspiration for years of painting was no longer there … it existed firmly in my head of course.

> *… her recording of landscape turned out to be far removed from any prosaic investigative exercise. Filled with that 'spirit of place' which means so much to her, the pictures which resulted from her quest constitute in themselves an important section of her oeuvre. Moreover, their landscape has become part of her consciousness, to be drawn upon at will in the creation of subsequent pictures …*

(Mary Taubman,
catalogue essay for Victoria Crowe's solo show at the Thackeray Gallery, 1994)

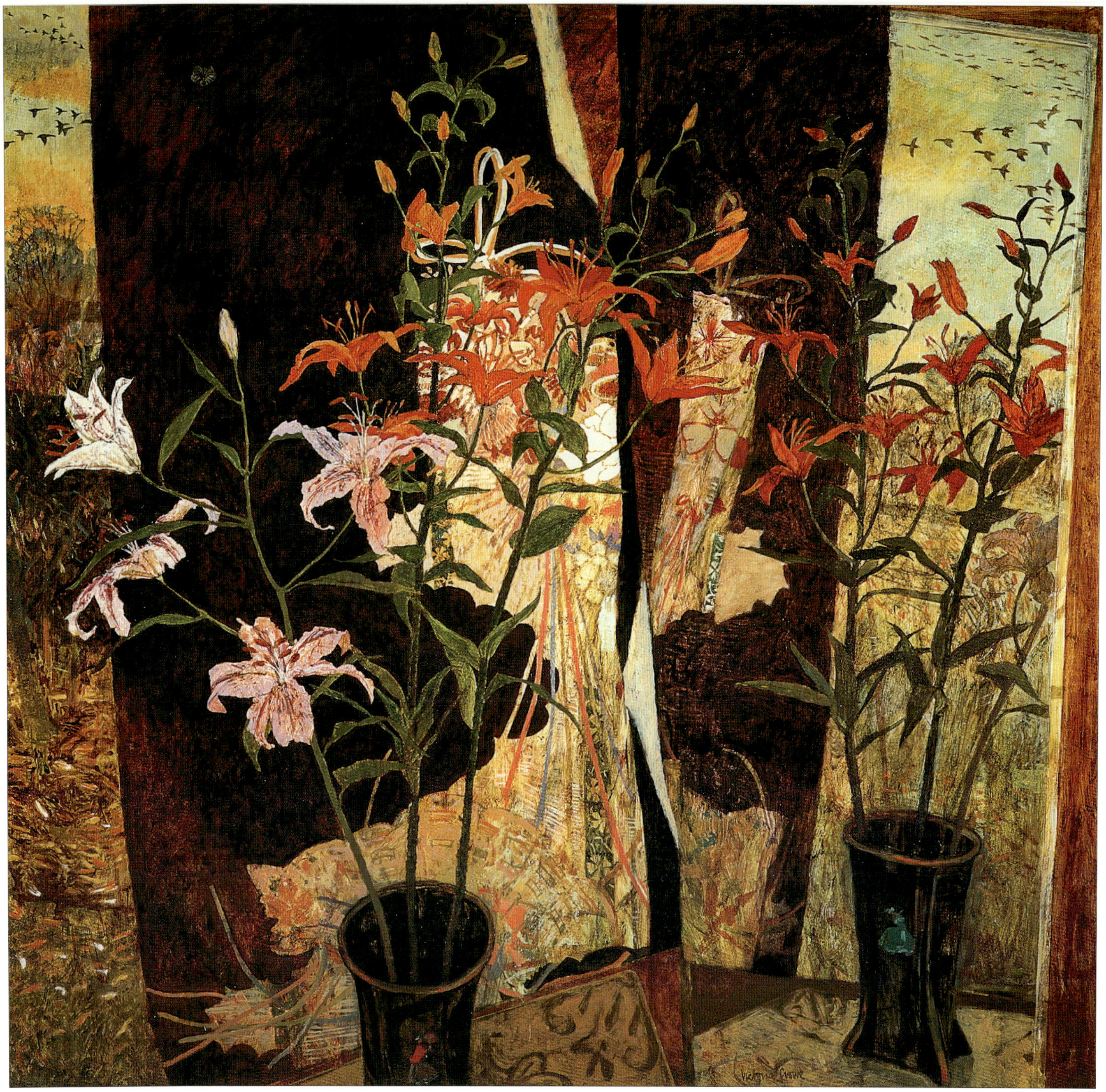

**RITES OF PASSAGE** 1991. Oil on board. 36in. x 36in. Private Collection

In the spring of 1990, in the throes of moving house, I was commissioned to take part in a series of half-hour films for Grampian Television. They were making a series called *Portrait of the Wild.* Four artists were each given a season and an aspect of wildlife to work with at varied locations throughout Scotland. Mine was 'Spring', the subject a Borders woodland and the chosen location was part of the estate bordering Kittleyknowe – a heavily wooded area with deep valleys. It was a very rewarding opportunity to work on this project and to pay a kind of tribute to the place I loved so much. An opportunity too to examine in detail the wild plant structures of mosses, fern, lichen and flowers which comprise the fabric of the greater whole. It seemed ironic that while uprooting ourselves, surrounded with packing cases, I was simultaneously recording in paint the rejuvenating return of spring to ancient landscape. The completed series was transmitted in 1991 by which time we were settled into our new home.

We moved about five miles to a house with wonderful space and light in the village of West Linton, still close to the Pentlands and the moorland plain. It's very difficult getting used to a new way of life, a new studio space, and this period of transition is clearly seen in such works as *Landscape Icon.* There's a reflected image of myself moving through a remembered landscape, seen against a dense interior with, on the extreme left, a strip of the view which had been my daily walk down to Carlops for the school bus – a painting of shifting scenes. There were times of real longing for the remoteness of Kittleyknowe – I missed the curlew, lapwing in the spring, and I celebrated our new home's location on the flight path of wild geese from reservoir to feeding grounds by including their straggling flight in such paintings as *Rites of Passage.* At that time I looked consciously again at earlier inspirations from the richness of Byzantine painting (fuelled by further visits to Russia and to Greece) to the pattern and formal two-dimensional quality of early Italian painting which I knew from UK galleries and in reproduction.

Images of our new surroundings eventually appeared in the work. I painted both the children – now almost young adults. Gemma is seen as a somewhat classical reflected head against the mirror full of Kittleyknowe snowy associations, while on the left edge the new view of the village makes its entry. Ben is also shown against a remembered view – an unnerving occurrence when the army held parachute practice exercises on nearby Auchencorth. At the time I painted the portrait the Gulf War was looming – one of Ben's contemporaries was to be drafted out there. I felt the image of Ben, a young man on the verge of adult life, appeared so vulnerable, with that threat of warfare and an undercurrent of potential danger.

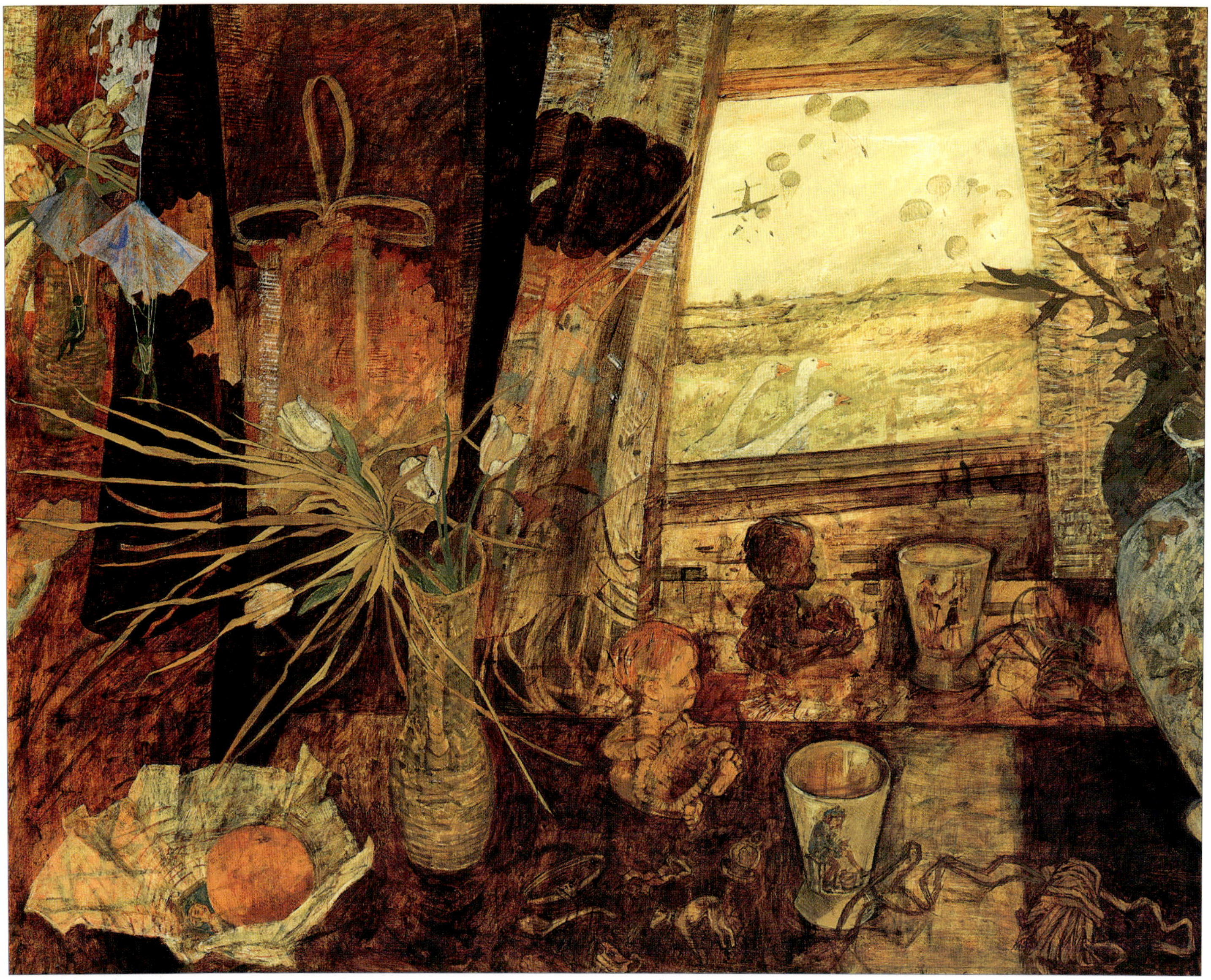

STRANGE OCCURRENCE AT AUCHENCORTH 1990. Oil on board. 30in. x 38in. Private Collection

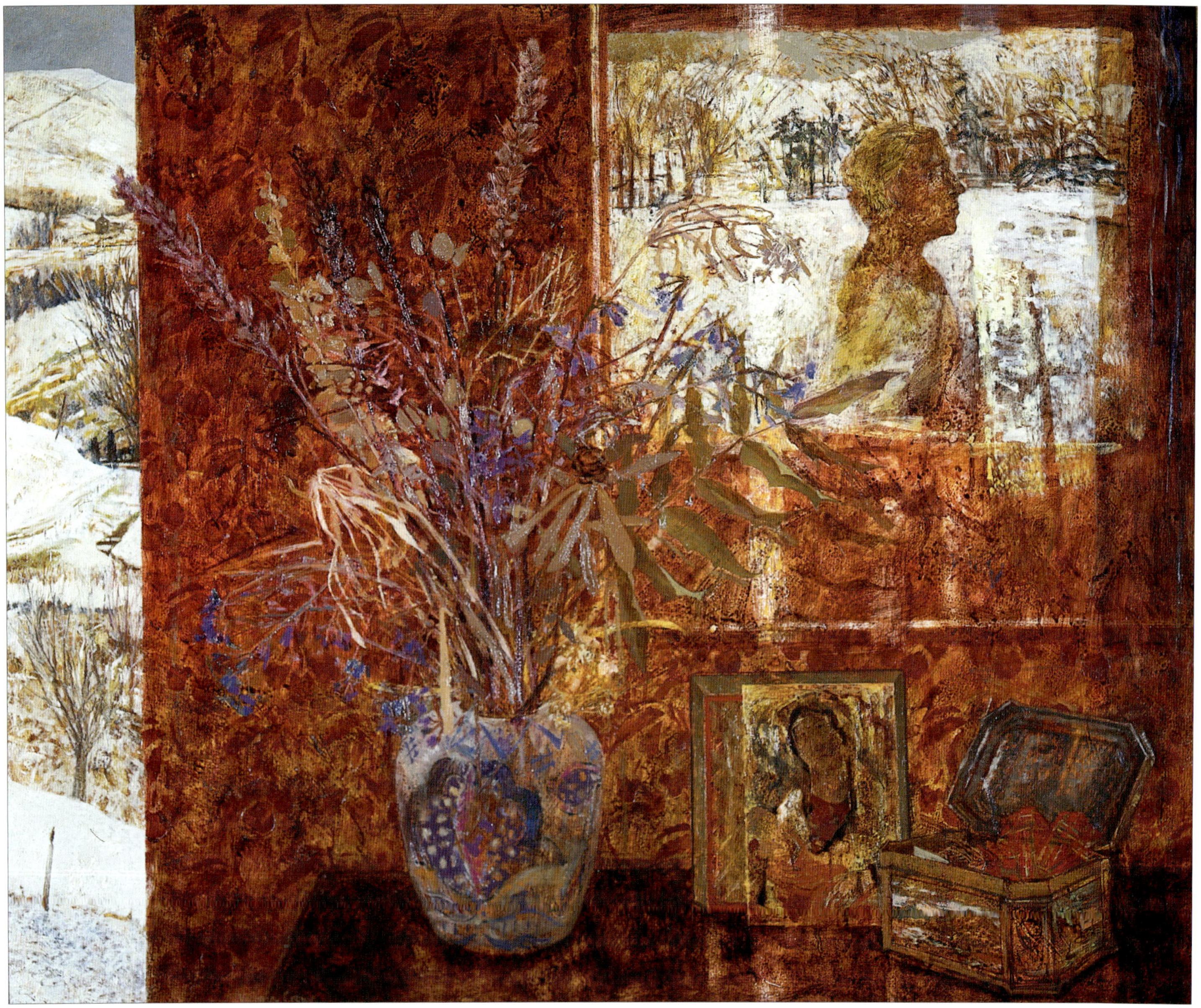

LANDSCAPE ICON 1991. Oil on board. 37½in. x 43½in. Private Collection

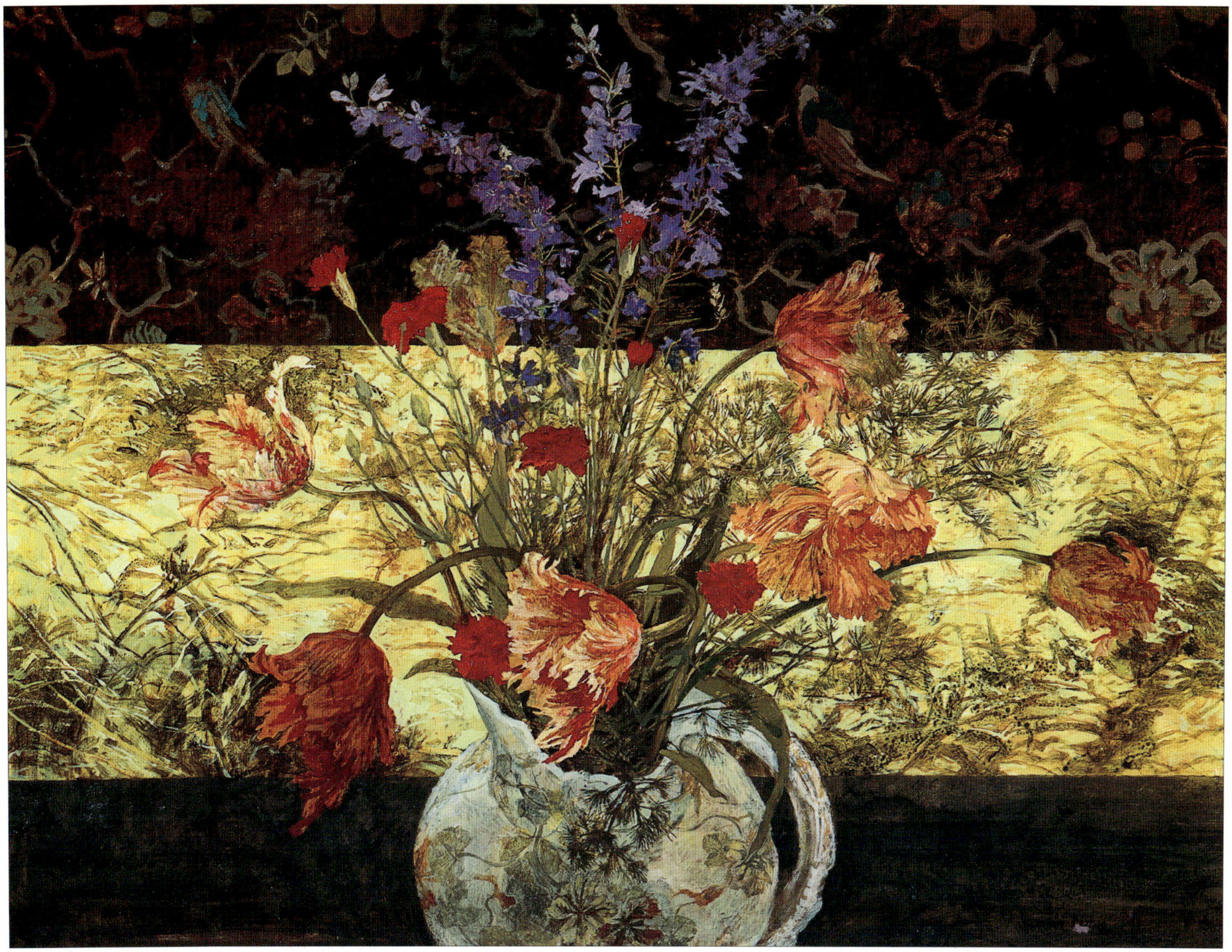

**AMAZING PARROT TULIPS WITH DRAWN BLIND** 1989. Oil on board. 28in. x 36in. Private Collection

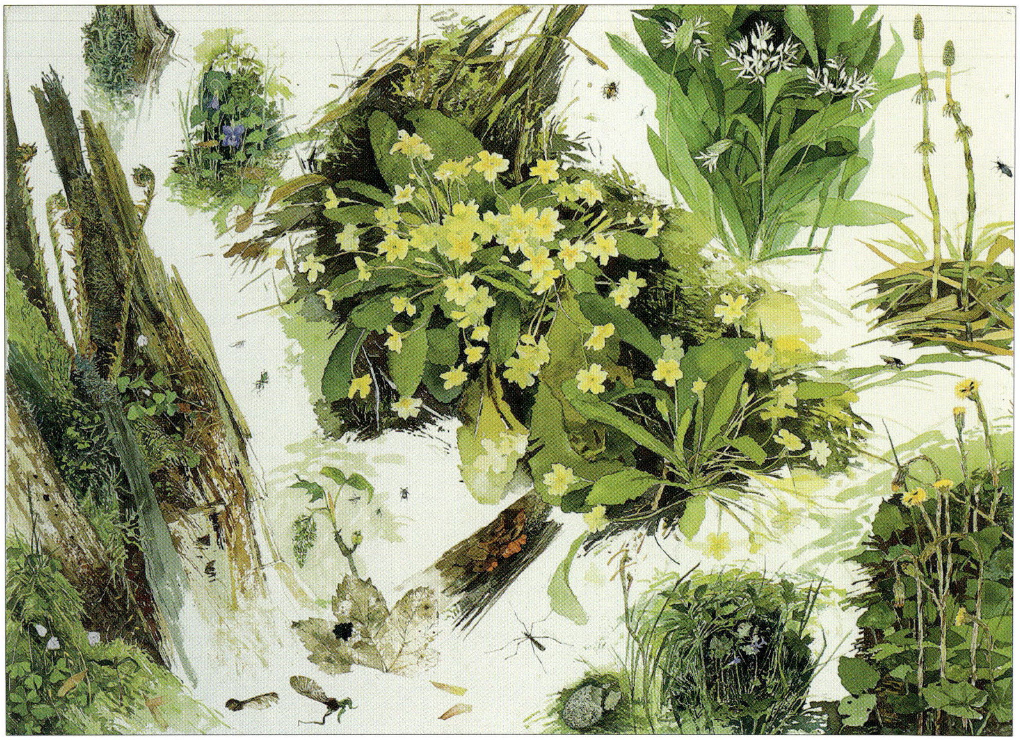

SPRING: FLOWERS IN A BORDERS WOOD. 1989. Watercolour. 22½in x 30in. Destroyed.
The making of the painting was the subject, one of four, in the series of half-hour programmes for 'Portrait of the Wild', produced by Grampian Television and broadcast in 1990. A limited edition reproduction 15in. x 20in. was produced in conjunction with the series.

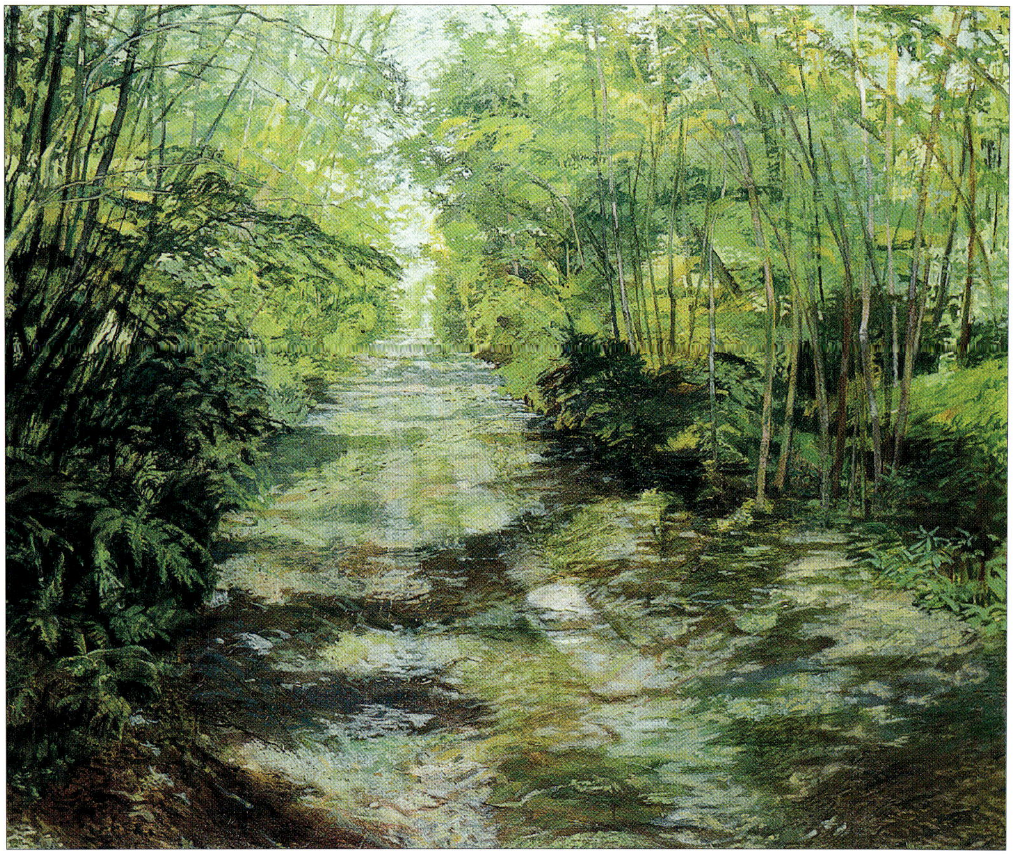

ENTRANCE TO ERCHLESS 1983. Oil on canvas. 38in. x 44in. Fleming -Wyfold Art Foundation

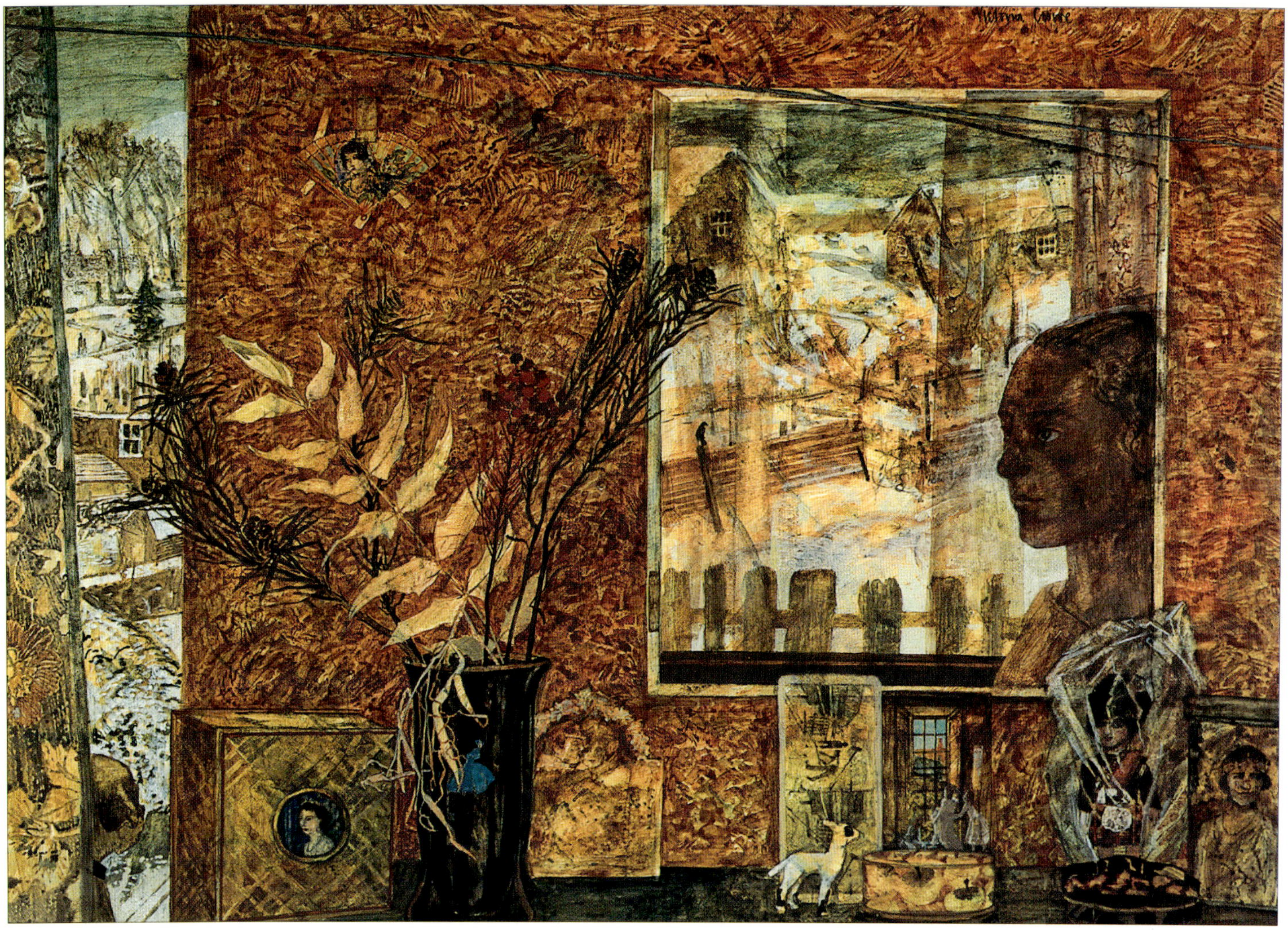

**TRANSITIONAL ARRANGEMENT** 1991 Watercolour. 22in. x 30in. Private Collection

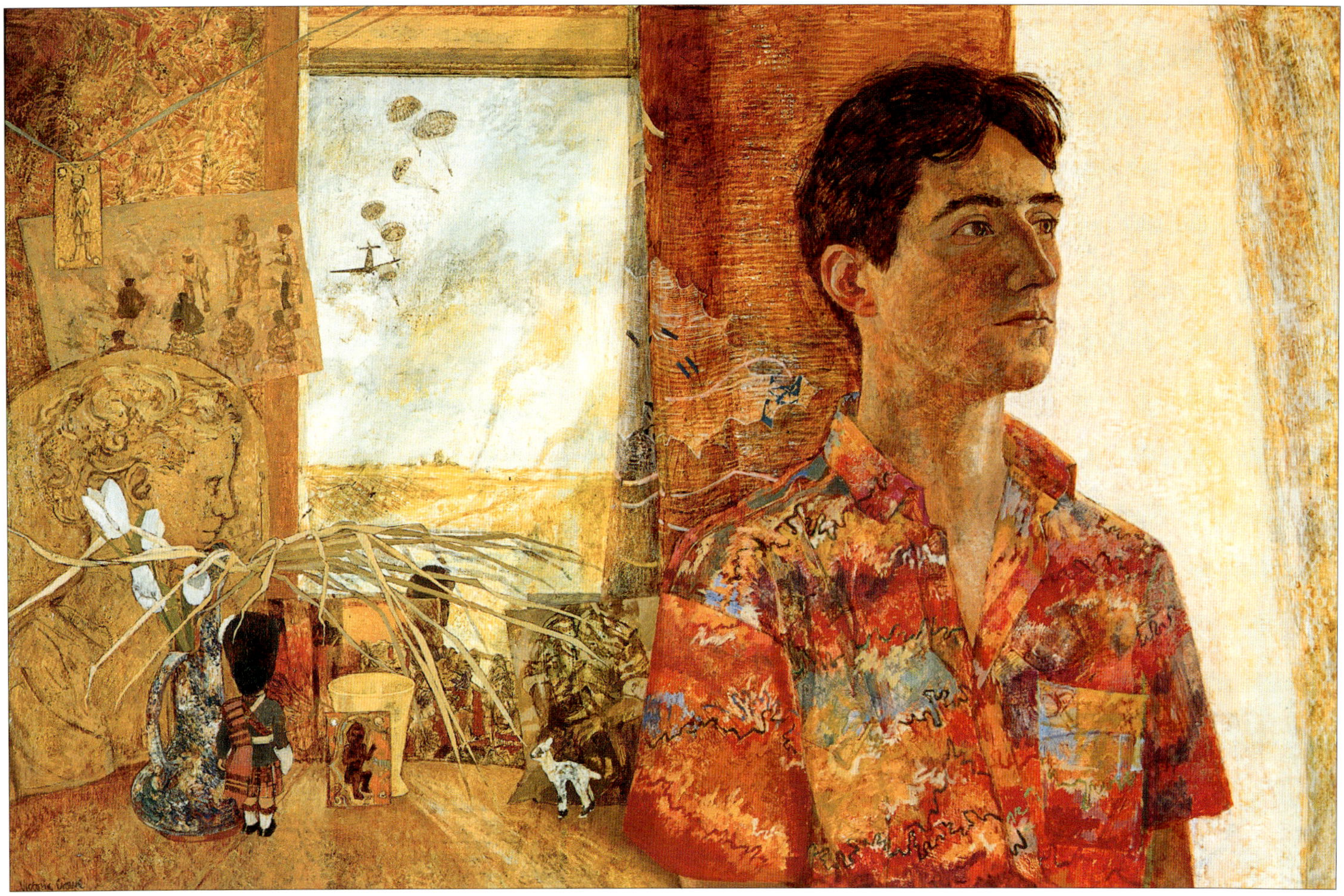

**HEROES AND VILLAINS** 1991. Oil on Board. 30in. x 43in. Collection of the Artist's Family

# 'THE EYE OF A FRIEND IS A TRUE MIRROR' – PORTRAITS

Throughout the '80s, my interest in portraiture had been growing. As a student, I had been interested in twentieth century figurative painting, particularly the single figures of Modigliani, Seurat, early Lucian Freud and the portrait work of my professor at the Royal College of Art, Carel Weight. His extraordinary paintings are full of psychological tension and an awareness of the essential 'aloneness' of every human being.

In the portrait of Kathleen Raine (overleaf) the artist uses imagery from Kathleen Raine's writings and excerpts from this poem

### THE MOMENT

Never, never again
This moment, never
These slow ripples
Across smooth water,
Never again these
Clouds white and grey
In sky sharp crystalline
Blue as the tern's cry
Shrill in light air
Salt from the ocean,
Sweet from flowers.

Here coincide
The long histories
Of forms recurrent
That meet at a point
And part in a moment,
The rapid waves
Of wind and water
And slower rhythm
Of rock weathering
And land sinking.

In teeming pools
The life cycle
Of brown weed
Is intersecting
The frequencies
Of diverse shells
Each with its variant
Arc or spiral
Spun from a point
In tone and semitone
Of formal octave.

Here come soaring
White gulls
Leisurely wheeling
In air over islands
Sea pinks and salt grass.
Gannet and eider
Curlew and cormorant
Each a differing
Pattern of ecstasy
Recurring at nodes
In an on-flowing current,
The perpetual species,
Repeated, renewed
By the will of joy
In eggs lodged safe
On perilous ledges.

The sun that rises
Upon one earth
Sets on another.
Swiftly the flowers
Are waxing and waning,
The tall yellow iris
Unfolds its corolla
As primroses wither,
Scrolls of fern
Unroll and midges
Dance for an hour
In the evening air,
The brown moth
From its pupa emerges
And the lark's bones
Fall apart in the grass.

The sun that rose
From the sea this morning
Will never return,
For the broadcast light
That brightens the leaves
And glances on water
Will travel tonight
On its long journey
Out of the universe,
Never this sun,
This world, and never
Again this watcher.

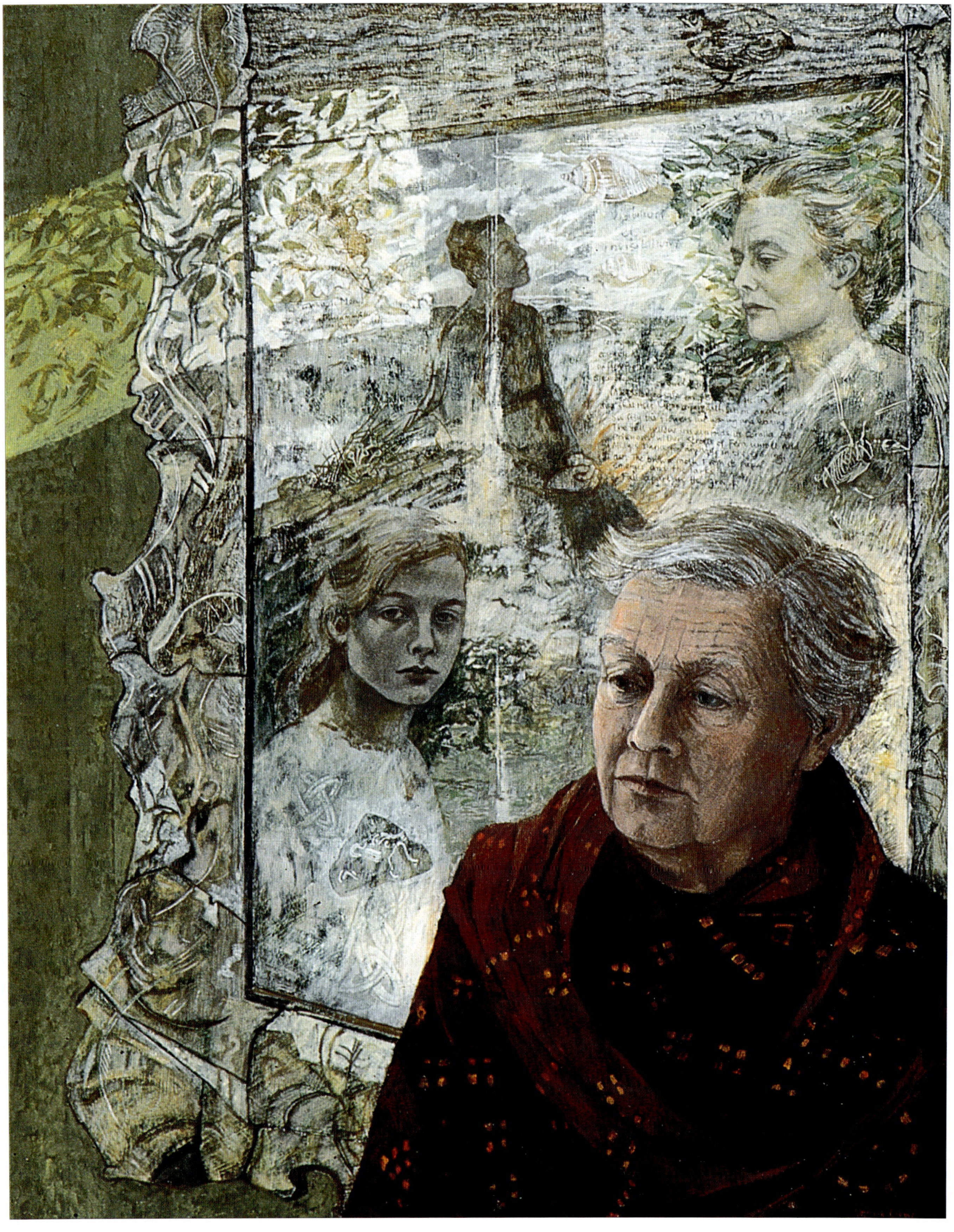

**KATHLEEN RAINE** 1986. Oil on board. 36in. x 28in. National Portrait Gallery, London

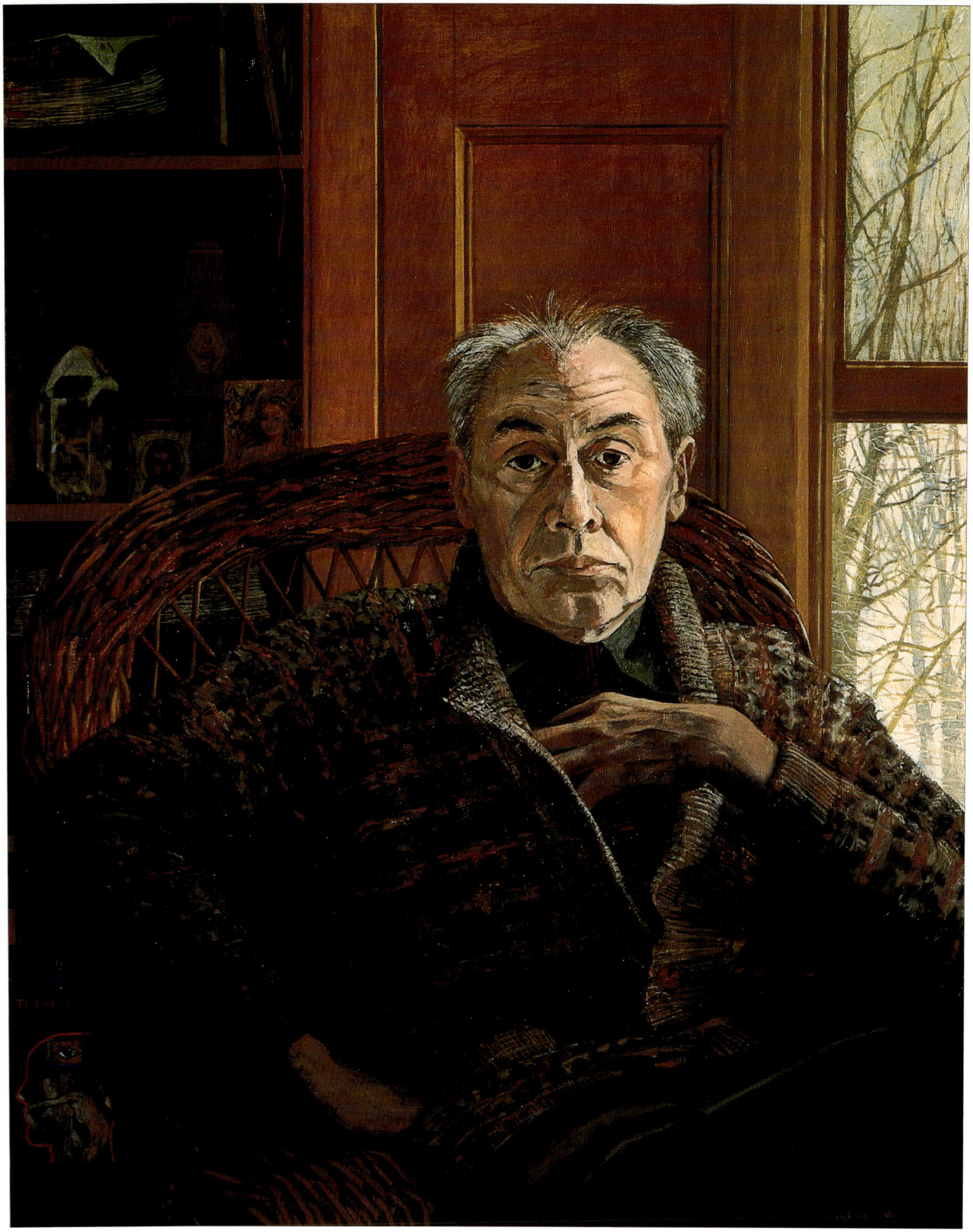

**R.D. LAING (1927-1989)** 1984. Oil on board. 36in. x 28in. Scottish National Portrait Gallery, Edinburgh

I loved the clarity of early Titian and Bronzino portraits and that powerful examination of the human condition we see in Rembrandt's lifelong series of self-portraits. Eric Newton's book *The Meaning of Beauty* suggests that each society produces its own image of human truth and therefore its own definition of beauty, and this made me look again at the magnificent Benin bronzes, Egyptian and early Greek sculpture.

I never cared for the fleeting expression, the 'swagger' gesture or the momentary smile.

I liked portraits which spoke of some kind of irrevocable image, a clear reflection of our human condition. Round about the time of our first travels to Greece I was reading John Fowles' book *The Magus,* and there is a wonderful description of a small carved head which has a sense of having survived all it has witnessed. The author's enigmatic fictional character, Conchis, shows the narrator a small, ancient cloth-wrapped head. It had neither predominantly male nor female characteristics; its nose had been broken, the hair simply parted. The face of this fragment had tremendous power – a timelessly intelligent smile, an acceptance and transcendence of all it had seen. The head is described not so much as having some aspect of divinity about it, but of having *known* divinity. Conchis says that on his deathbed he would like this little head near him – it's the last image of humanity he would want to see.

This idea seemed to echo what I had responded to in the icon paintings by Andrei Rublev which I had seen when I was a student travelling in Russia. These paintings, which despite, or because of, their restricted iconography produce images of a profound and lasting spirituality – transcendent of time and place, here and now – an eternal unchanging image of humankind. These notional ideas were a background to my interest in painting people. Portraits of Jenny Armstrong evolved through long knowing and observing and resolved themselves into almost archetypal images.

In the mid-'80s I met Winifred Rushforth at her ninety-fourth birthday party in Edinburgh, and I was immediately invited to one of her 'dream' groups. This was the beginning of an interest in dream and its imagery and the related symbolism of myth and archetype within a Jungian framework. Winifred's many groups, her wisdom and her healing abilities were legendary. The two portraits I did of her were tributes to this strong woman. The smaller version has a subtitle – a quote from Winifred herself – 'Age is not measured by the fragility of the body, but by the strength and creativity of the psyche'. The painting was purchased by the Scottish National Portrait Gallery and a commission to paint R.D. Laing, whose written work I had known since student days, followed. So, portraiture started out for me as a painted tribute to friends' ways of life, to their philosophy or to their commitment to their own life's work.

Throughout the last twenty years I have undertaken a limited number of commissioned portraits. Through this work I have come into contact with fascinating people from the worlds of politics, medicine, the arts and academia. Portrait painting, for me at least, involves much commitment and scrutiny and I also hope for a reciprocal

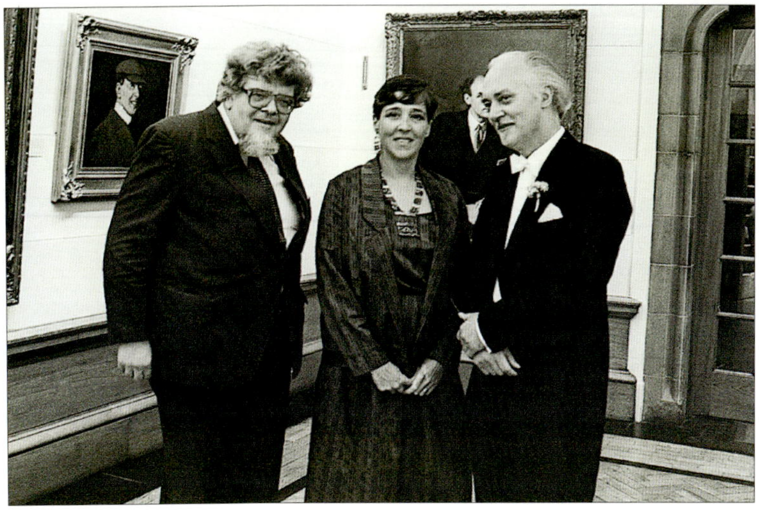

**JOHN OGDEN, VICTORIA CROWE AND RONALD STEVENSON** at the recital and presentation of his portrait at the Scottish National Portrait Gallery, 17 August 1984. Photograph © Antonia Reeve

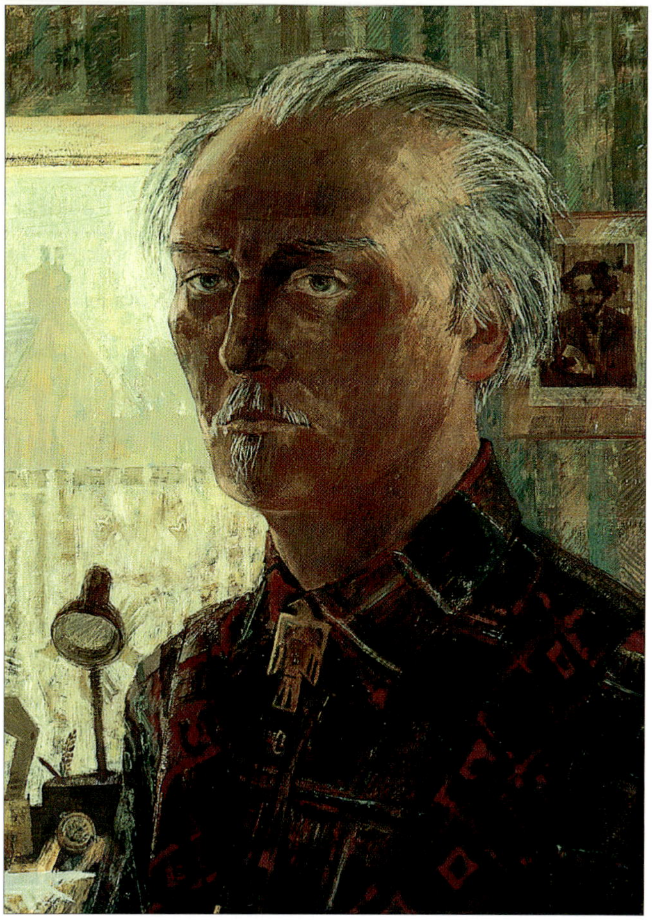

**RONALD STEVENSON (detail)** 1984. Oil on board. 28in. x 36in.
Scottish National Portrait Gallery, Edinburgh

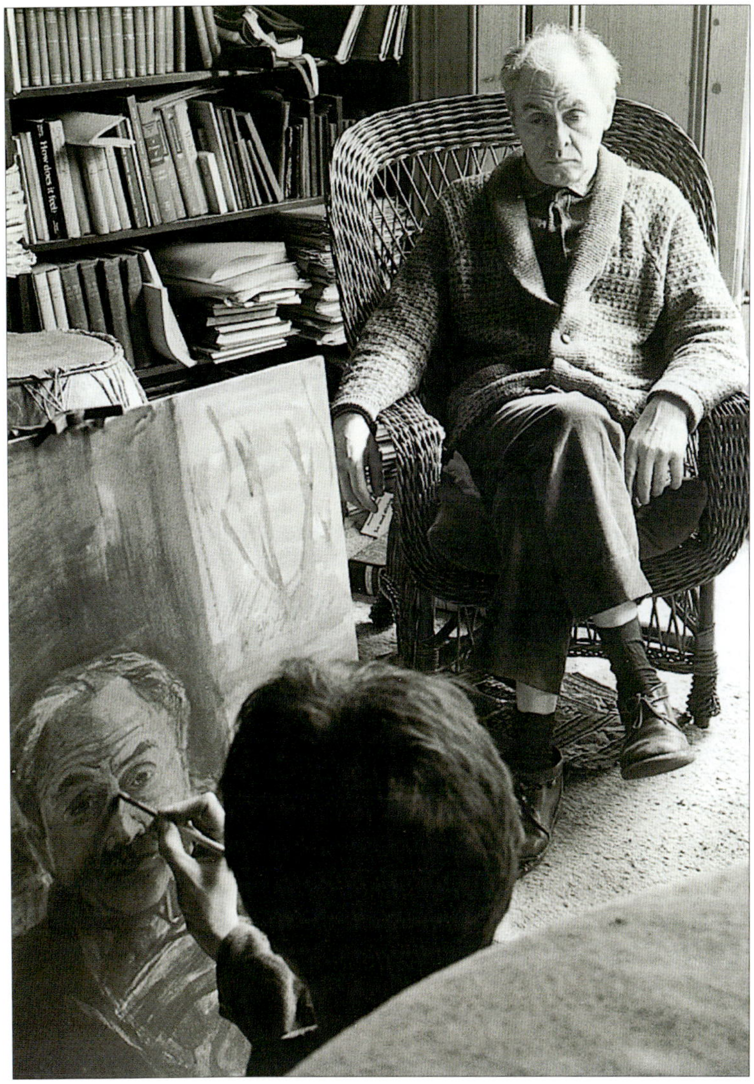

**VICTORIA CROWE PAINTING R.D. LAING** at Eton Road, London, 1984.
Photograph © Michael Walton

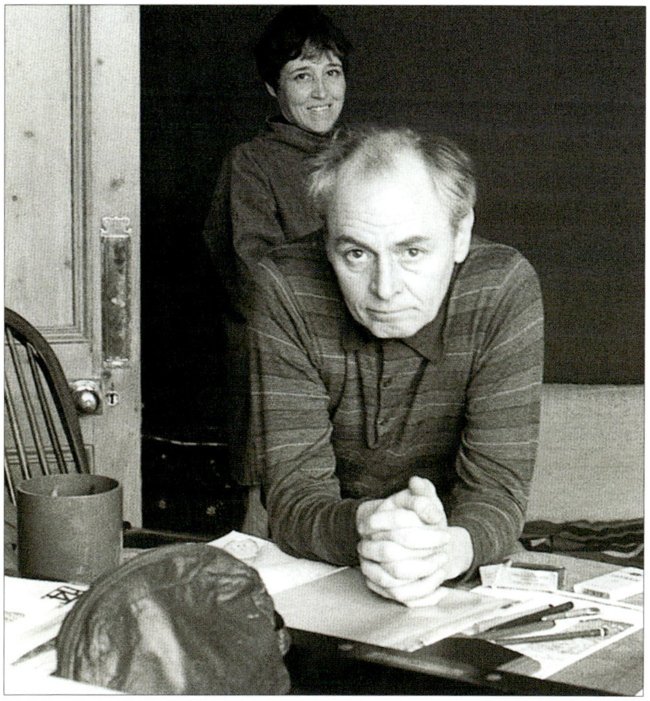

**VICTORIA CROWE AND R.D. LAING** during a break in sittings, at Eton Road, London, 1984. Photograph © Michael Walton

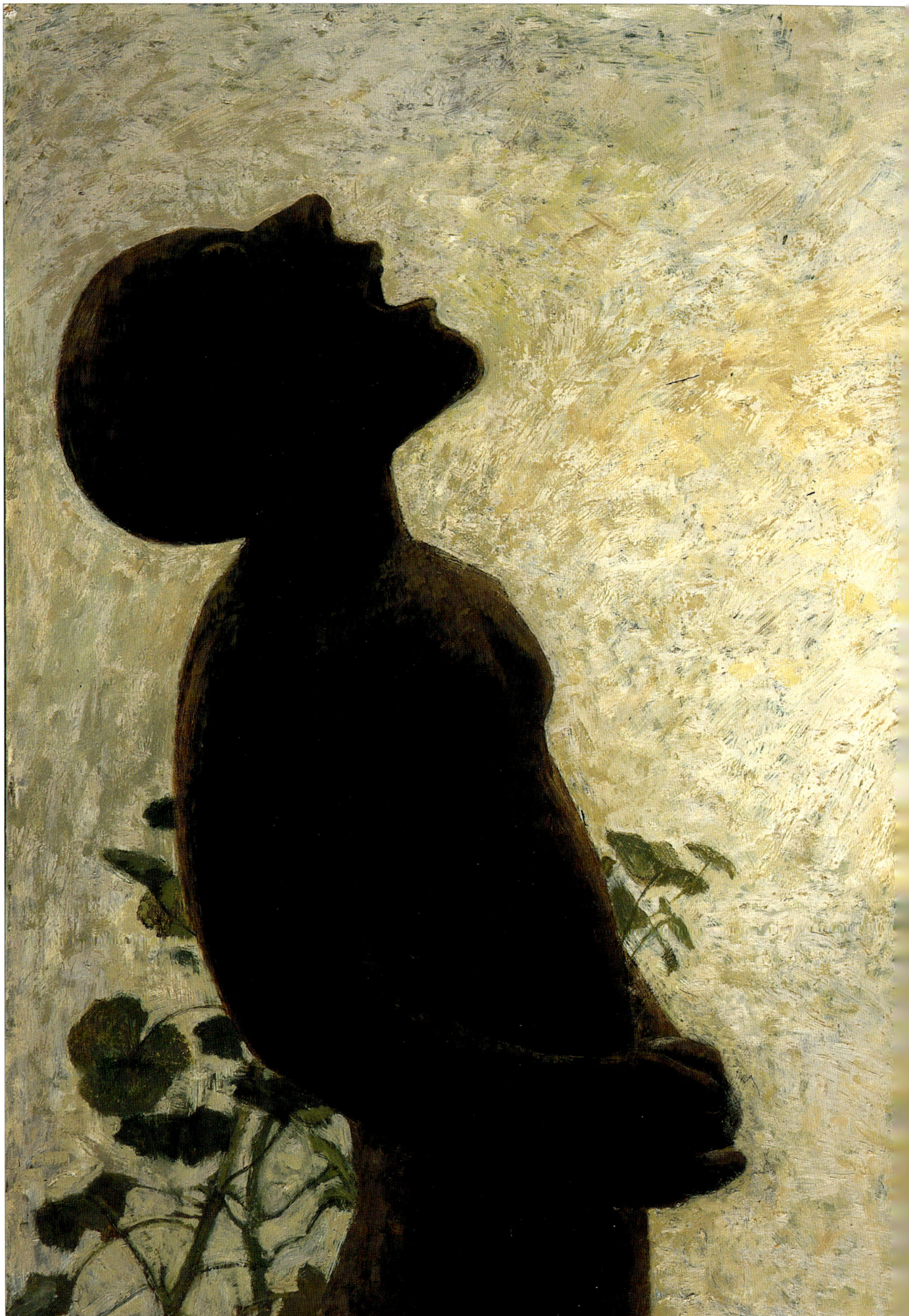

DR. WINIFRED RUSHFORTH
1982. Oil on board. 24in. x 28in.
Scottish National Portrait Gallery, Edinburgh

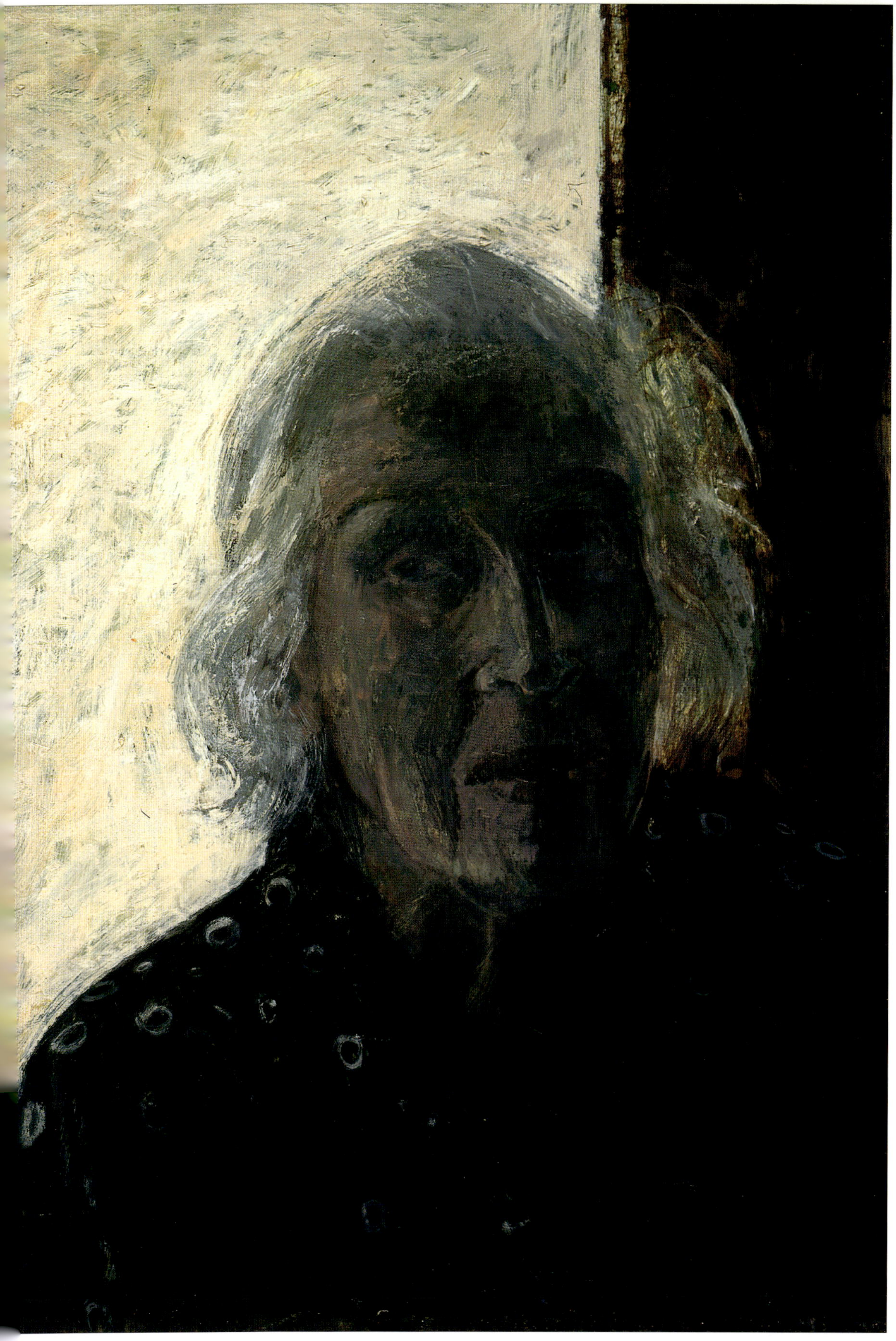

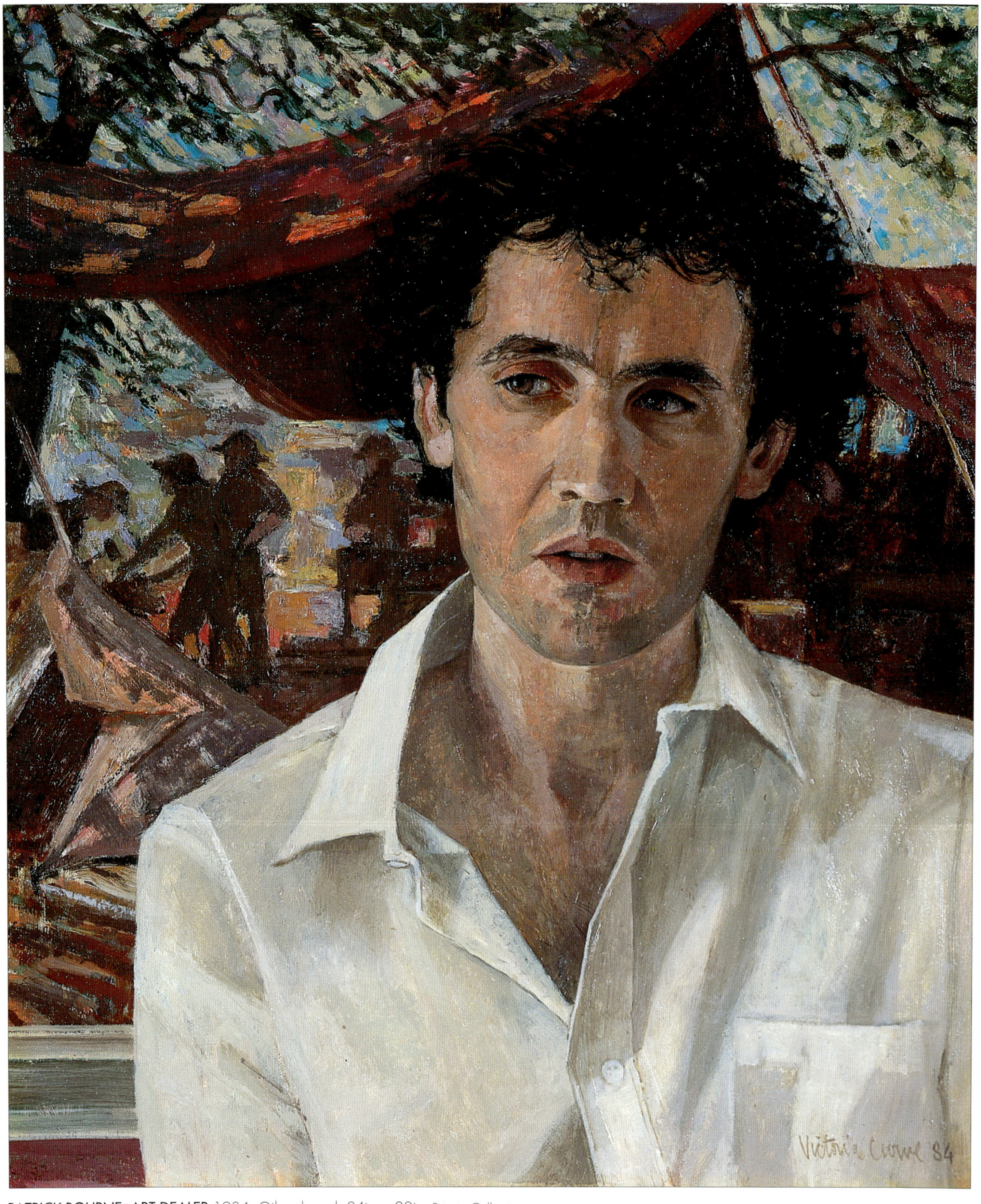

PATRICK BOURNE, ART DEALER 1984. Oil on board. 24in. x 20in. Private Collection

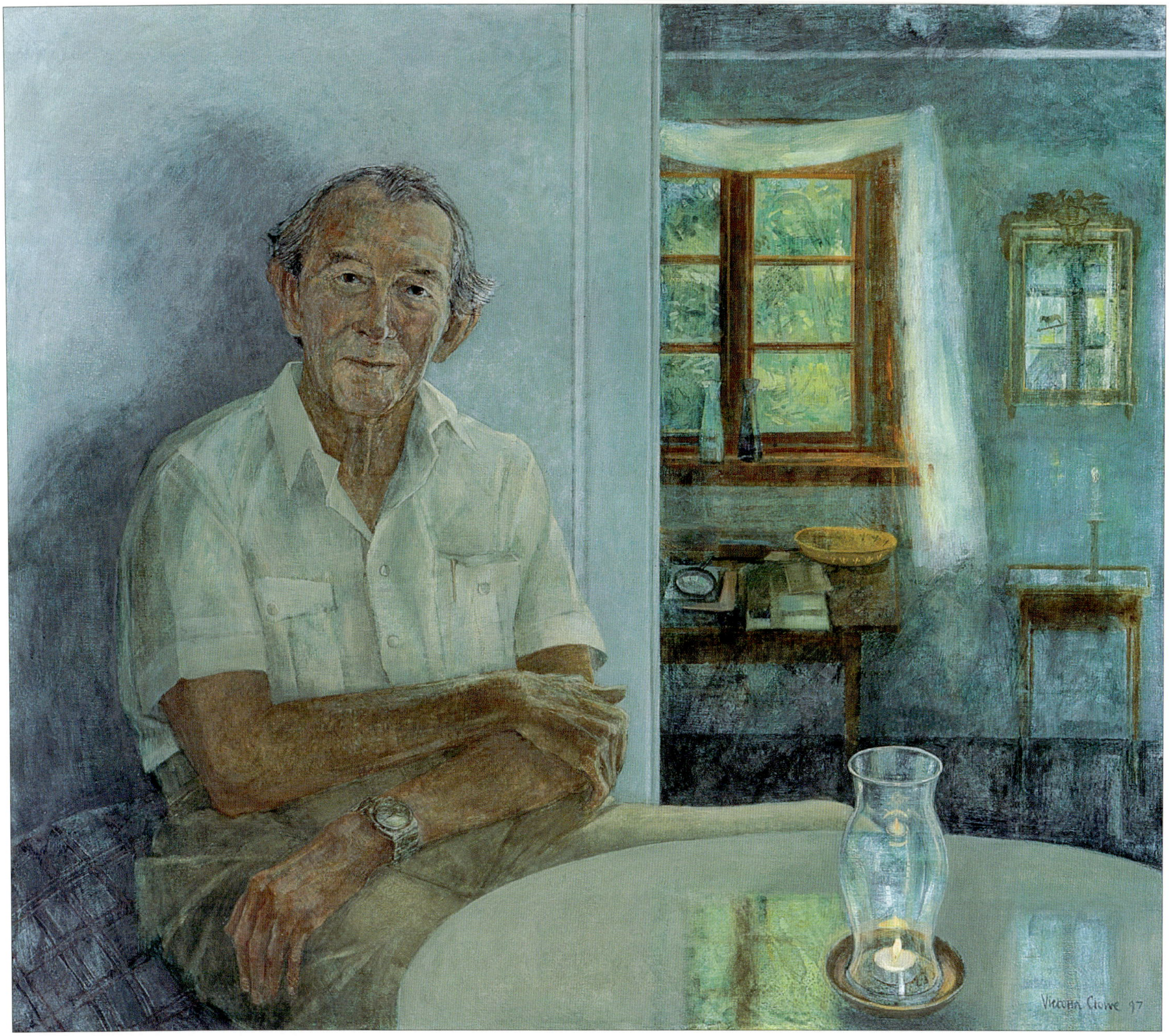

**OLE LIPPMANN, HEAD OF SOE DENMARK** 1997. Oil on board. 36in. x 40in.
Danish National Portrait Collection, Frederiksborg Castle

commitment by the sitter to be open and communicative! I meet and get to know the sitter before accepting the commission; it's a two way process and the chemistry has to be right. By the end of the sittings many lasting friendships have developed as I usually feel I have met and known these people on quite a deep level.

It's the balance between the personality of the sitter, a sense of what they are, revealed through work and conversation, and the objective reality of 'what they look like' that I find so intriguing. Portraiture contains the delights of rigorous drawing and observation with an imaginative response to the sitters – an opportunity to recreate them in my own terms and in accordance with my understanding of them. It's an

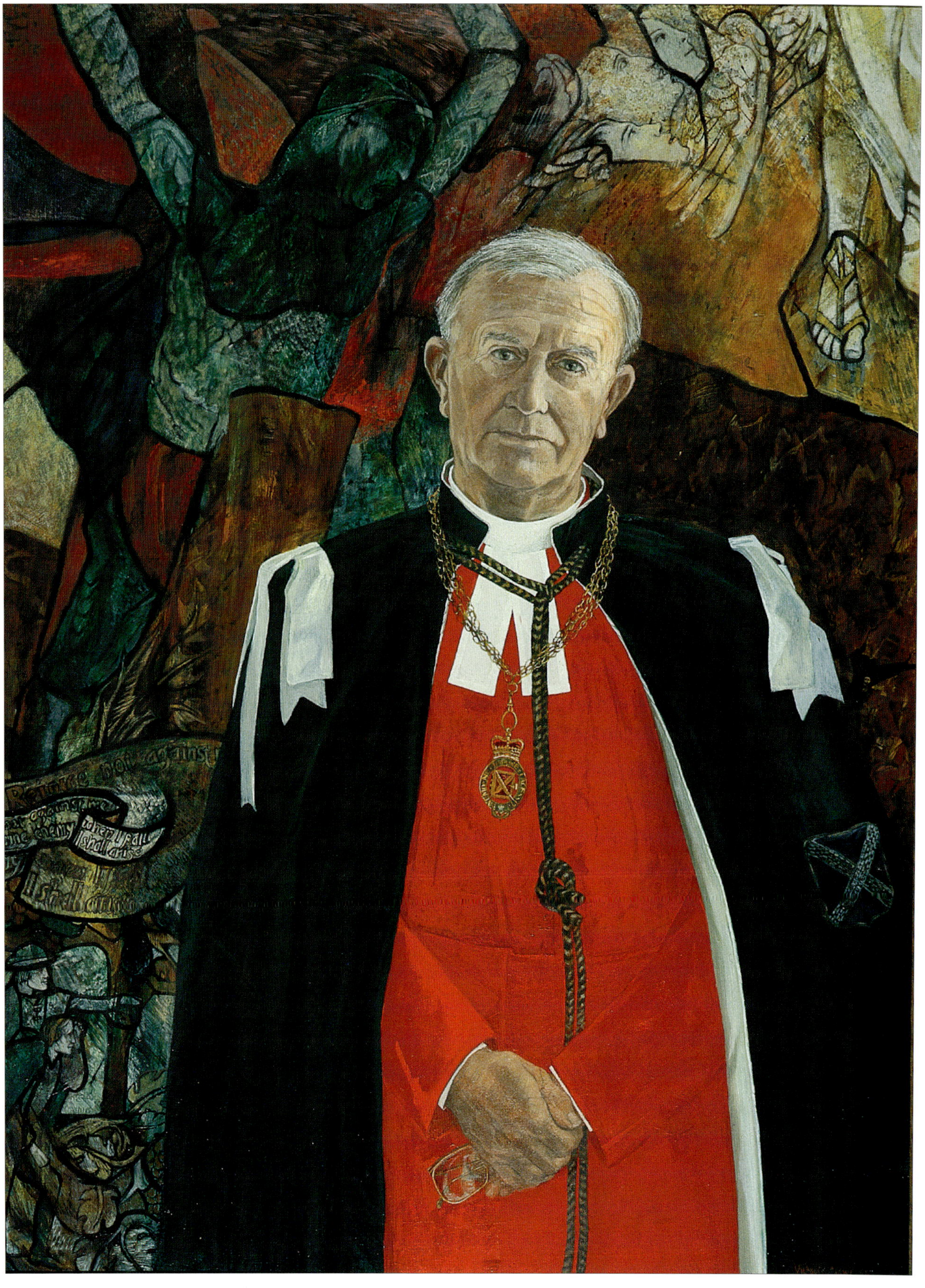

THE VERY REVEREND PROFESSOR JOHN McINTYRE 1986. Oil on board. 48in. x 38in. New College, Edinburgh

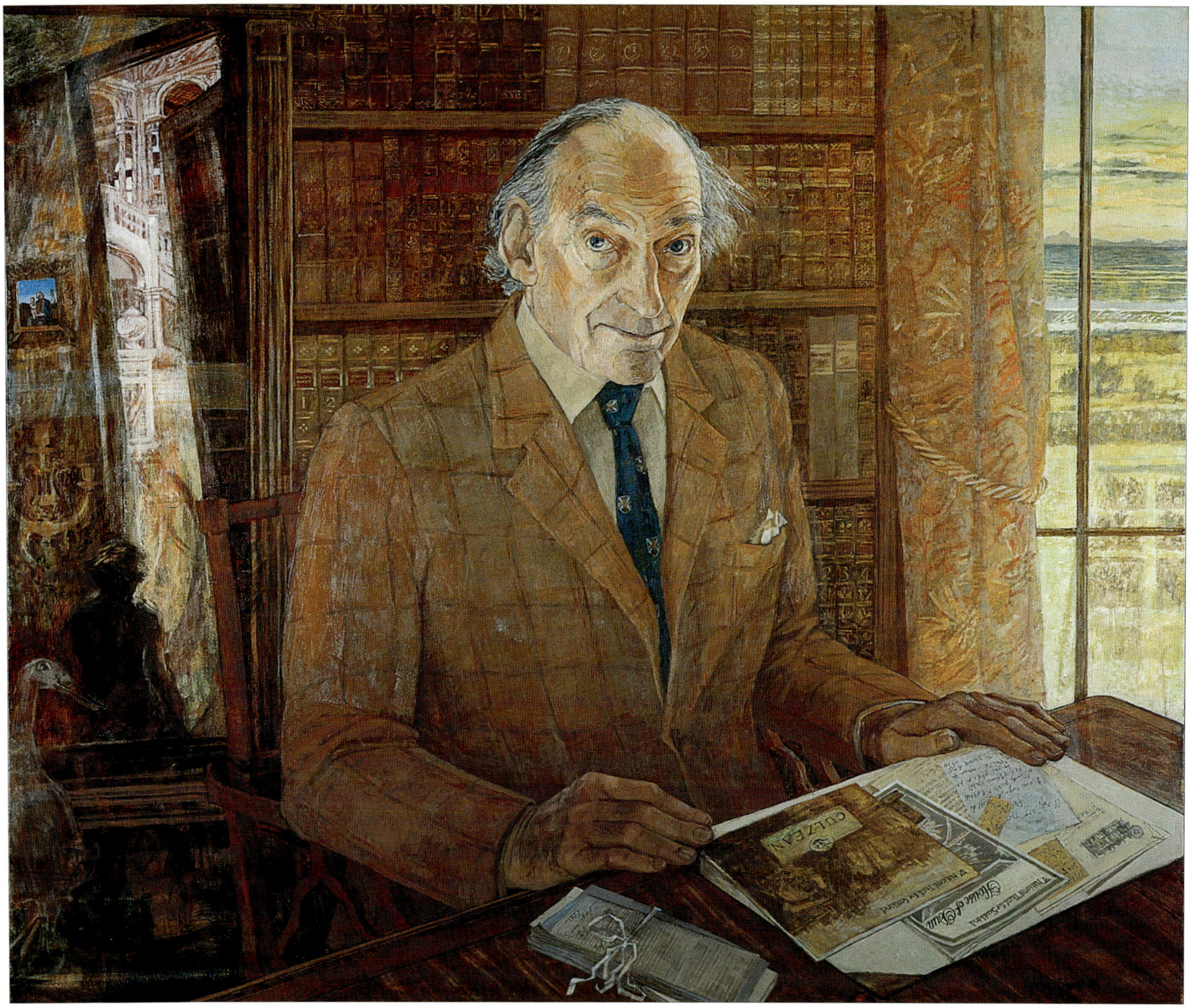

**THE EARL OF WEMYSS AND MARCH KT.** 1989. Oil on board. 38in. x 44in. The National Trust for Scotland

indulgence in a fascination for the uniqueness and separateness of each of us, and yet a point of contact – a way of touching another's life.

I have also painted many of my personal heroes and friends: Ronald Stevenson the composer, who lives in our village; Kathleen Raine the poet, whose work was a revelation to me; Dame Janet Vaughan, part of the first medical team into Belsen after the war; and the actor Graham Crowden, whom I painted for my son and who is now a close family friend.

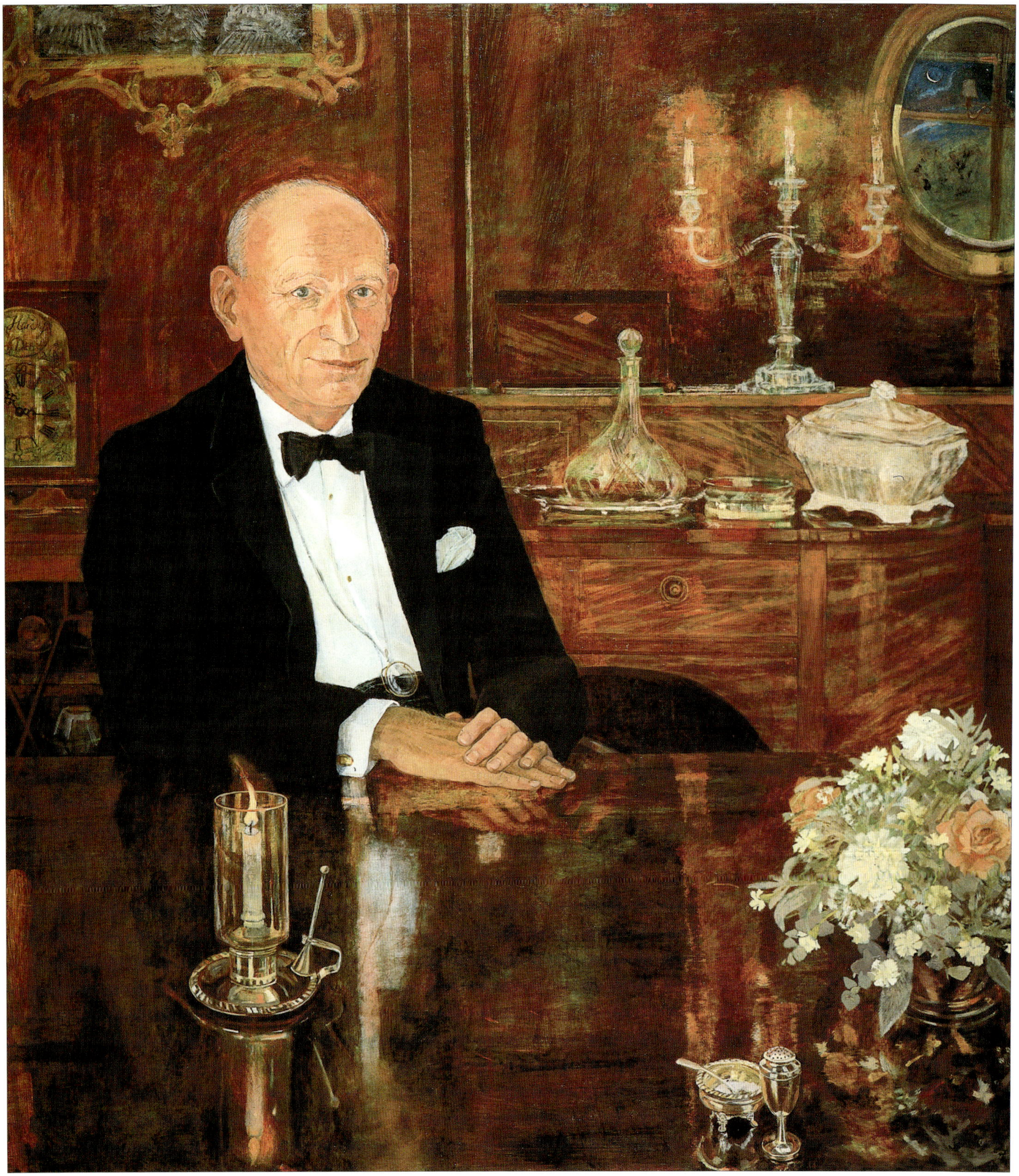

**PRINCIPAL, GEORGE MCNICOL** 1990/91. Oil on board. 44in. x 38in. Aberdeen University

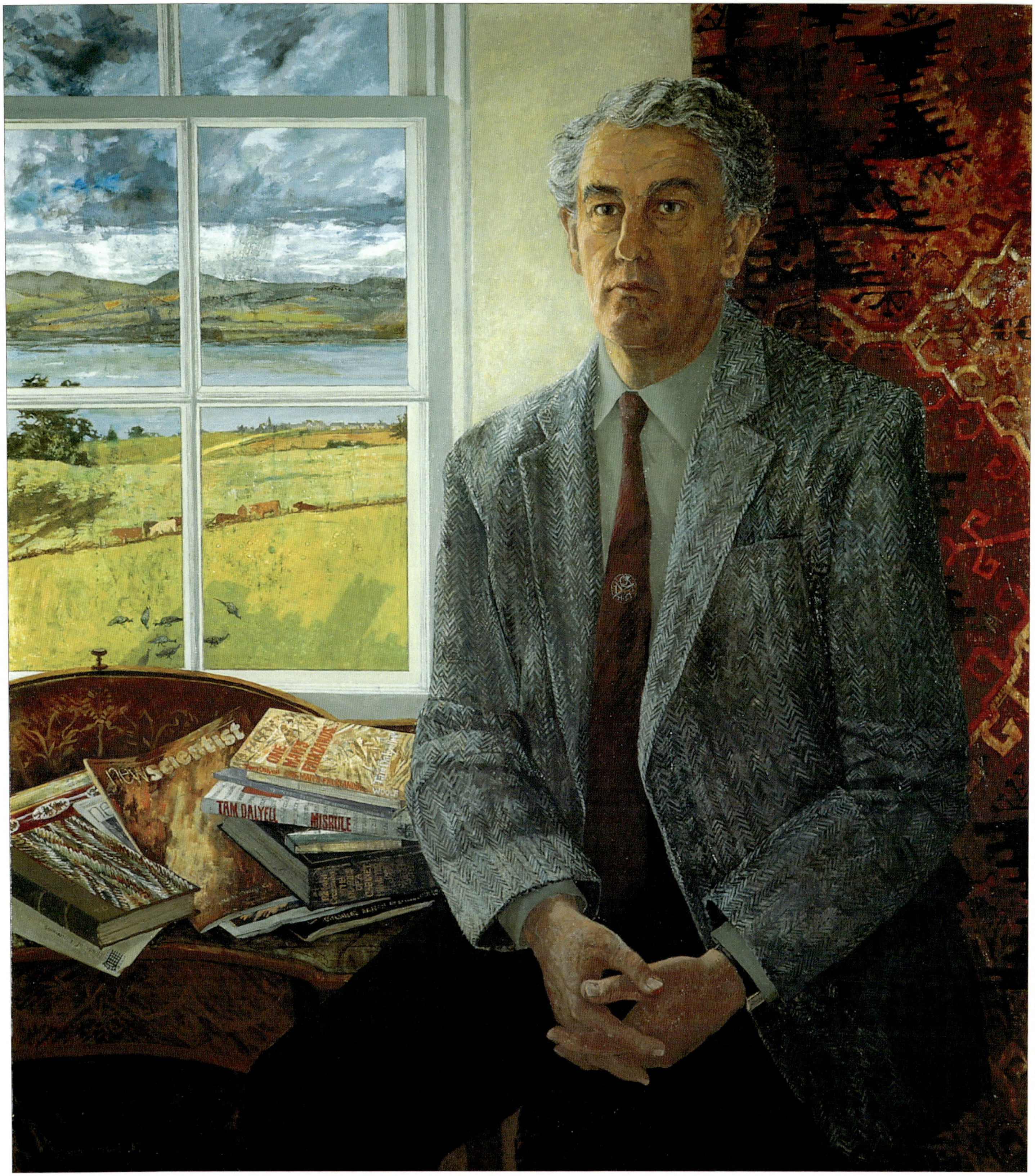


**TAM DALYELL, M.P.** 1987. Oil on board. 48in. x 40in. West Lothian District Council

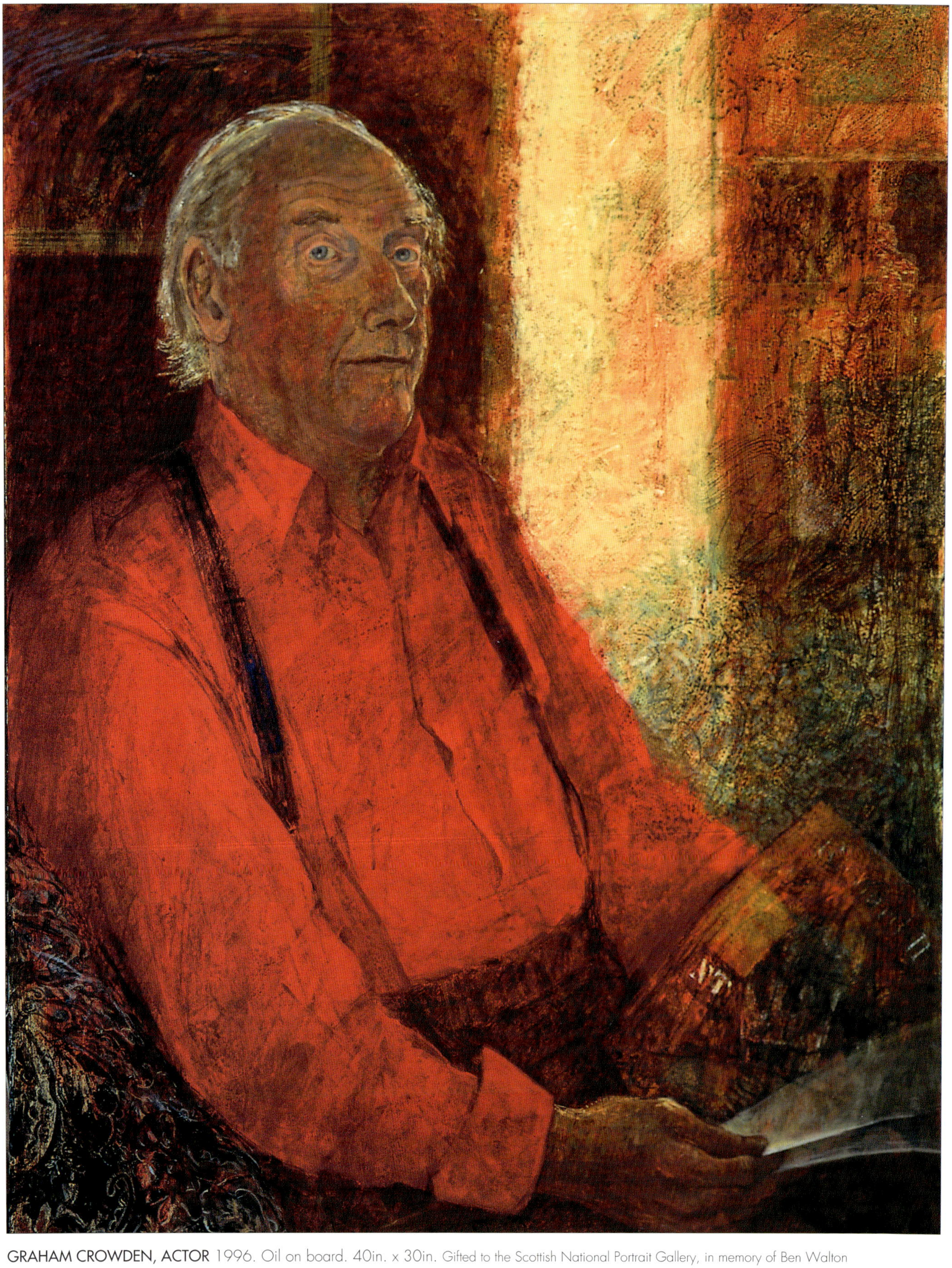

**GRAHAM CROWDEN, ACTOR** 1996. Oil on board. 40in. x 30in. Gifted to the Scottish National Portrait Gallery, in memory of Ben Walton

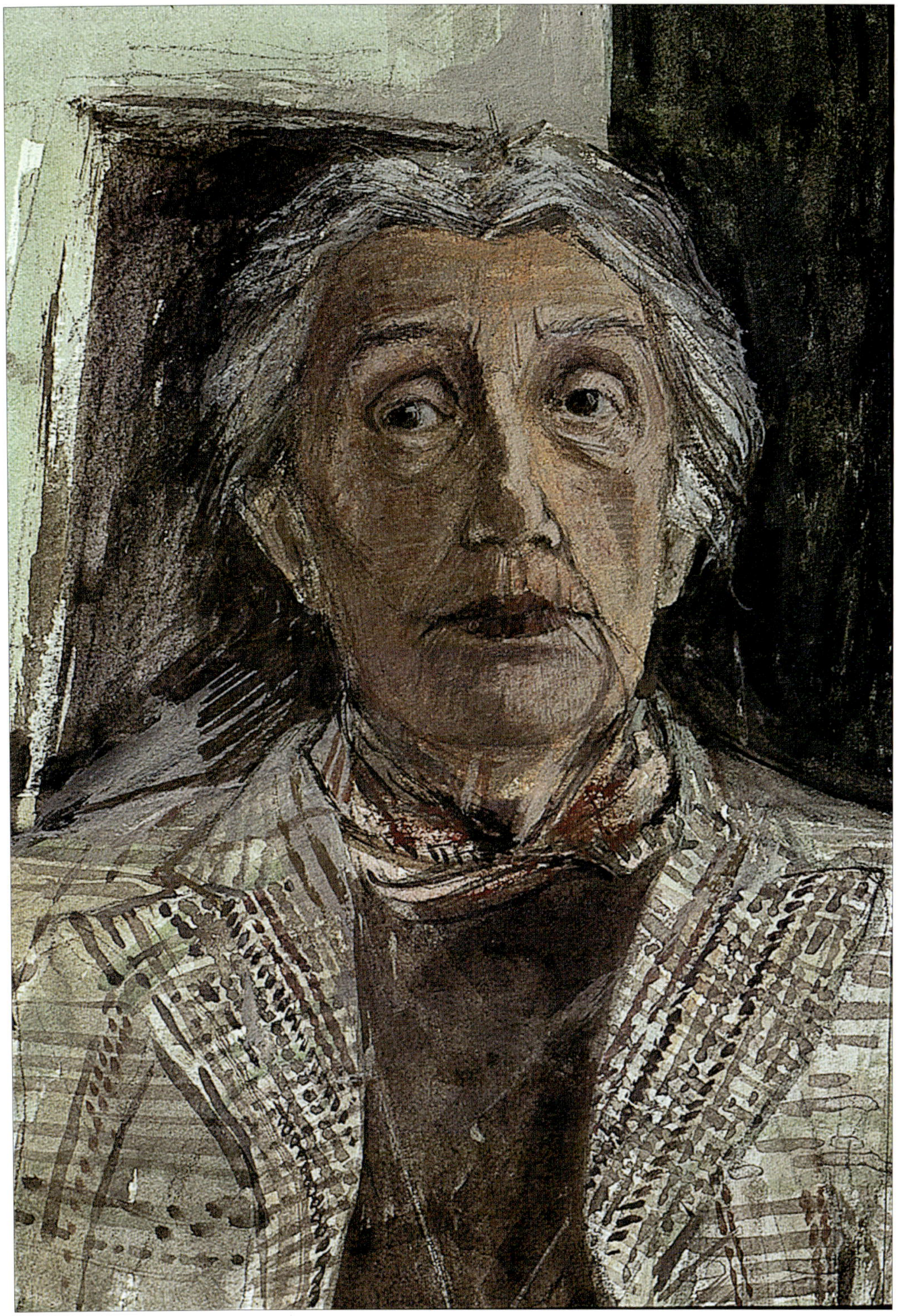

**DAME JANET VAUGHAN, F.R.S.** 1986. Watercolour with drawing. (Detail) 9in. x 5in.
Private Collection (Study for portrait in the collection of NPG London)

Janet Vaughan told me that she was sent into Germany in 1945, just before the war had ended. She went with the army as part of the medical team into Belsen. Her work was to develop a treatment for extreme cases of starvation, using a liquid form of concentrated protein. She told me 'the trouble was that the protein hydrolysate was such foul stuff to take, and I soon ran out of things to flavour it with. One day I had found some onions, which helped – frightful excitement! But when I had to give the solution intravenously they would cry out: *'Nicht crematorium!'* – you see, their previous companions had been injected with paraffin to make them burn better '.

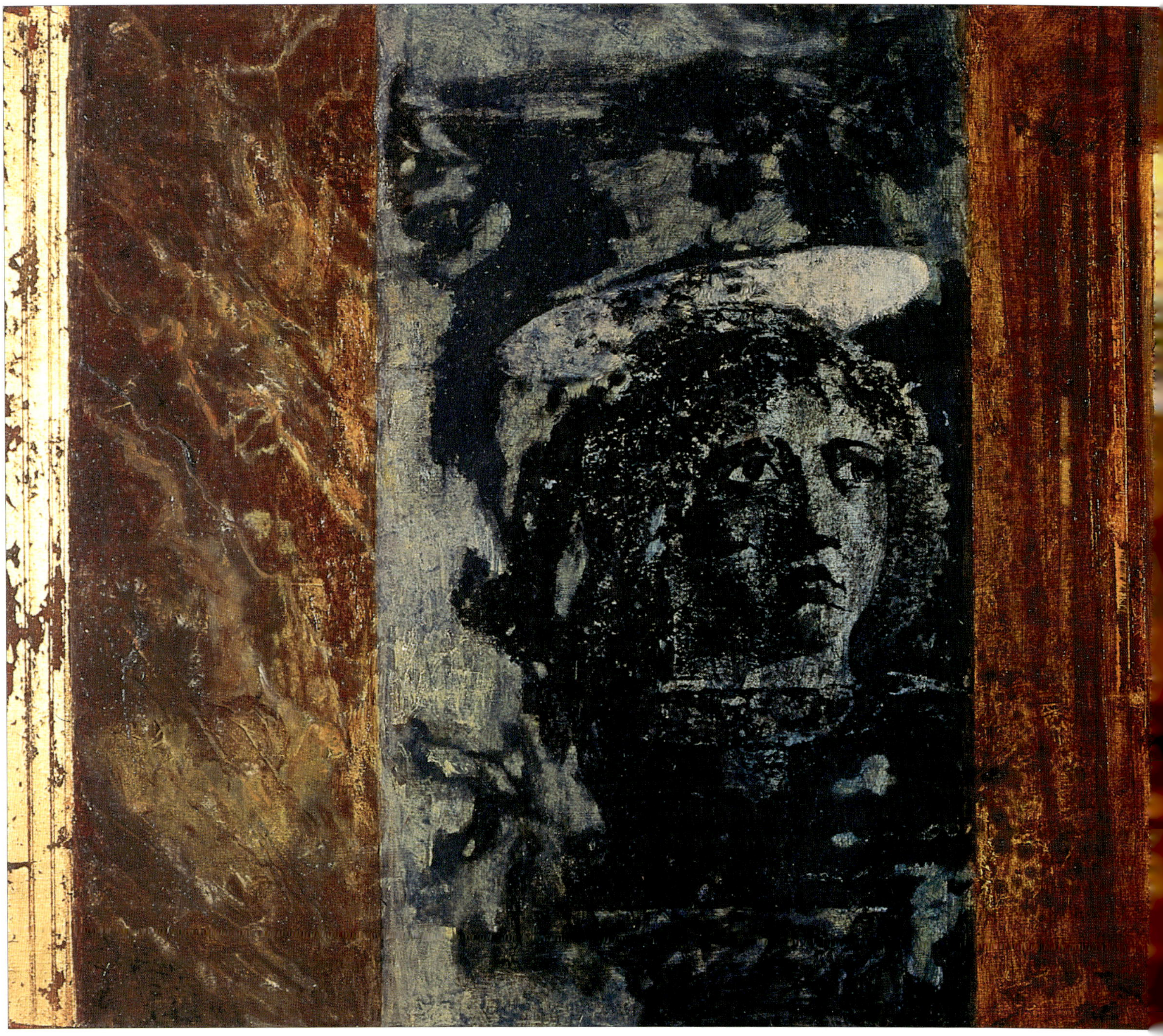

# THE IMPACT OF ITALY

**DIALOGUE IN SAN SEPULCRO**
1994. Oil on board with gold leaf.
14in. x 32in.
Private Collection

With the William Gillies Travel Bequest from the Royal Scottish Academy, and a term's sabbatical from the College, I eventually visited Italy in 1992.

This first visit was to Tuscany and Umbria; so many aspects delighted me – the landscape, architecture, interiors, paintings and artefacts of the region – the cultural clash of modern Italy with its past.

Italy reaffirmed my interest in unexpected juxtapositions. Compositional devices in

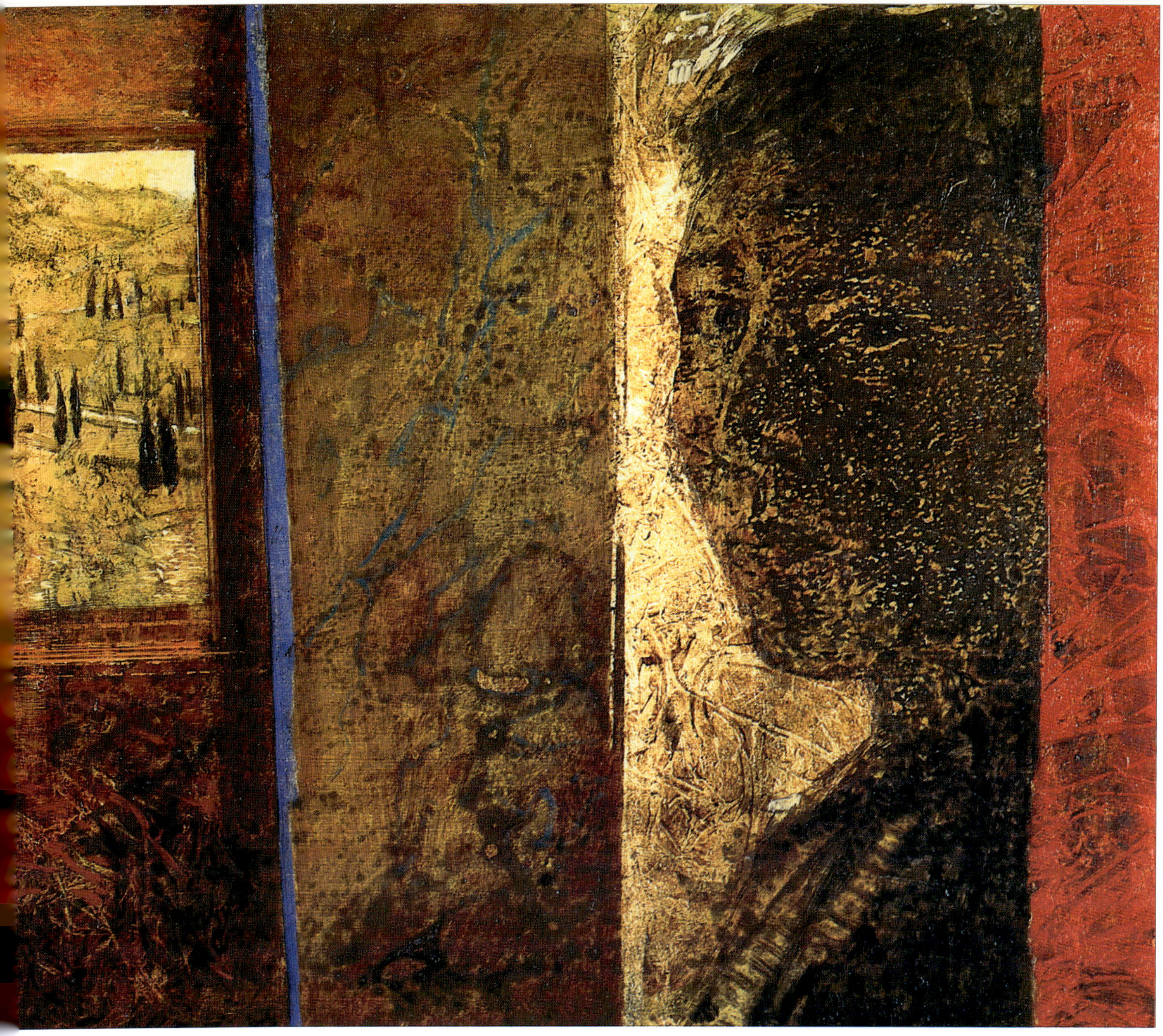

paintings stretched time and subverted logic. The physical reality in our world, glorified in later Renaissance art, was questioned in earlier works through symbolic use of colour, and compositional harmonies, resulting in static, highly contemplative images. Images which freed the imagination by refusing to tie us to physical reality. The profundity of the portraits affected me too – the intensity of the gaze, so present for that brief time.

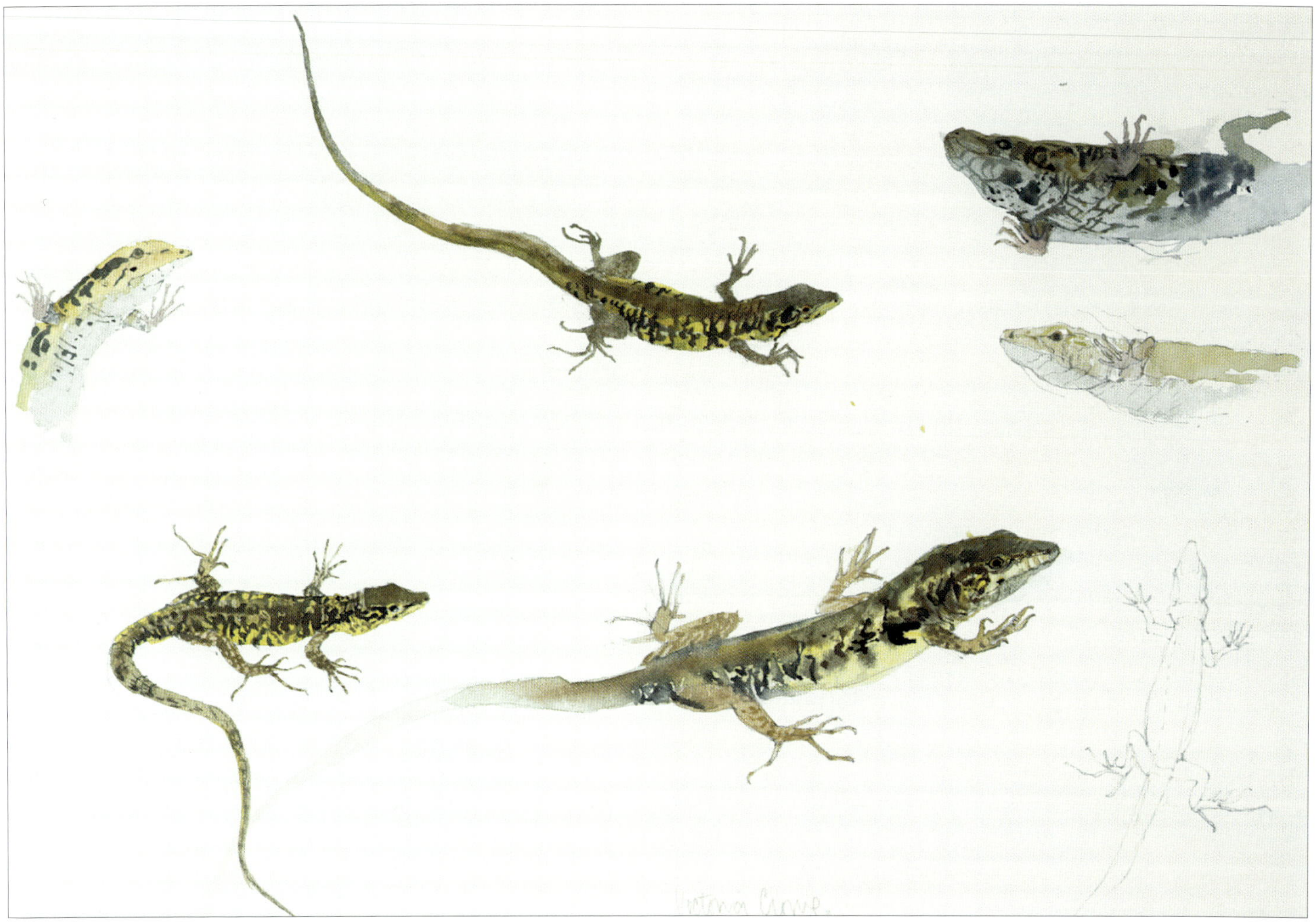

**STUDY OF A LIZARD, APECOLLE**
1993. Watercolour. 10in. x 14in.
Private Collection

The following diary extracts from that time show more vividly the full impact the country and its art made on me.

### Day 2: Florence

Today I stood in the cloisters of Santa Maria Novella – the wondrous Uccello 'flood' fresco three feet in front of me, and just about equidistant from my back, the rain poured down into the central square in torrents and this amazing, timeless and mysterious image was just *there* on its cold wall, with damp air all around it. Two great slabs of the arc and a corridor almost to infinity, shadows of trees and men thrown on to one side, incessant perspective of ladders, receding figures and forms – Stanley Spencer *must* have seen this ... A figure – Noah? – is framed in the perspective of a window, a dead baby among the drowned figures and a scavenging crow ... The lower fresco – drunkenness of Noah ravaged by the 1966 floods – is dominated for me by the central figure seen in profile against the vine trellis – pale translucent green on the leaves, grapes a burnt orange and the blue purple background. There's a line of deep tonal contrast around the head. The fading and weathering has led to a combining of different stylistic moods – resulting in great power and mystery – a kind of contradiction of reality which provokes and intrigues.

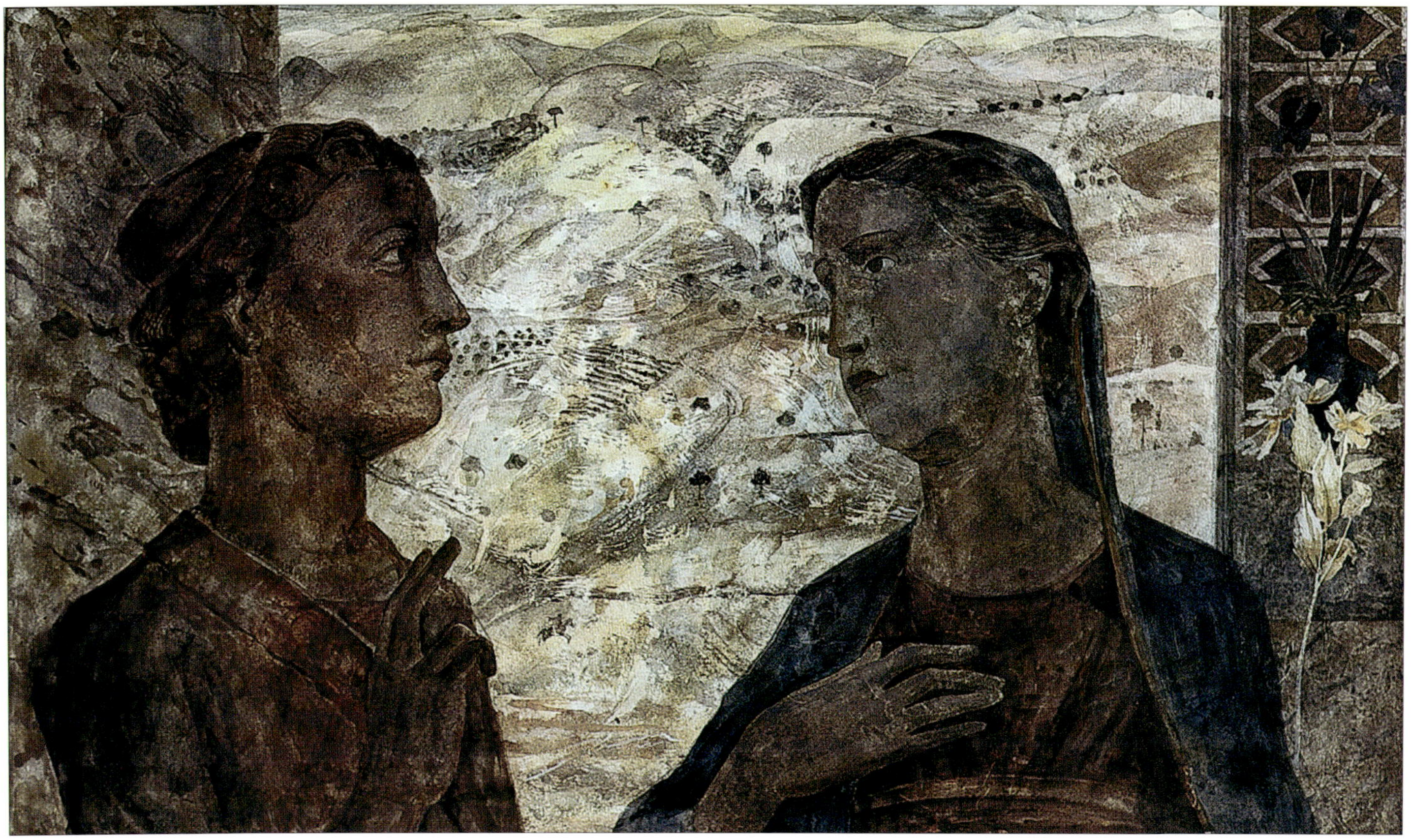

DIALOGUE IN VOLTERRA
1993. Watercolour. 20in. x 32in.
Private Collection

### Day 4: S. Trinita

I drew three crucifixes here (totally different realities) – one a really beautiful glowing crucifix with painted figure, early 1200s (said to be miraculous and to have bowed – I can well believe it!). Then an almost erotic smoothly carved one, lit from beneath its toes and casting huge distorting shadows on to the arch above, and losing itself in places in the black and white streaked marble behind it. The third was an early fourteenth century carved wooden figure against a red material background, dimly lit and encased behind glass. The background was hung with a vast array of votive hearts. They looked like great gold pincushions with lace surrounds, or metal with filigree decoration – some fat, pale and dusty, some gleaming sleekly. Also, one large votive hand and part of an arm – an echo of Byzantium in sophisticated Florence? Just outside I saw some superb Armani suits – 18,600 lire, about £900?

### Santa Croce

Wonderfully deserted and devoid of groups!

The Giottos were beautiful, much has been lost, but still that power and monumentality from what remains. Some interesting mixes of images here, from pale, undefined and patched fresco, to brilliant stained glass, to the pure kitsch of the electric light bulbs around the halo of the painted plaster virgin in the side chapel.

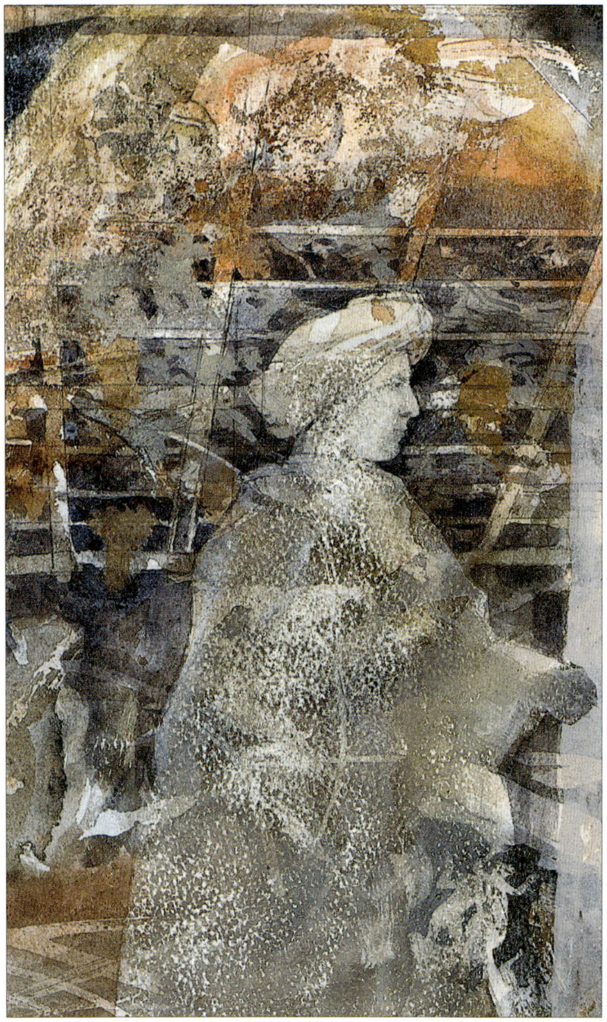

STUDY FROM THE CLOISTRE VERDE
1992. Watercolour. 12¼ in. x 7in.
Private Collection

## Day 5: Florence

Strangest thing of all was the Cappella dei Principi; great marbled octagonal mausoleum, with tombs around the walls, but because it was Good Friday, a huge array of candles and white flowers, great tubs of hydrangea, orange blossom, white roses and a curious collection of sprouting shoots, all white and limp like little pots of thick flowing hair. I was told that it was mustard seed sprouts (like mustard and cress) and it was forced in the dark and then brought out on Good Friday to represent the body of Christ lying under the ground for three days.

## Day 6: Siena

While walking around Siena all the Palio and contrada business starts to impinge. I keep seeing contrada badges and squares with their particular fountain and emblem – she-wolf, porcupine, eagle, owl, ram, etc. These respective flags are everywhere and one sees in card shops and vendors' stalls references to them on ceramic tiles and coloured postcards of the contrada costumes – like their medieval counterparts, some wonderful legs in quartered, striped and patterned stockings.

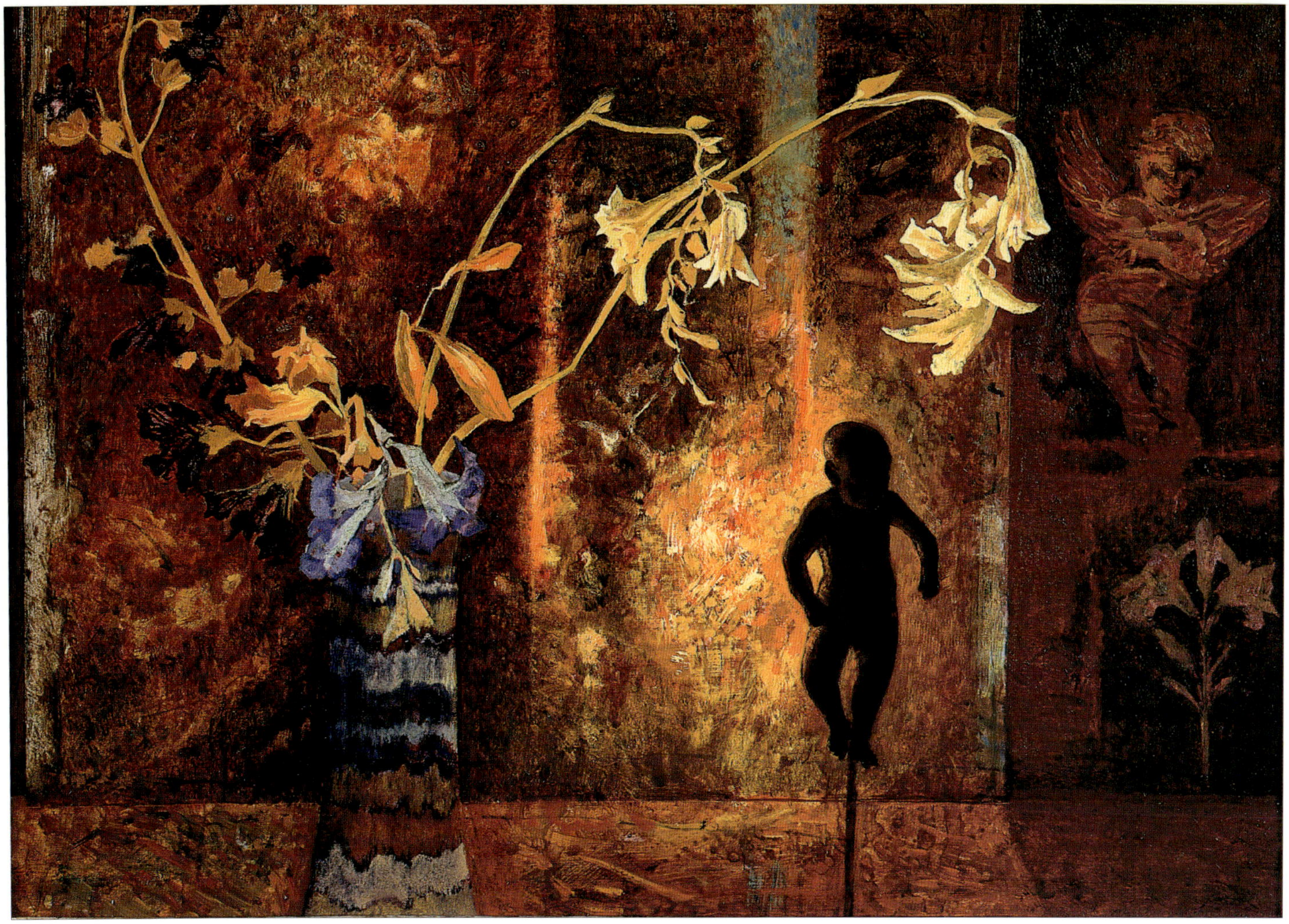

TRANSFIGURED
1993. Oil on board. 11in. x 15in.
Private Collection

### Day 7: Siena

Sunday: Today I saw people carrying olive branches back from church – everyone was out in the sunshine – a lovely feeling, families strolling round, palm and olive branches waving. I heard the beat of drums and a procession emerged – one of the contrada houses. There were about a dozen youths and older men in costume with great flags and those amazing leggings, some in armour and a couple on horseback. One guy had a gold and green brocade hat – a smaller version of Niccolo da Tolentino's red and gold one in the Uccello *Battle of San Romano*. I followed the group along to San Domenico where one gets that first glimpse of Siena – a medieval city with winding terracotta roofs leading up to the black and white tower and the duomo beyond.

A very haunting experience because these twentieth century men in costume assembled against an unchanged backdrop, their horses snorting and jostling. I could have been watching a mixture of fourteenth century events; it could really have been like that – a six hundred year old view ...

### Day 8: Siena: the duomo

Some of the most interesting things were the pavements – marble sgraffito filled with pitch and in some cases with coloured marbles – religious and mythical scenes with

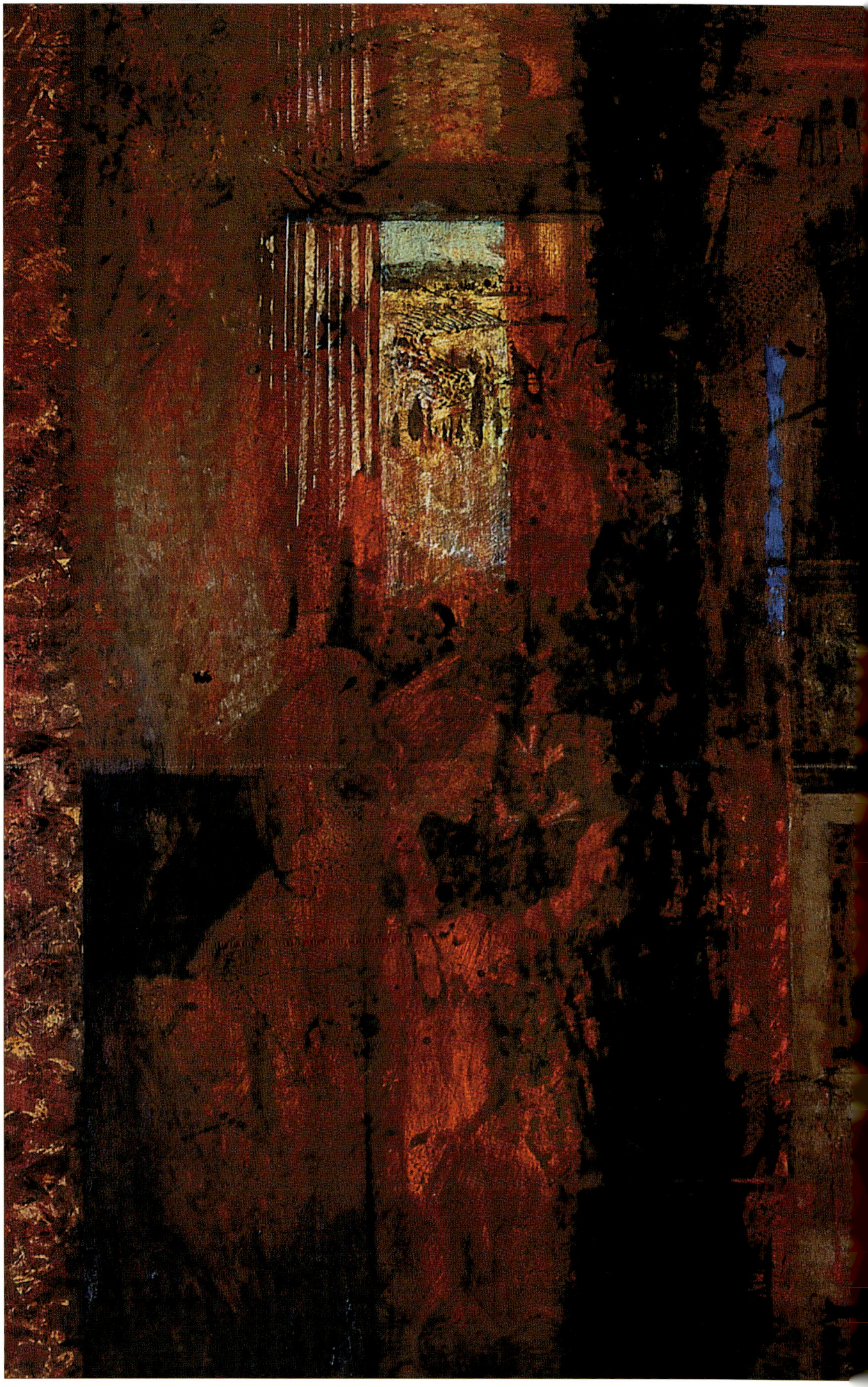

BEING IN ITALY
1993/94. Oil on board. 32in. x 48in.
Private Collection

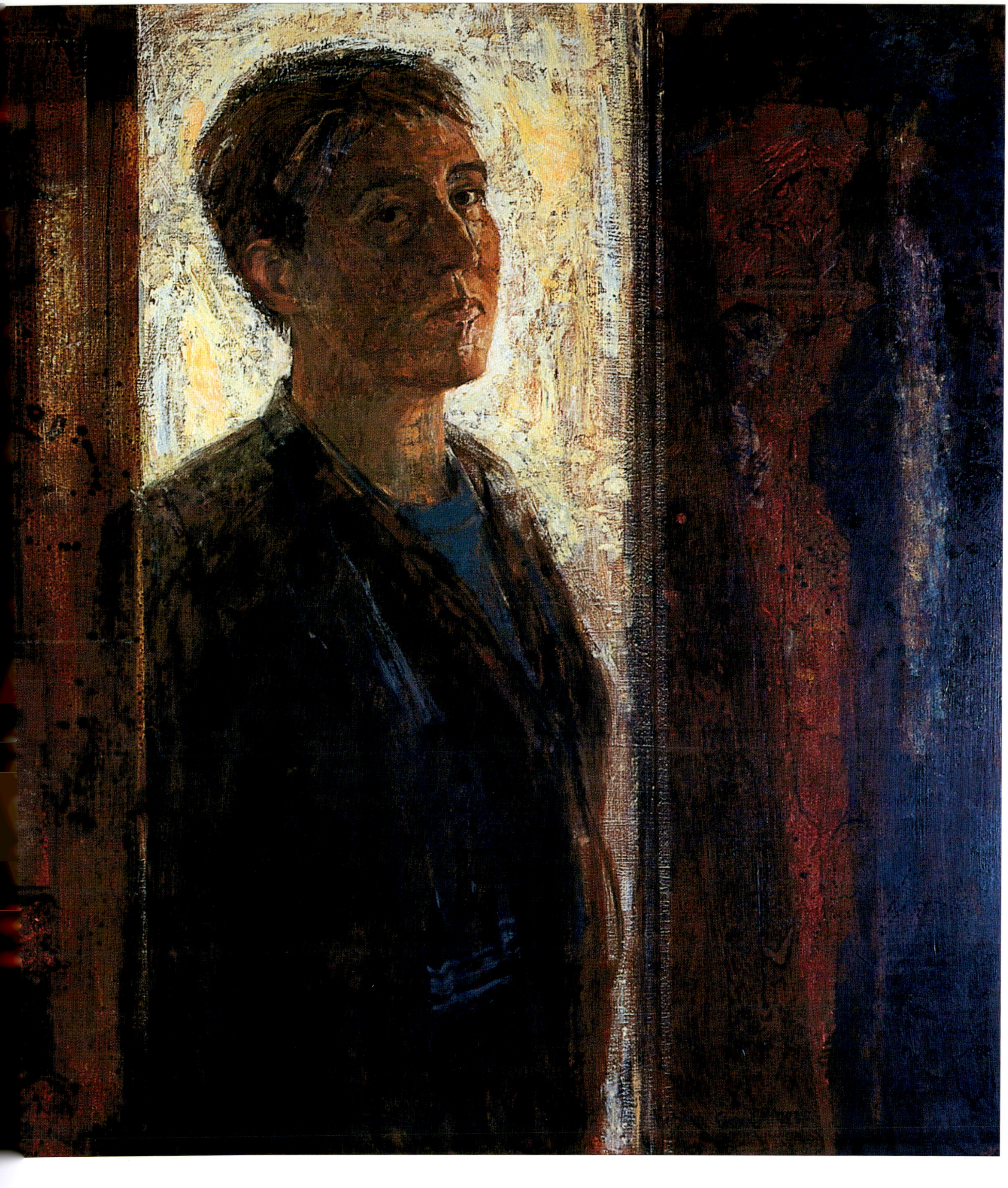

geometric borders. Artists over two centuries apparently contributed to design a panel on this gleaming floor. Intriguing to imagine each artist thinking 'Well, I've made it now, along with the Italian greats on the duomo floor!'. The Beccafumi bronze angels high above the altar were lovely. When one stops to look through binoculars, one sees the real quality – he must have realised it would go largely unseen … (it's the same Beccafumi I saw in the Pinacoteca yesterday, and that rather compelling painting was rejected by the Cathedral here and instead he had to provide a more conservative version for the frescos above the altar).

I found the votive offerings of motorbike helmets and contrada hats interesting, also the real flowers which looked like fakes beneath the icon.

### Day 9: San Gimignano, the duomo

The Cathedral with the most heavily frescoed interior, with old and new testament on each side. Old testament: Bartoldo di Fredi 1367. Wonderful narrative detail, costumes, landscape (pure Tuscan – just like what I've been looking at) in background and particularly the Creation lunettes where the colour is still brilliant. A love of describing fruit and flowers, animals and birds. Parting of Red Sea – great drama and composition all the struggling and abandoned figures and the cool group of women and children calmly walking on. Other side, new testament by either Barna da Siena or, now they think, Lippo Memmi (1350s) with wonderful crucifixion and the drama of the betrayal is great – real eyeball to eyeball contact between Judas and Jesus – one's eye moves around the whole composition but becomes riveted by that look and returns again and again. Also the head of Christ carrying the cross with a rope tether around his neck and a long sideways glance – all this within the black and white painted pillars and arches.

Cappella di Santa Fina was closed. I could only peer through the iron pierced screen into the gloom beyond to see the Ghirlandaio frescos which look superb. I never knew about all these really fine Ghirlandaios.

### Day 12

Went to Pisa – expecting it to be a sort of Tourist-tat experience, but it was astonishing. I think that the first view of all three buildings together on that flat grassy plane, inside the hectic, touristy market square, had the most impact. The impossible baptistry like an abandoned Pope's crown, the marble and mixed façade of the Cathedral looking rather more real and functional and beyond it, this crazy beautiful sloping tower. It's the unlikely relationship between all three and this green space all around them which is so curious.

The Cathedral is a mix and match of recycled marble on the façade with upside-down lettering and unrelated carving used on the face. Some Egyptian porphyry too. Inside there is the surviving Cimabue mosaic, Renaissance ceiling, gilt and blue Medici symbols, as well as the great chandelier supposed to have been watched by Galileo, as it swung after one of its oil lamps was knocked by the lamp lighter.

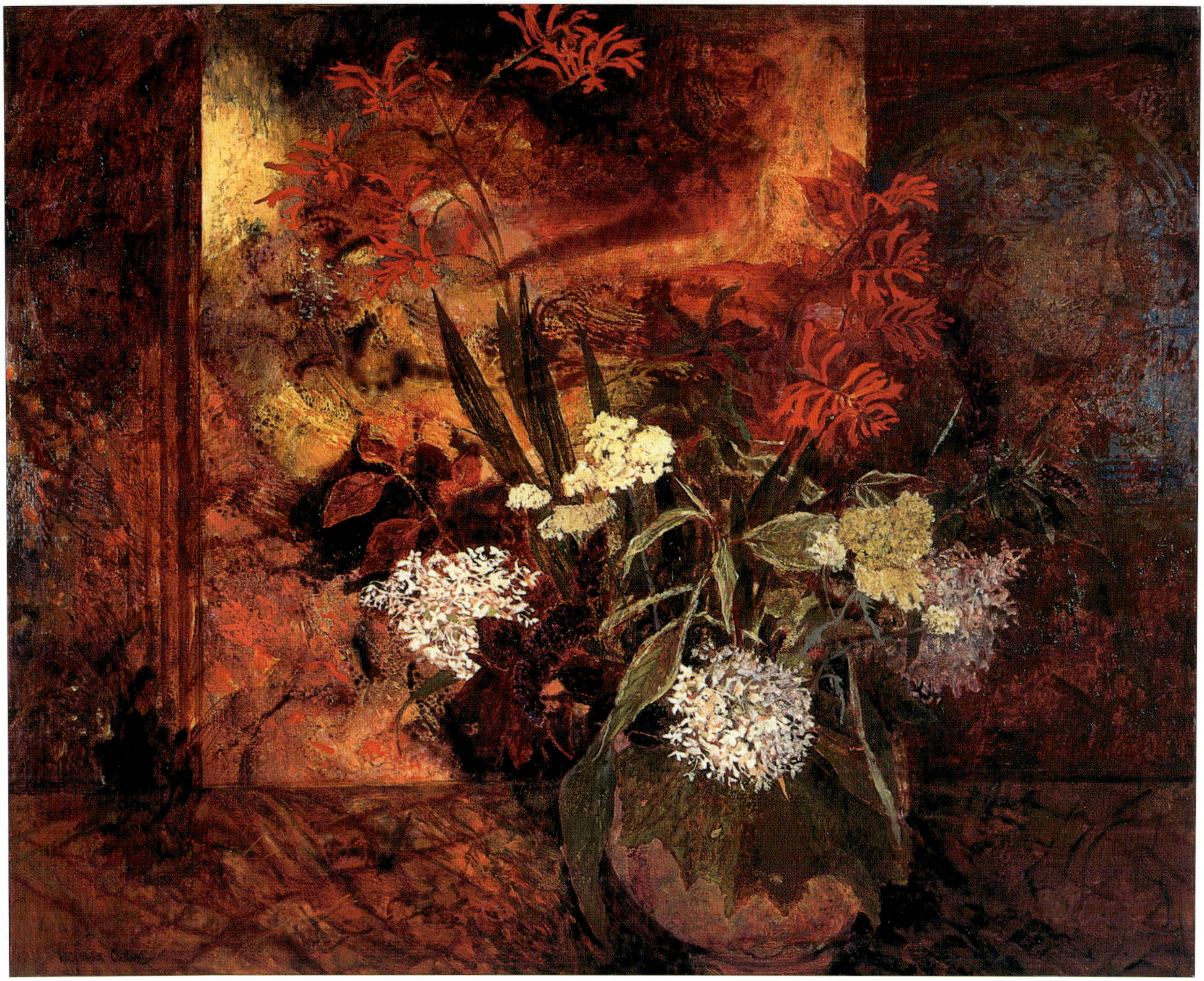

VIGIL IN SIENA
1995. Oil on board. 30in. x 36in.

## Day 13: Volterra

Through magnificent landscape towards Volterra, another high plateau town, mediaeval centre and walls and gateways with Etruscan lower blocks. I particularly liked the unpretentious Duomo and small baptistry, both of which were swamped by a huge Saturday market – fish, fruit, vegetables, cheese, meats, tapes and records, clothes, tourist tat etc. Inside the little Cathedral it reeked of being a used holy place, not the vast museum-like spaces I had become used to!

The Pinacoteca – a lovely, calm building with cloisters – a polychromed group of the annunciation – tremendous dialogue and play of hands – also Ghirlandaio and Signorelli and curious Rosso Fiorentino's descent from the cross. Vibrant colour, monumental blocks of it and a horribly haunting, almost laughing, head of Christ.

The Uffizi had its own rewards for me and I spent many hours with those great, sublime paintings.

I was intrigued by the religiosity of the church interiors, memories from my own Catholic past well and truly stirred … I was reminded of the ideas of sacred and profane – for every truly spiritual transcendent image there were the many accompanying sentimental golden-haired Jesus figures. Plaster virgins, their blue painted eyes gazing devotedly heavenwards as haloes flicked on and off like Christmas trees and, for the truly devout, plastic statuettes made of the luminous material of children's bedroom stars …

The Annunciation was a theme which was forcibly brought home by the variety of approaches that I saw, both painted and in three dimensions. In Volterra in a square stone room, there were full sized polychrome wooden figures of the Angel and the Virgin, standing in endless dialogue while through the opened window the sun shone on an archetypal Tuscan landscape beyond. The hand raised in blessing, the passive 'receiving' hand gesture, the purity of the lily – just exactly what was that exchange about?

Not only the joyous announcement, but, by implication, the shadow of future grief.

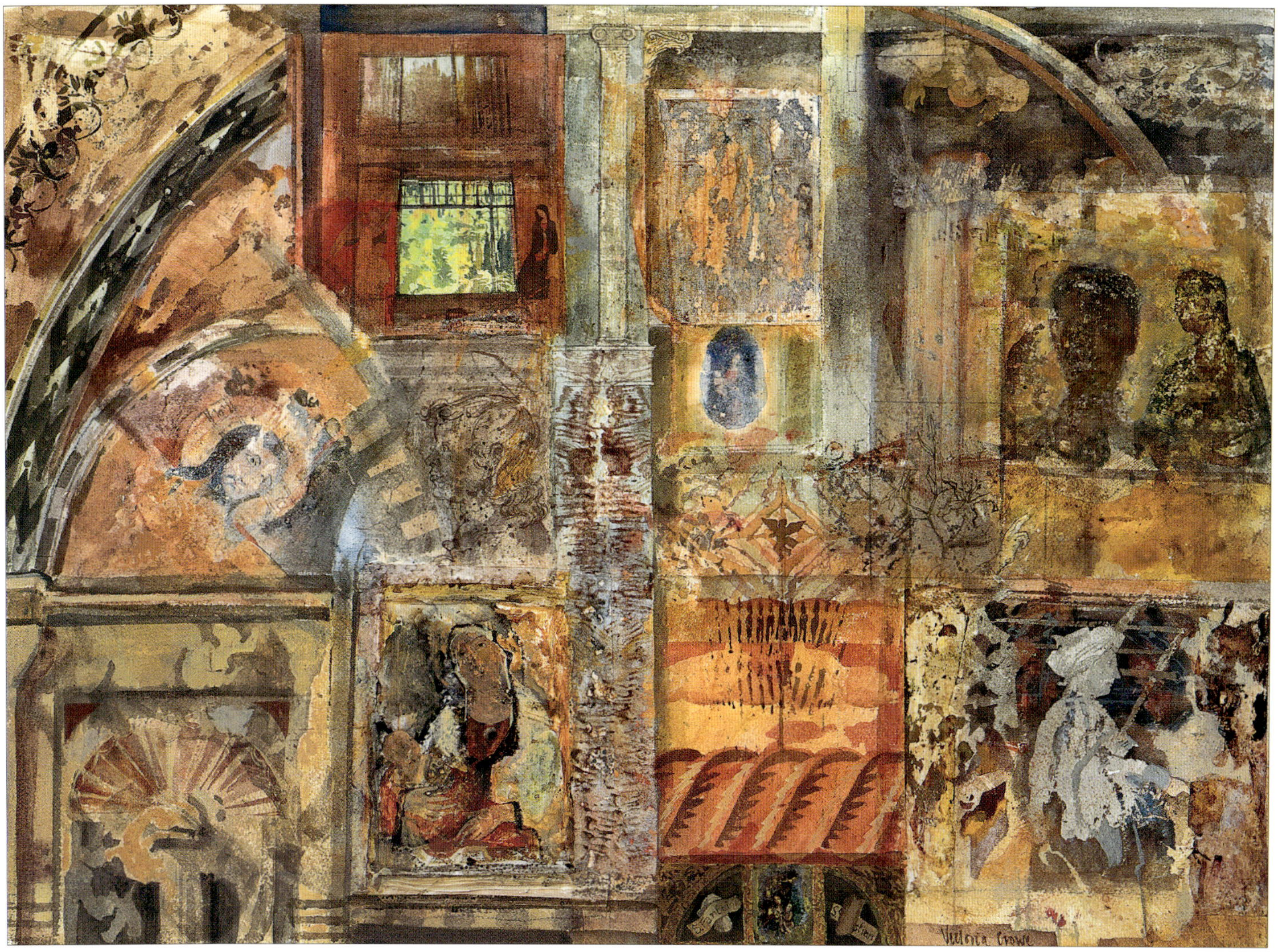


**INTERIORS TRANSFORMED** 1993. Watercolour and acrylic. 22in. x 30in.

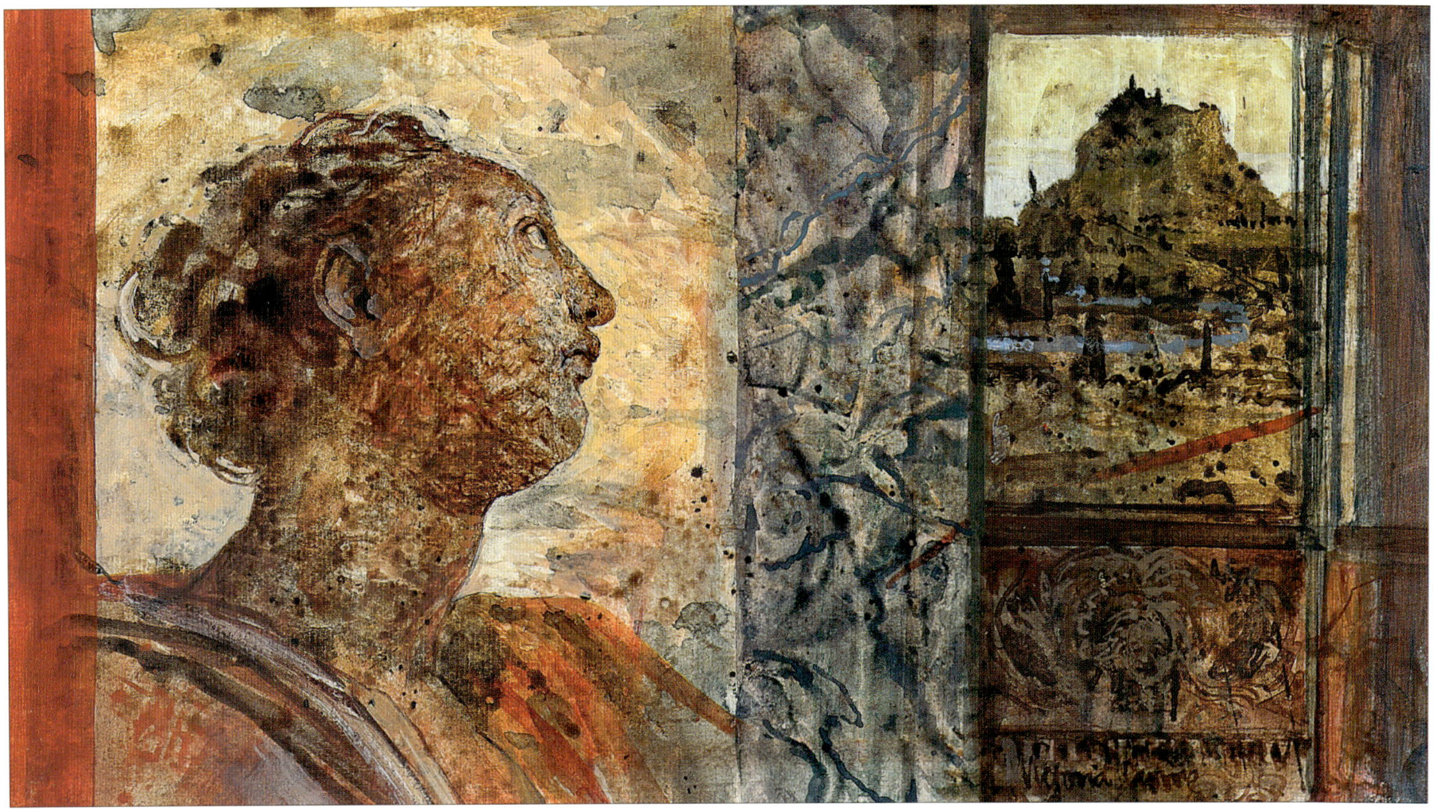

**PAINTED ROOM WITH A VIEW** 1994. Watercolour. 10½in. x 17½in. Private Collection

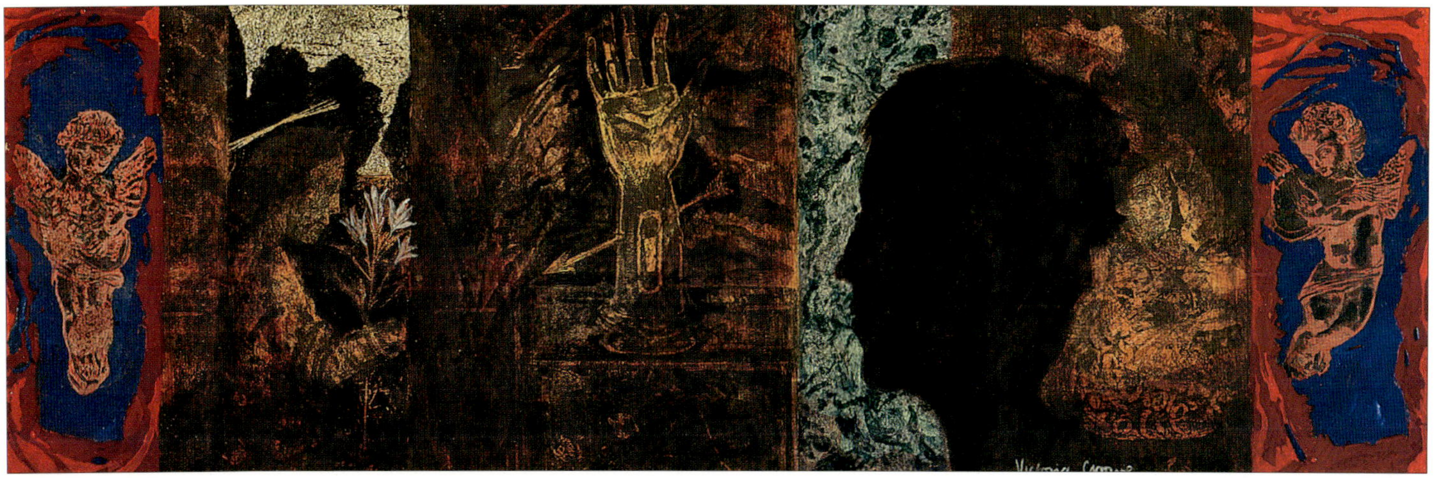

**WHILE IN ITALY** 1993. Variation: Capella dei Principi. Silkscreen print, oil, gold leaf. 8in. x 22in.
Private Collection

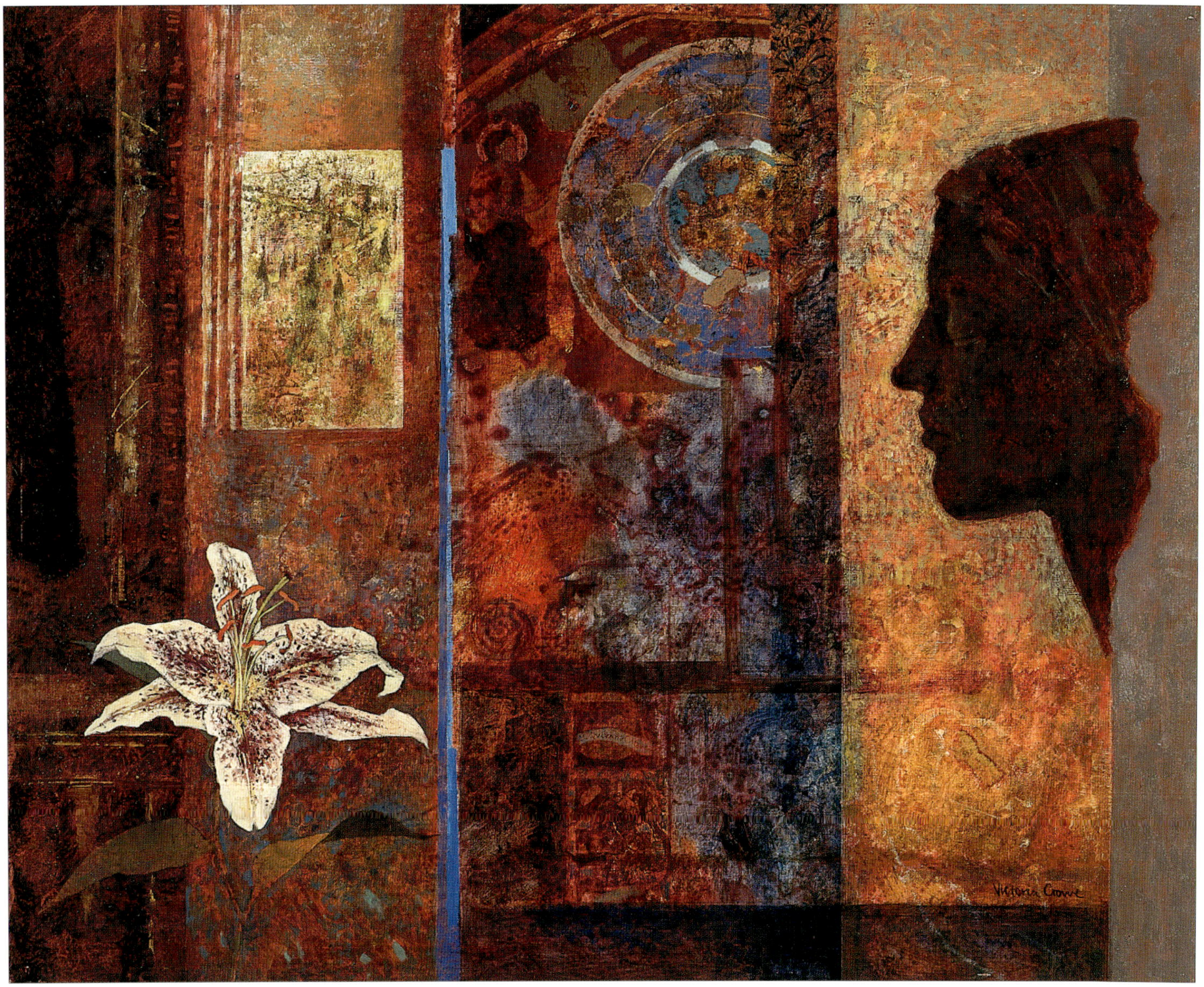

**WITHIN AND WITHOUT** 1993/94. Oil on board. 20in. x 24in. Private Collection

# SHADOW

After the northern light and imagery of Kittleyknowe, the sabbatical term in Italy and subsequent work in the studio opened up many new possibilities for me. I began using stronger and richer colour; my composition was freed from direct observation and my subject matter moved towards more personal themes with a greater use of symbolic and archetypal imagery.

I painted several self-portraits around this time – the Italian experience had felt very much like a self-defining one. In many of these paintings the human presence of myself acts almost like an anonymous observer while in other instances it is used as a direct connection with the viewer. Many of the fourteenth century Italian frescos contained narrative scenes wherein one of the characters confronts the viewer by turning away from the action being played out and looking directly beyond the painted reality to the observer. Ghirlandaio paints himself looking out in the crowd gathered around Santa Fina in the Cathedral in San Gimignano. The direct look of the artist subverts the illusion of that particular reality. The questioning, yet assertive gaze of the artist's self-portrait contains the knowledge that his painted eyes will meet those of travellers and visitors over hundreds of years, and there would be that spark of instant contact – the recognition of our own common human state. In my paintings at that time I juxtaposed images of myself with those of classical artefacts, references to Piero della Francesca's work, early frescos, Pompeiian wall painting and ex-votos.

It was a time of experimentation with new techniques – particularly with aspects of printmaking – and using collage, applying gold and metal leaf to embellish surfaces, using marbling, glazing and various mixed media. Concurrent with these departures into new ways of working and structuring a painting was the breakthrough to more personal imagery. I mentioned that the annunciation theme had particularly interested me while I was in Italy. Now I painted several works based on my responses to that subject matter, from direct compositions of two figures to the more circumspect self-portrait images with gessoed angels, lilies against pagan and Christian imagery and landscapes with sculpted angels and carved hands raised in blessing. Well, what was this fascination with this imagery all about? In 1994 while working on this body of work I too had an annunciation of sorts – a reverse annunciation, my angel being an oncologist in Aberdeen telling me my only son had cancer. It was at this point in my life that I realised why I was an artist. A strange thing to say, but I knew then that if I didn't have a passionate commitment to painting, if I hadn't evolved for myself a personal language which was able to deal – on a metaphorical level – with issues in my life, then I would hardly have survived the trauma of the following months. Mike, Gemma my daughter, our many friends, and I watched Ben valiantly fight his oral cancer for a year; we were told in June '95 that his illness was terminal, and he died in December of that year. As a family we hung on together, hardly believing, hardly accepting what our fate was to be. And I painted – I painted about my own sense of disbelief in this new reality, I revisited in paint the landscapes of my children's childhood alongside dark reflections of the present or with objects arrayed like protective votives against the snowy ground.

The portrait I had painted of Ben in '91 became in my mind almost iconic in its new relevance – the epitome of youth on the verge of life – so drastically changed in a few short years. I used that image of his youthful portrait in a series of prints, oil and mixed media pieces. In *Votives for Male Children* that image of Ben is set against a classical Italian sculpted head and a Greek ex-voto of a male infant. His portrait became almost as distant in time as the other images – he seemed in my perception already to be withdrawing from the real world.

Many of the works around this time became, for want of a better word, painted prayers – not so much pleas to change the outcome, as meditations recognising the process we were all going through – to value it in all its intense highs and lows. I was able to channel my hope, energy, questioning; the painting process contained my despair and grief, my remembering and my determination that in the face of such loss, all that was good and eternal and true must somehow be held on to and celebrated for Ben's sake. I realised, through the work, how our sense of time – the present, the here and now – can be so disrupted and how memory and imagination are unfettered. The last painting in this section is the large *Travelling By Moonlight*. Duncan Thomson wrote in the catalogue of my Scottish Gallery exhibition in November 1995:

> *... And themes of passage and time again in* Travelling By Moonlight, *virtually a triptych in form and a bringing together of the most powerful experiences in a night journey out from Edinburgh, Ben the artist's son – a proud warrior of the moment – and a thin blue vase of flowers, tropaeolum, clematis and berberis that break into the thicket of forms beneath the encircled moon in the right section of the picture, where the moth from Lindisfarne flutters again, towards the unassailable light ... the sense of yearning like a line from the poet Kathleen Raine, whom Vicky has painted: 'I would be with you as star with distant star.'*

That unreal time, the long journey for us as a family and the heroic one made by Ben, converged with my exhibition in November. Ben came to the private view – the last and greatest gift he gave to me was the memory of him standing by that portrait. He died a month later.

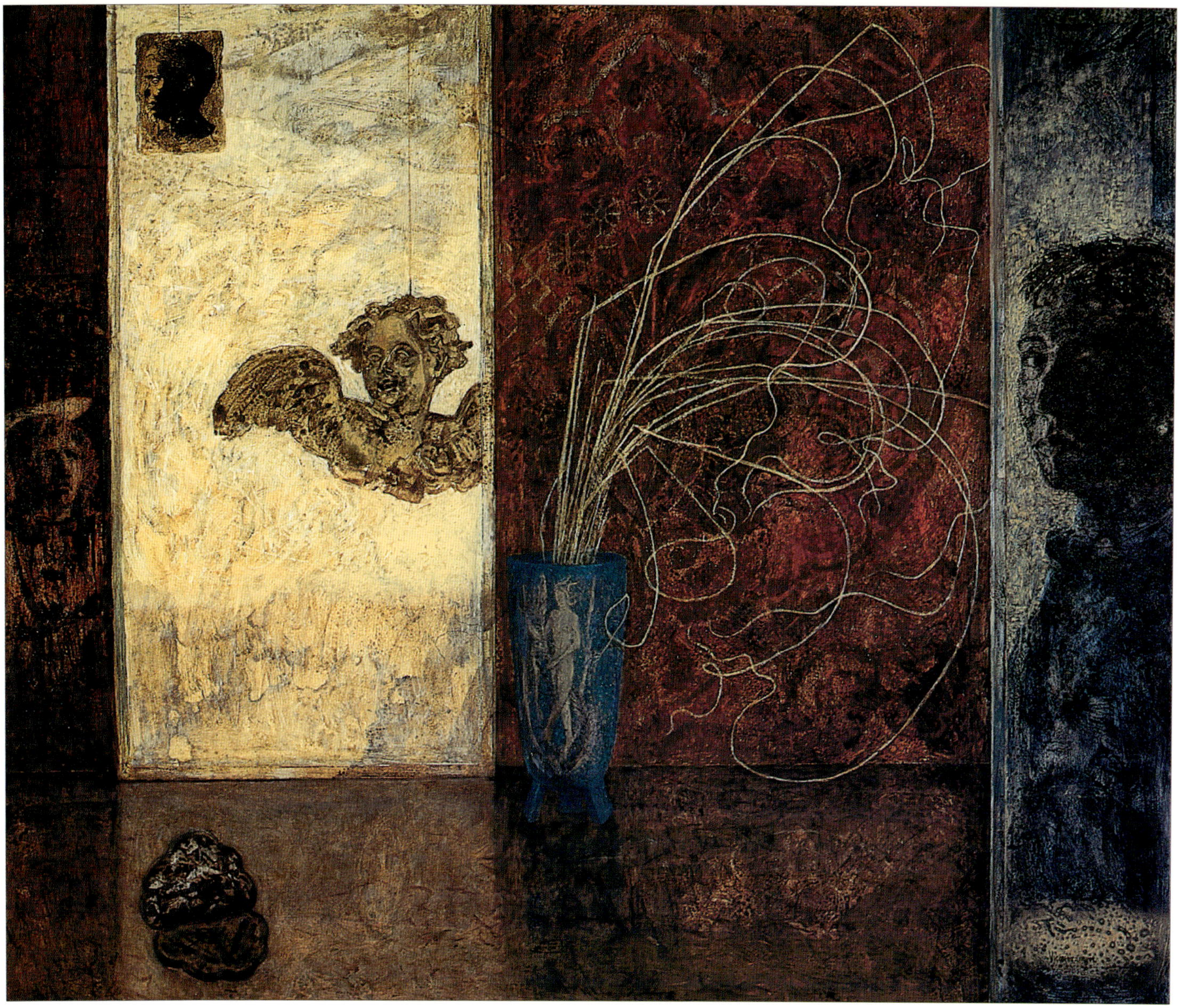

**DO NOT DISTURB THE DREAMING WORLD** 1995. Oil on board. 37¼in. x 43in. Private Collection

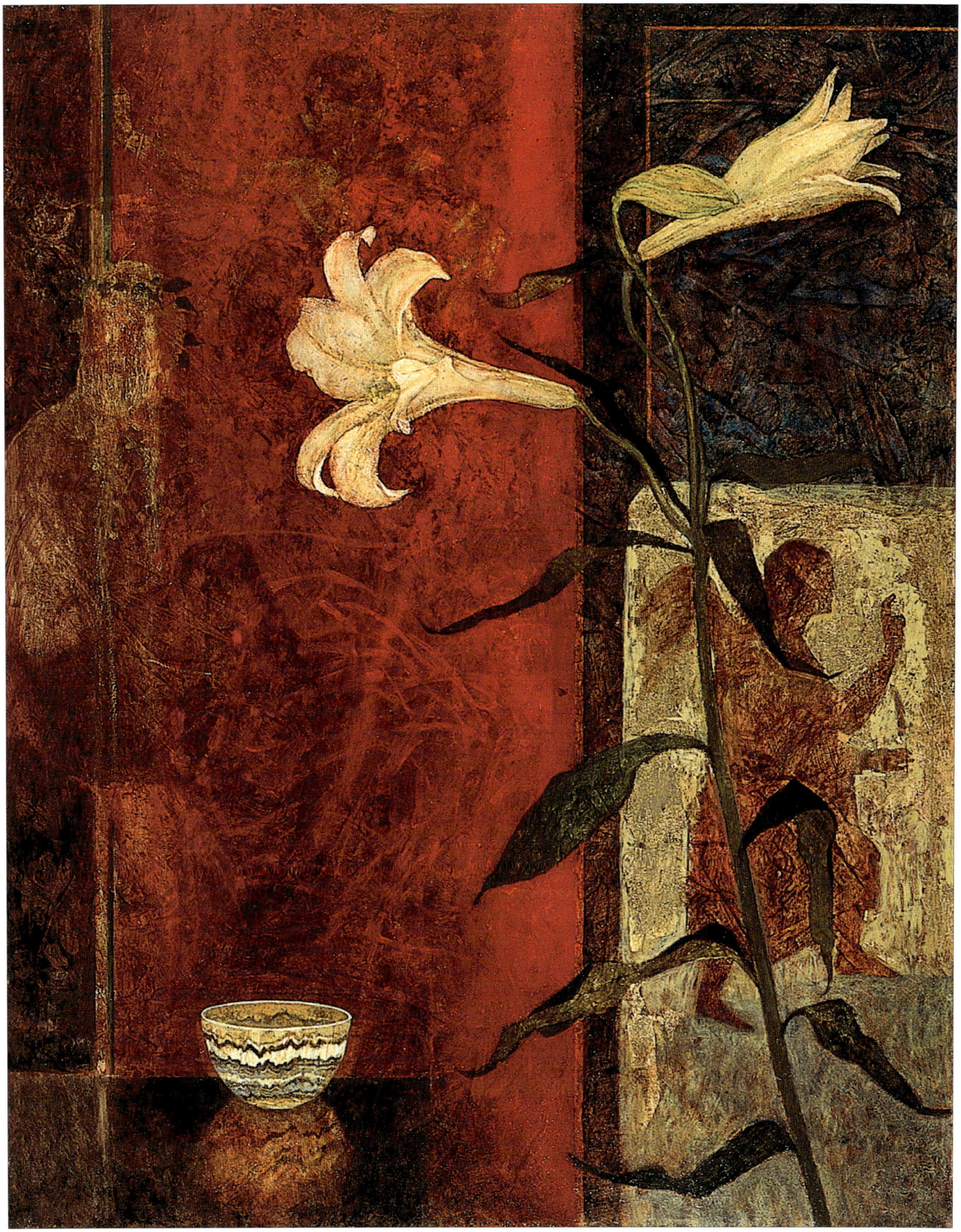

HOUSE OF MYSTERIES 1995. Oil on board. 34½in. x 27in. Private Collection

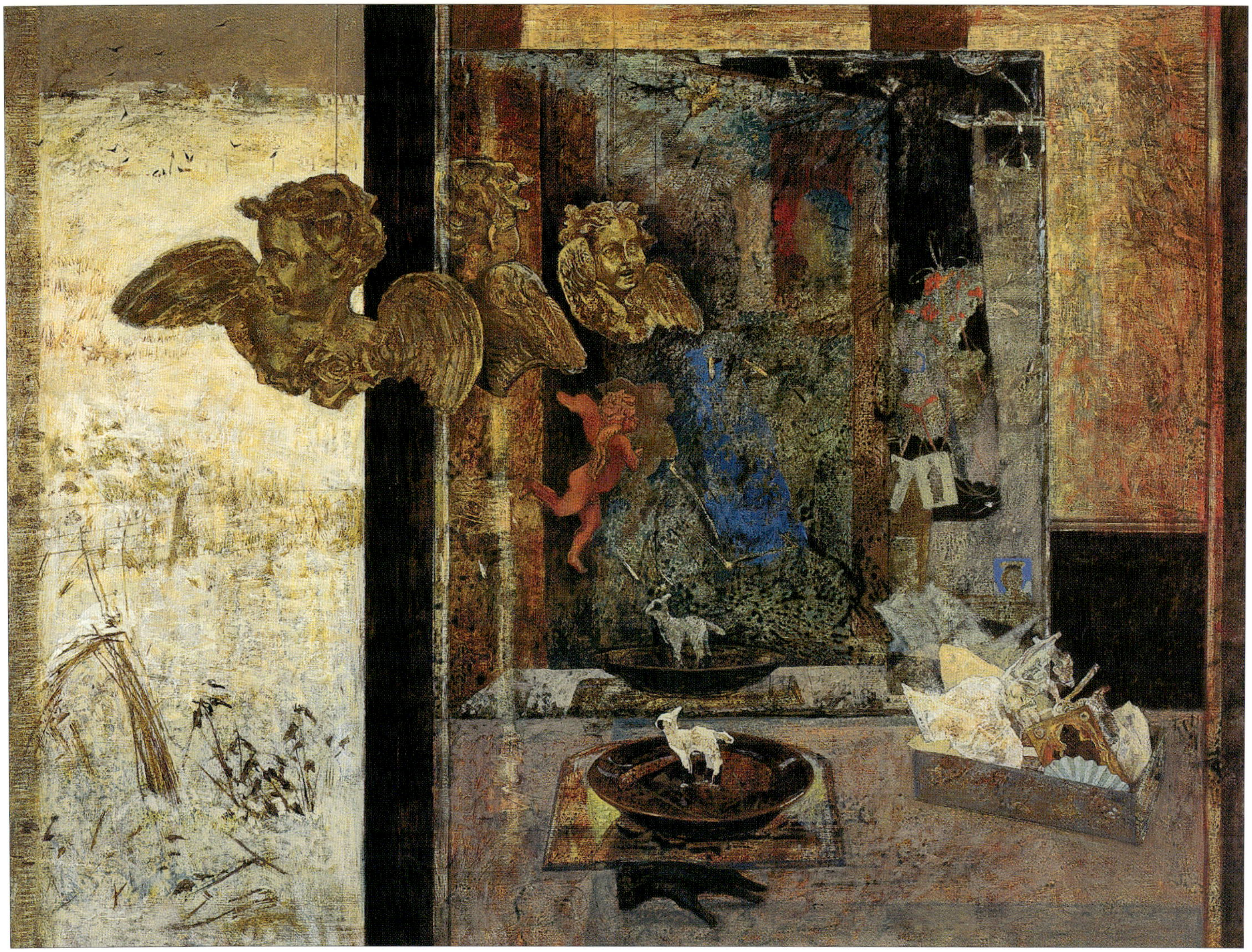

**DARK GLASS AND DISTANT LANDSCAPE** 1995. Oil on board. 28in. x 36in. Private Collection

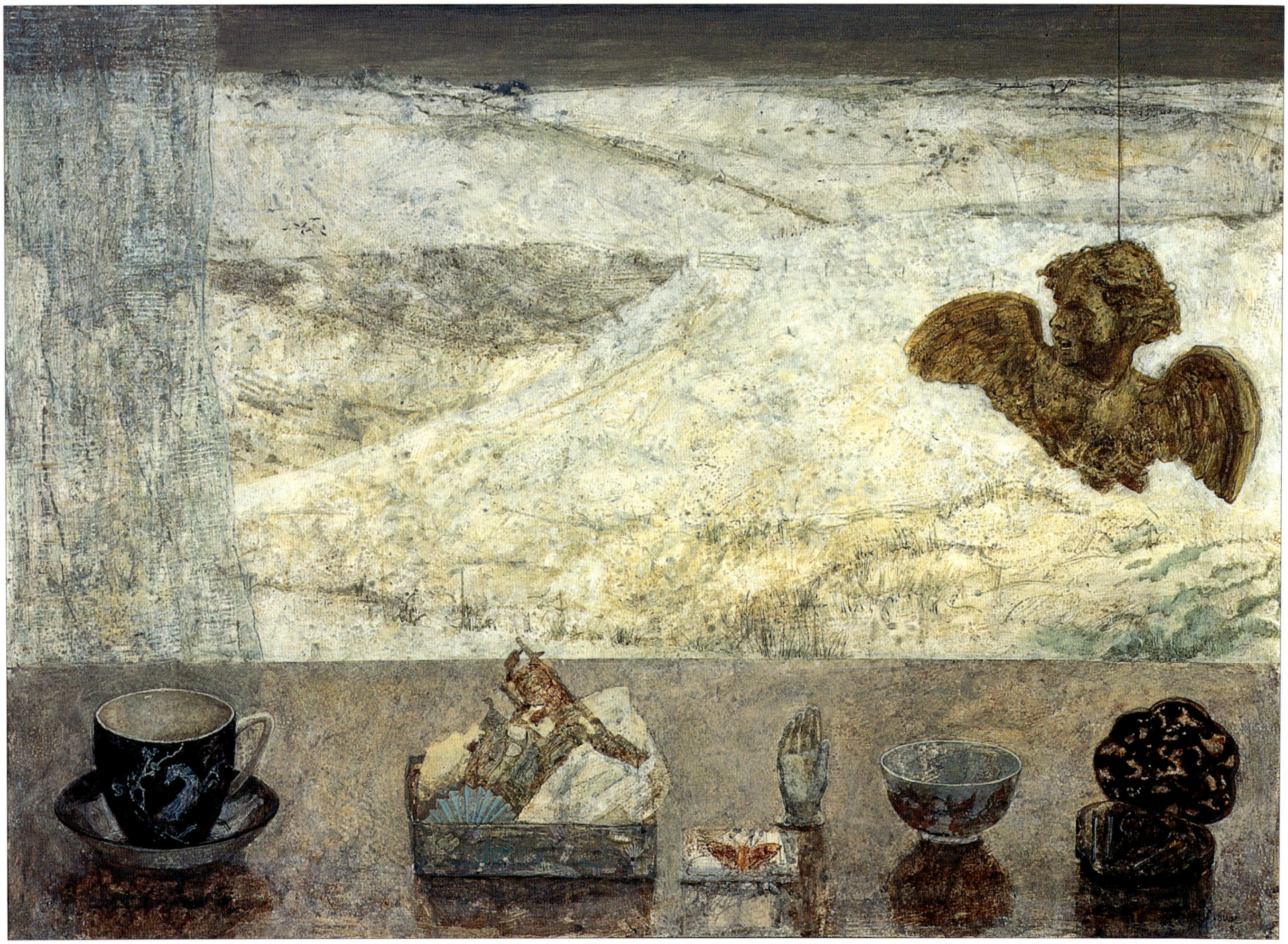

**SNOWLIGHT AND POWERFUL OBJECTS** 1995. Watercolour, 30in. x 40in. Private Collection

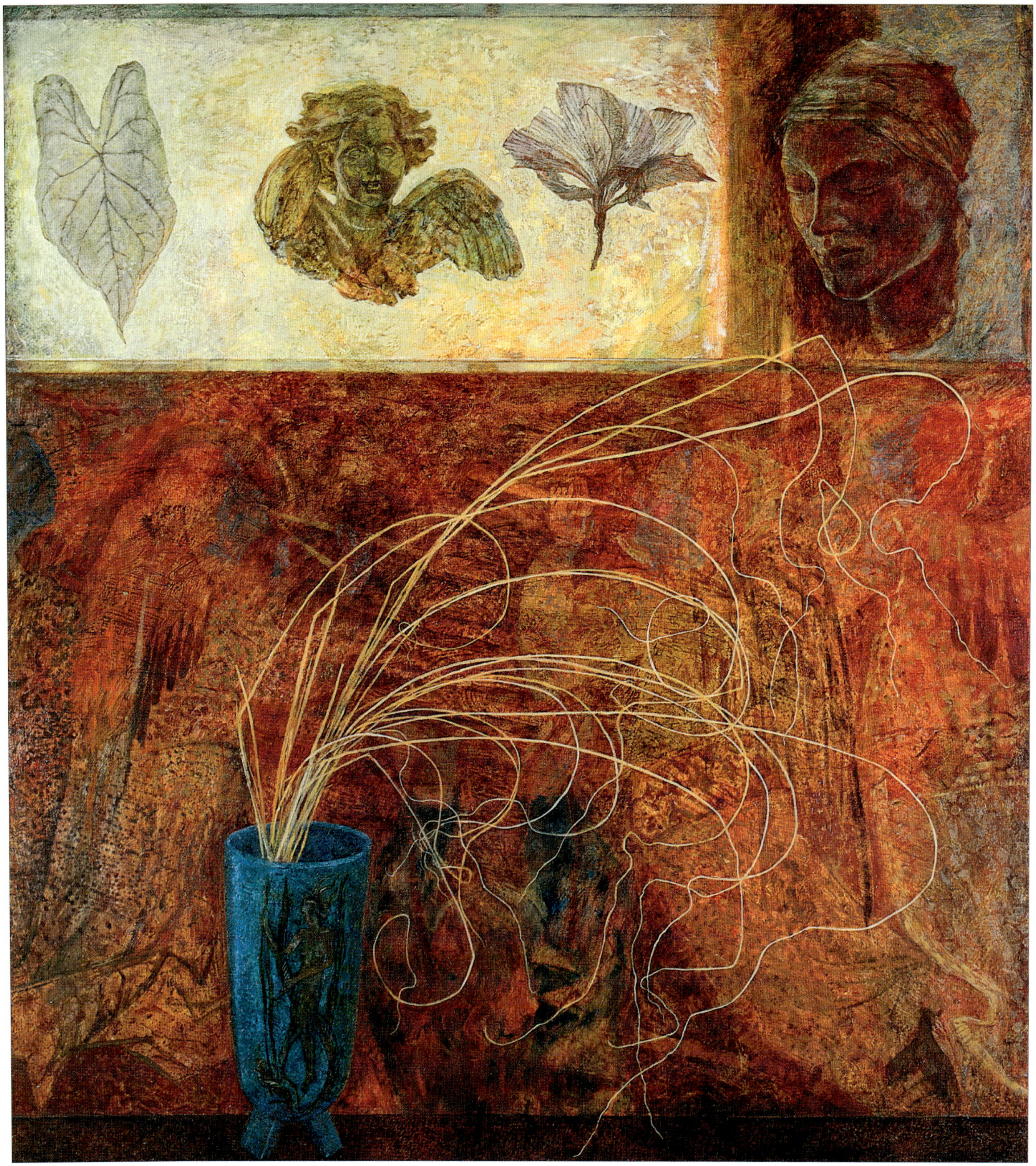

**DREAMING WORLD** 1997. Oil on board. 40in. x 36in. Private Collection

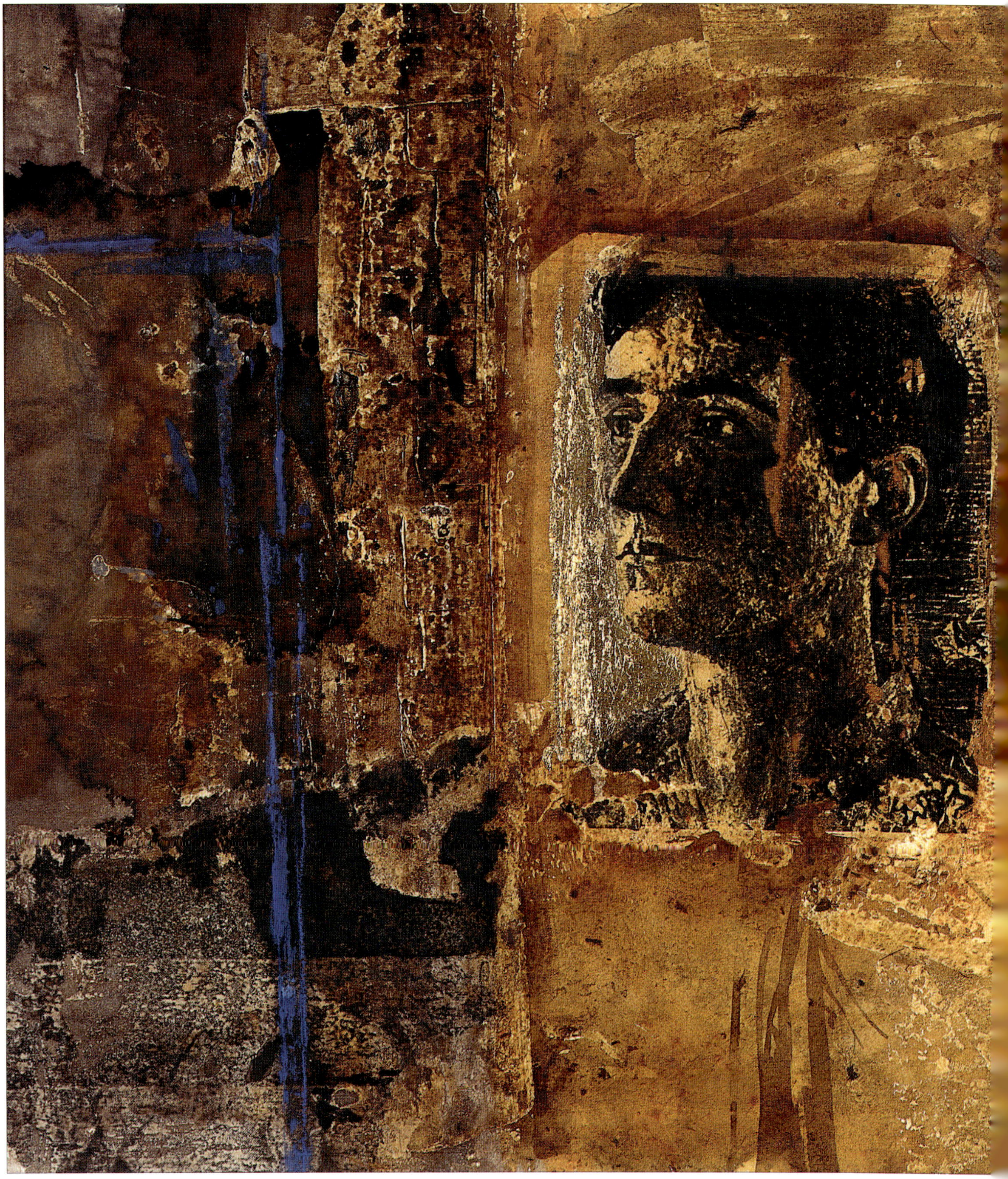

VOTIVES FOR MALE CHILDREN 1995. Mixed media on paper. 11in.x 18¾in. Private Collection

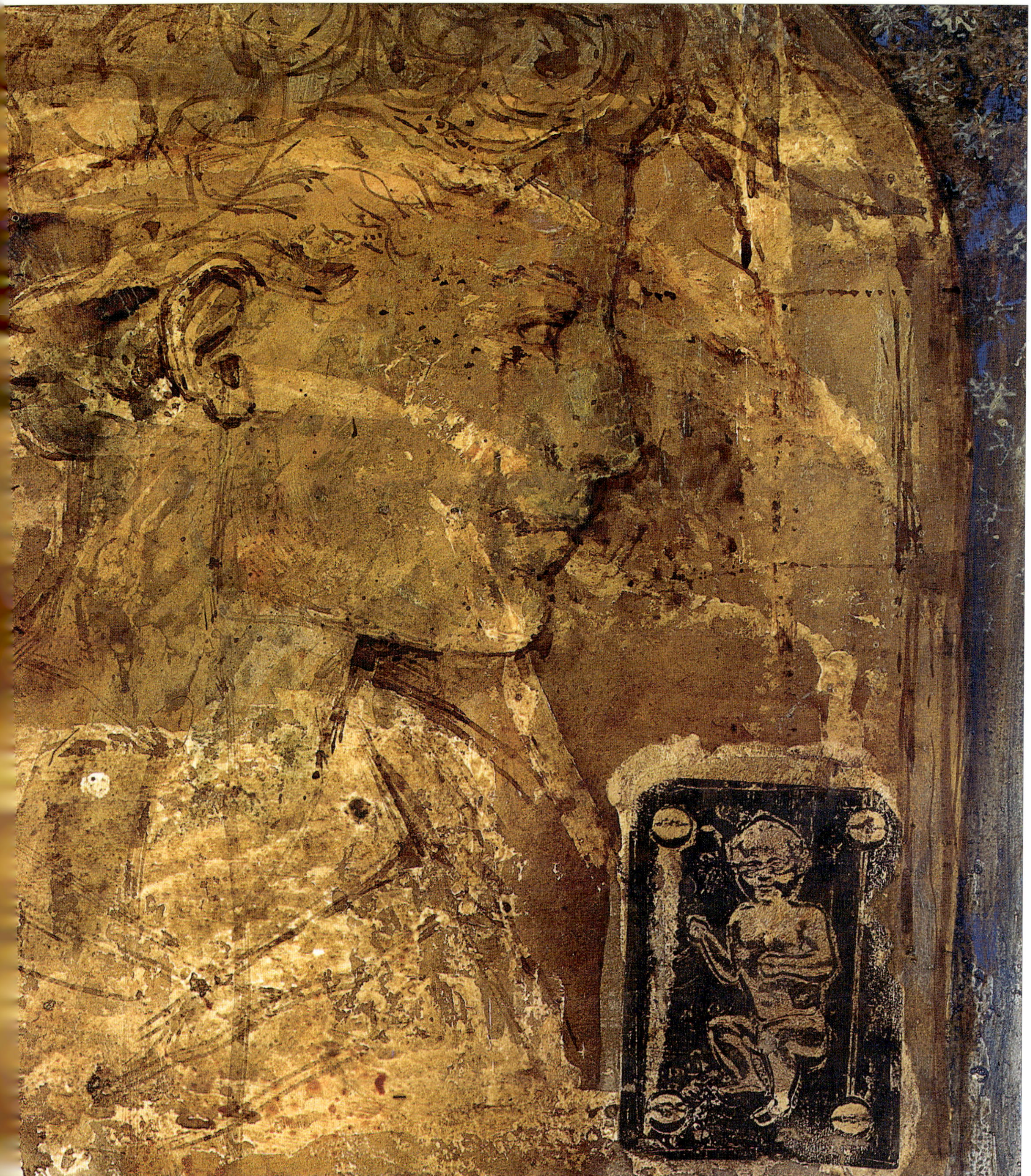

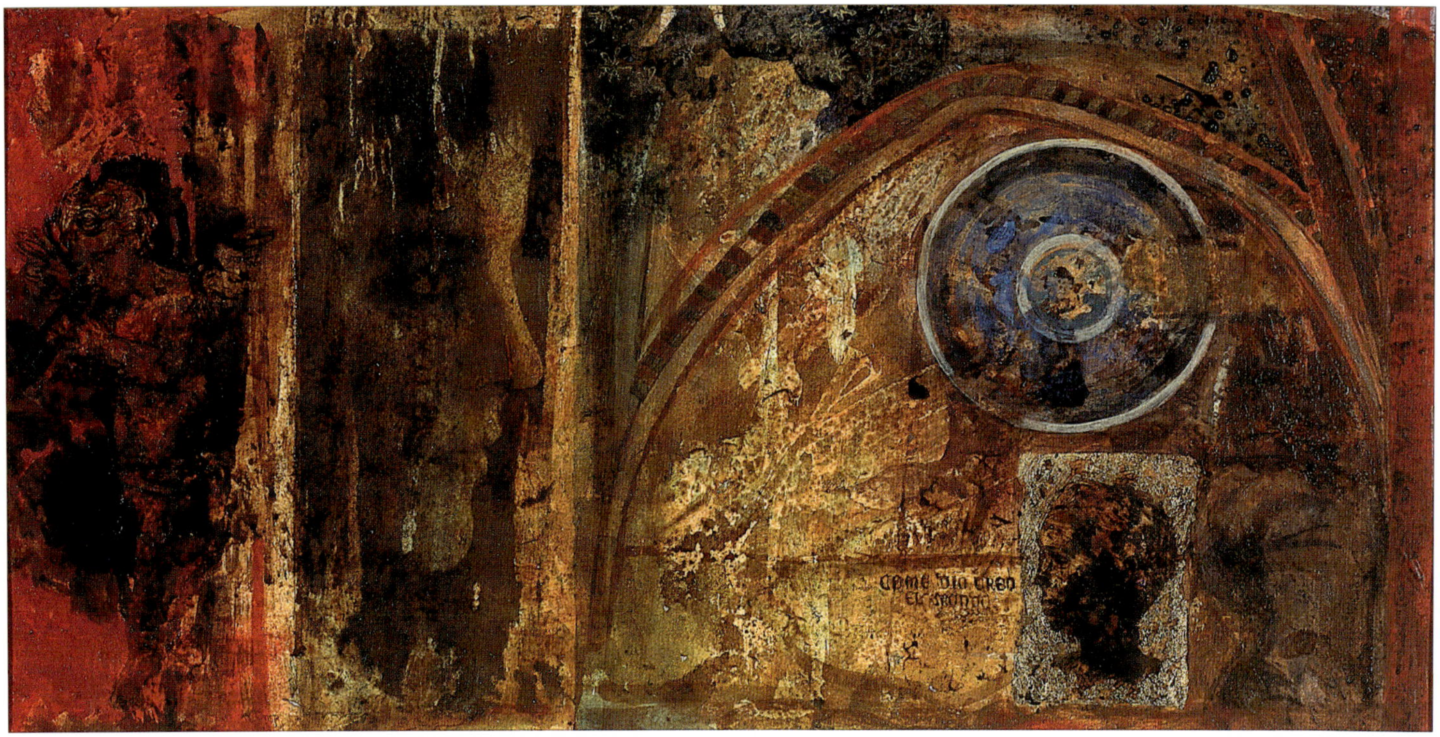

**CREATION OBSERVED** 1995. Mixed media on paper. 10in. x 19in. Private Collection

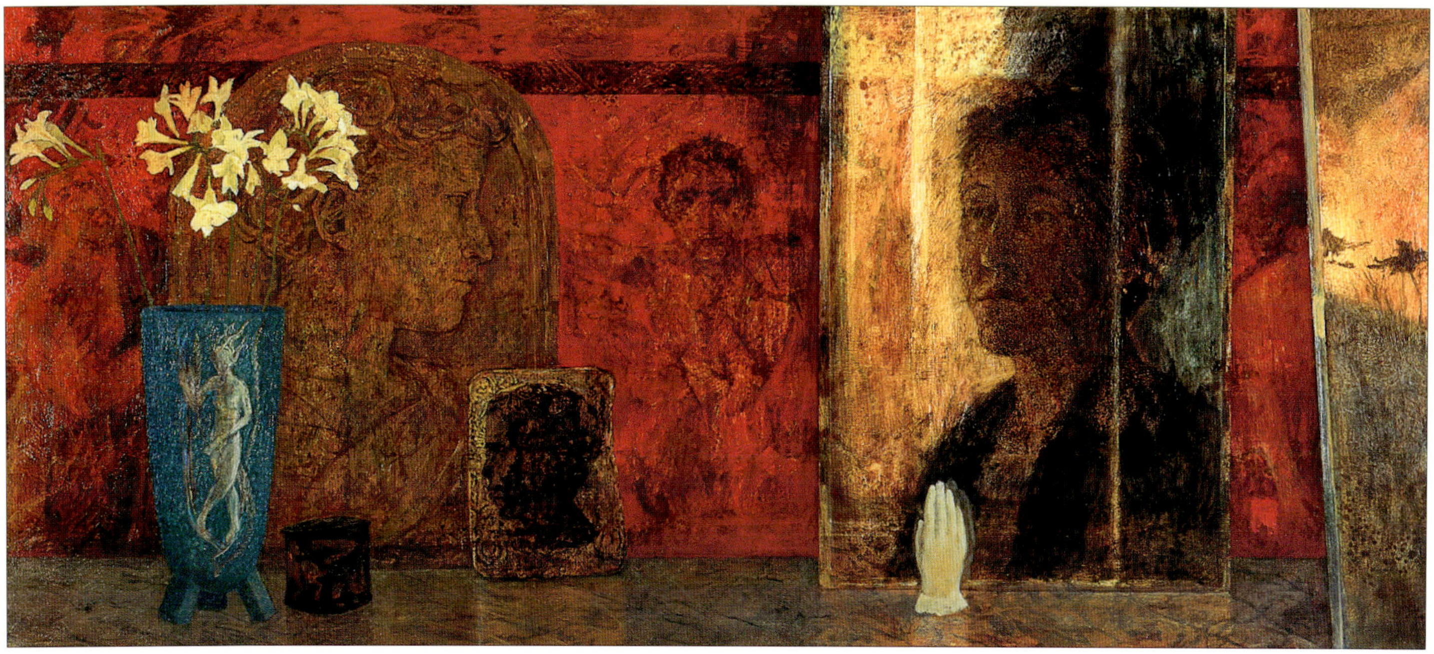

TIMES OF TWILIGHT AND RICHES 1995. Oil on board. 20in. x 48in. The Bank of Scotland

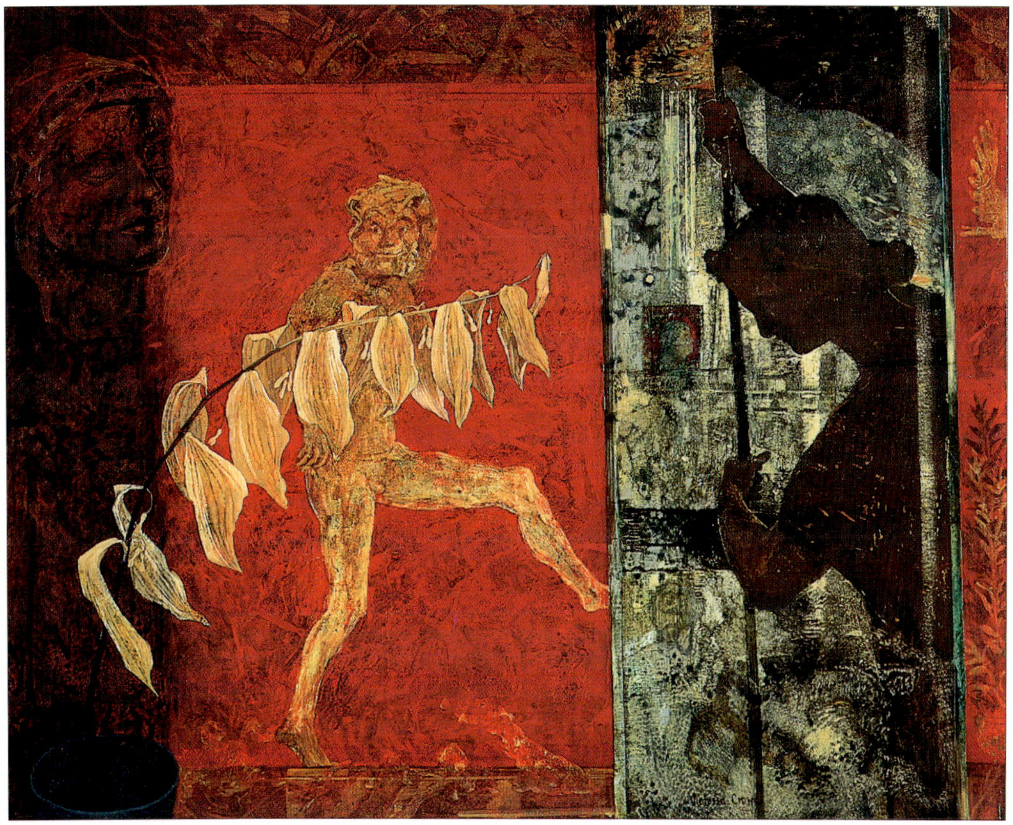

INTERIOR WITH UNHEEDING DANCER, POMPEII 1994. Oil on board. 30in. x 36in. Private Collection

## Spell of sleep

Let him be safe in sleep
As leaves folded together
As young birds under wings
As the unopened flower.

Let him be hidden in sleep
As islands under rain,
As mountains within their clouds,
As hills in the mantle of dusk.

Let him be free in sleep
As the flowing tides of the sea,
As the travelling wind on the moor,
As the journeying stars in space.

Let him be upheld in sleep
As a cloud at rest on the air,
As sea-wrack under the waves
When the flowing tide covers all
And the shells' delicate lives
Open on the sea-floor.

Let him be healed in sleep
In the quiet waters of night
In the mirroring pool of dreams
Where memory returns in peace,
Where the troubled spirit grows wise
And the heart is comforted.

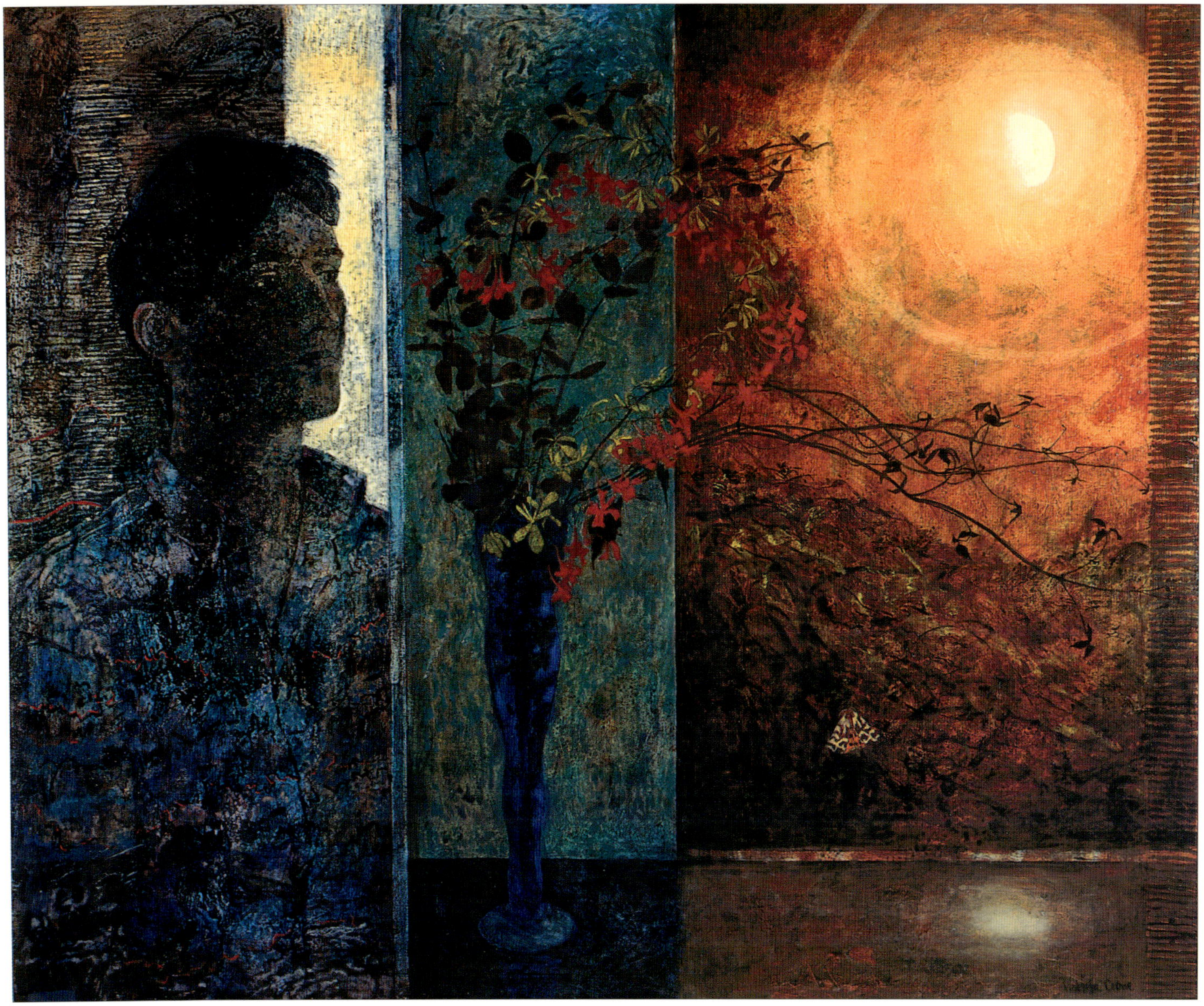

**TRAVELLING BY MOONLIGHT** 1995.Oil on board. 37¼in. x 43in. Private Collection

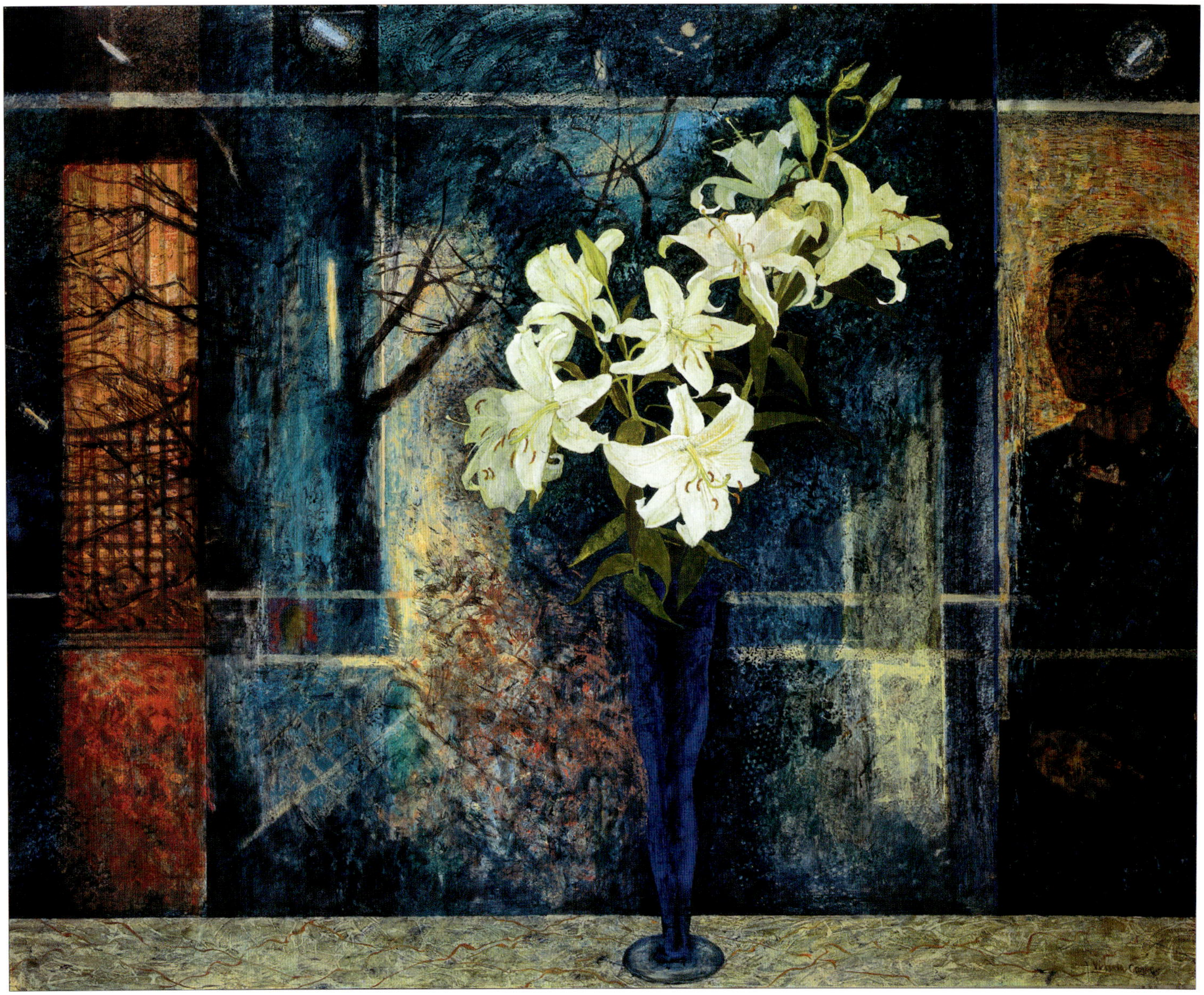

# RESOLUTION

NOVEMBER WINDOW, REFLECTING
1996. Oil on board. 40in. x 48in.
Private Collection

In some ways I feel I hardly remember '96 and '97, so many normal constraints seemed cut away. We travelled a lot – Madeira, Egypt, Italy – we worked at college, my daughter continued at university, we went through the motions of day-to-day living.

I remember a feeling of vertigo, of flying in uncharted space – nothing certain, everything possible – because my sense of reality itself had been so challenged. As well as painting and drawing, I wrote – mostly a sort of prose-poetry – dealing with similar subject matter and drawing on my daily thoughts and experiences, my memories and dreams. I think the writing, a kind of parallel activity for me, made it possible to work towards touching some deeper knowledge. Compositionally

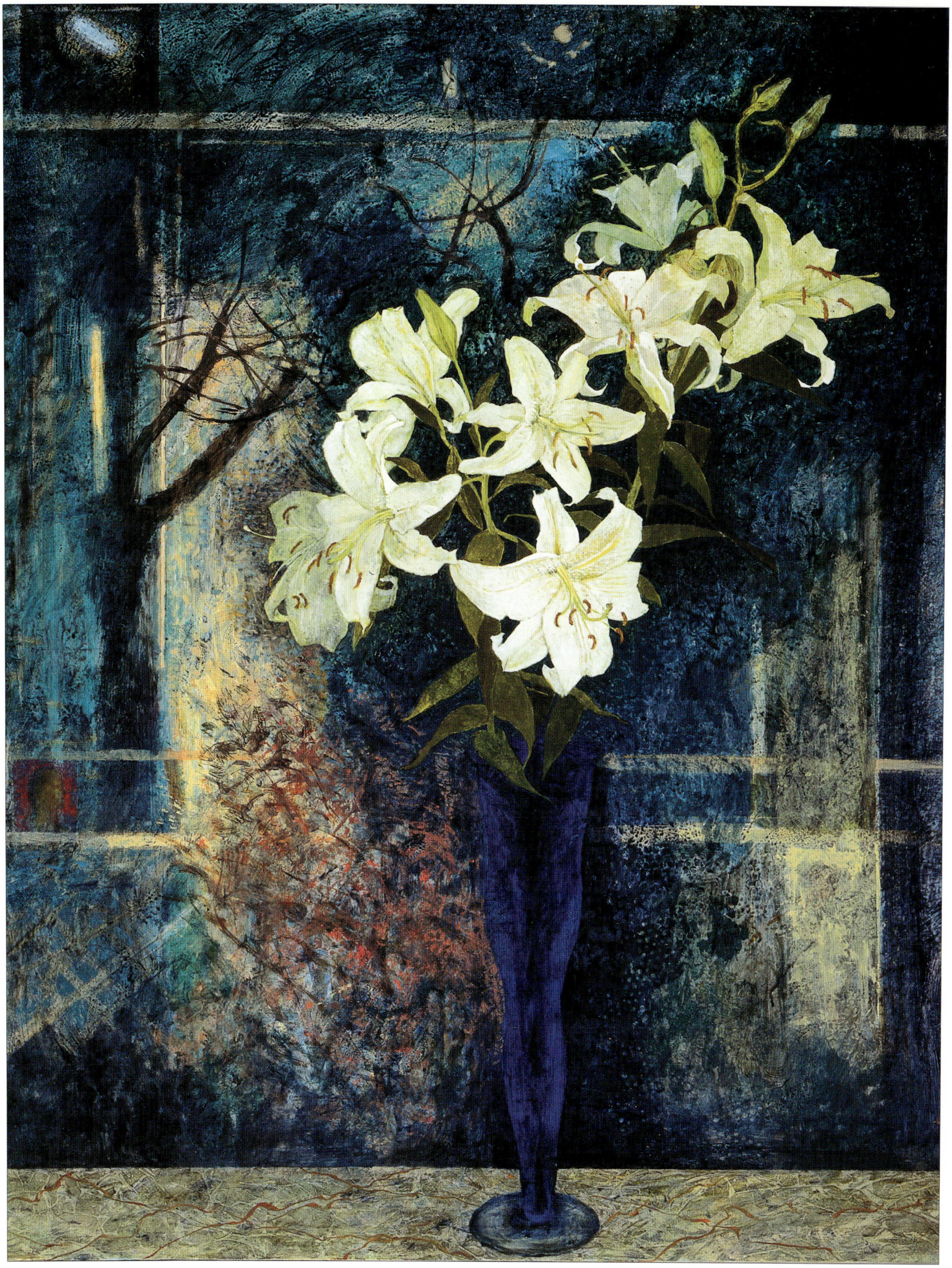

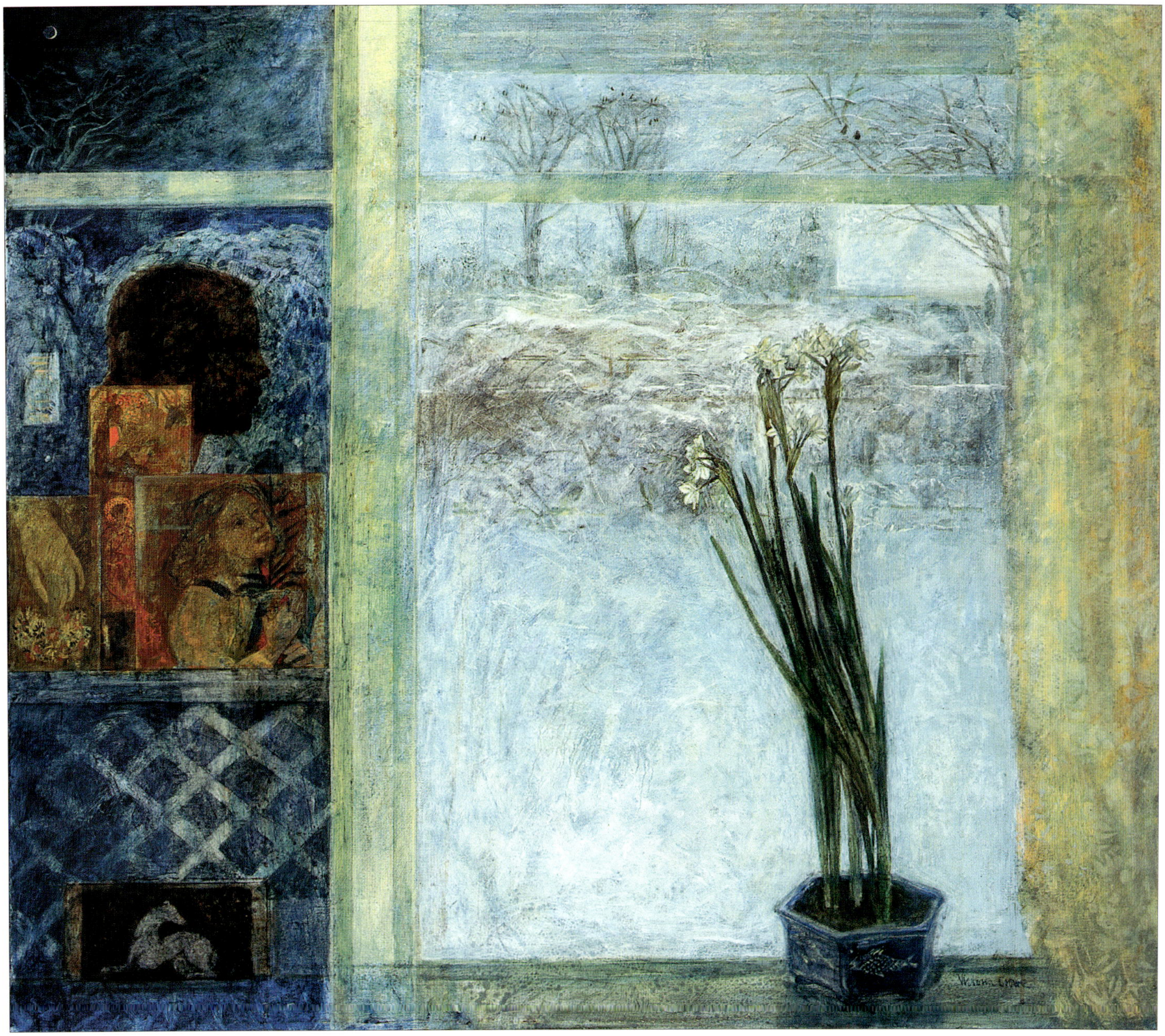

**TURN OF THE YEAR** 1996. Oil on board. 36in. x 40in. Private Collection

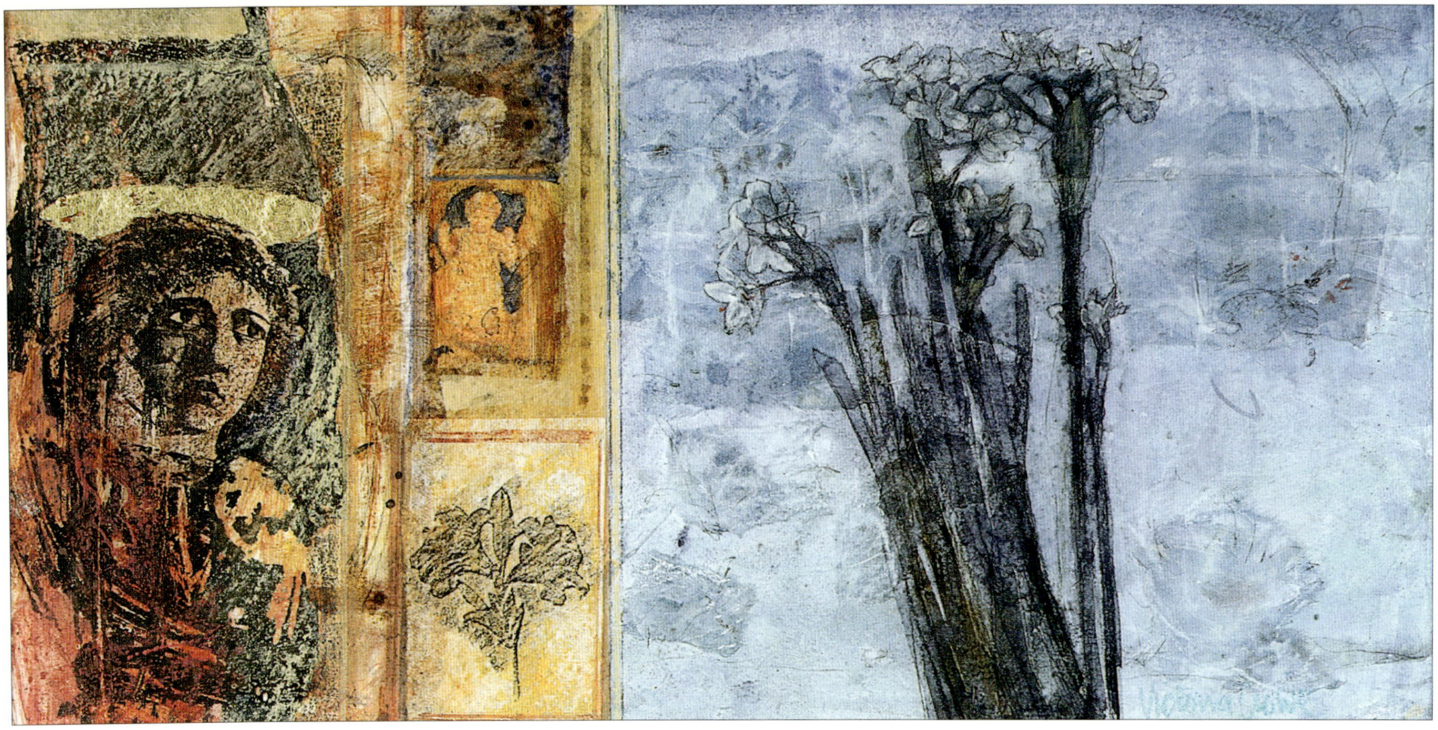

**THE YEAR'S TURNING**
1997. Mixed media on paper.
8½in. x 15¾in.
Private Collection

elements combined effortlessly. I felt no constraints at simultaneously depicting day and night, inside and outside, movement and stillness, the archaic and the immediate. To juxtapose is to underline the deliberate cross-reference and, as I had discovered in student days, as with Eisenstein's theory of montage in film making, the merging of two contrasting images produces a powerfully-charged and unexpected third image or sensation. However, I couldn't start out with logical deliberation of the end results (head + mirror + moon = x sensation), but with an intuitive response to write, draw or paint about certain images.

My subject matter broadened to include plant form, the subtle traces or shadows of the natural world remaining in dried leaf or petal tissue, in stem and dried grass growth patterns and in delicate, translucent D.N.A. tracings. I combined such images with the vastness of landscape, sky, back-lit spaces and reference to the human presence through reflections and painted and sculpted forms. The natural world, its patterns of growth and decay, the renewing cycle of seasons became a thing of mystery to me. I was drawn towards examining aspects of the eternal – the moon, the sea, an ancient artefact against the tiny lifespan of a flower's blooming or an insect's flight.

I continued working with printmaking, mixed media and collaged pieces. Some of the screen-printed self-portrait heads were worked over, sand-papered, waxed until they became traces and suggestions of their former selves, shadows of an existence. Votive plaques became worn fragments; I used the torn and deckle edges of the paper support to enhance the feeling of impermanence, and also to give the image a sense of being an object in its own right – something that was nevertheless surviving the ravages of time.

I found the complexity of many of the large oils with their divided compositions and densely worked surfaces called for a wider response, from me, to the tensions set up within the picture plane. When I'm painting all I'm really thinking about are the abstract qualities within the work – the interplay of transparent and opaque paint, the drama of saturated or muted colour and an overall tonal control. Each surface and passage of paint is considered and refined until its weight within the whole piece seems right. I enjoy paintings which can be read from a distance and yet reveal more and more as you get nearer. I don't mean in terms of literal detail but in the rewarding nature of the quality of paint itself, the subtlety of harmony, tone and texture – relative to nothing other than itself. I build my paintings up physically in layers – the end result of the colour, tone or image is reliant upon the last bit of glazing, the last scratched-through surface. I want to draw the viewer into the work, reveal the contents slowly and let them have time to find their own responses.

*Extract from the catalogue essay by Mary Sara for Victoria Crowe's exhibition at the Corrymella Scott Gallery, Newcastle, 1997:*

It is easy to be so seduced by the sheer beauty of paint, colour and imagery in a painting by Victoria Crowe that the eye alone is engaged. Yet even as the eye feasts, fastening on a detail here, a glorious passage of colour there, we are being directed onwards into the heart of a mystery. Beyond the picture surface, behind the glass, what questions are being asked, of the visual world, of the nature of existence – and of us? She looks at the world and finds that all that she is, thinks and feels has, potentially, an analogous form in nature, in art, or in the objects around her. The manner in which she arranges and suggests connections between these diverse forms reflects the complexity of her observations and the subtle interplay of personal and universal ideas and experience.

We are inarticulate in front of the biggest questions and essays at answers reveal that our knowledge can only be imperfect – and temporary. This artist shows us why it is vital that we should ask. She depicts objects not only for their own sake – out of delight in their colours, shapes and personal associations, but as signifiers for states of mind. Nothing so direct as symbol, allegory or metaphor is intended, instead it is as if she is a writer deploying hieroglyphs – pictures of objects that represent a word, or, mute, she makes gestures that stand for rather than explain. By elliptical yet urgent means she leaves us to search out the implications for our own lives. Images of angels like messengers between worlds float into her recent paintings. In addition to the received cultural and religious associations they bring with them they function as similes for the purpose of the artist – which is to attempt to make visible the invisible and inexplicable …

… There is sympathetic magic in the small votive plaques of children left by mothers in churches for the protection of children but we all practise similar rituals. We endow objects with associations and through juxtapositions cause them to resonate with meanings beyond appearances. We know ourselves and express what we know through our intuitive selection and organisation of objects in our domestic interiors. Put them together and paint them as Victoria Crowe does, time and time again trusting her instincts rather than her intellect, and we enter the realms of dreams. In

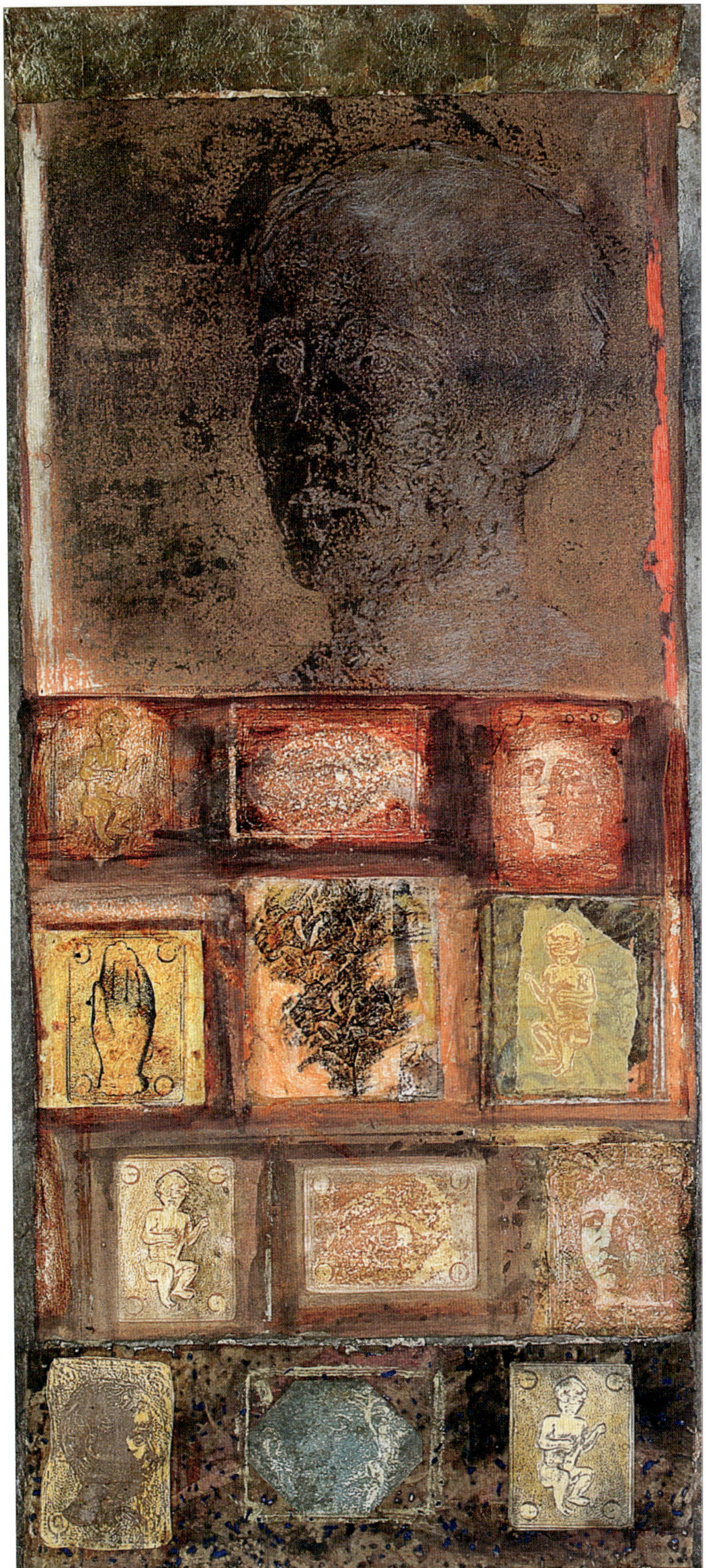

ASSEMBLED FRAGMENTS – GOLD
1997. Mixed media on paper. 30in. x 16in.
Private Collection

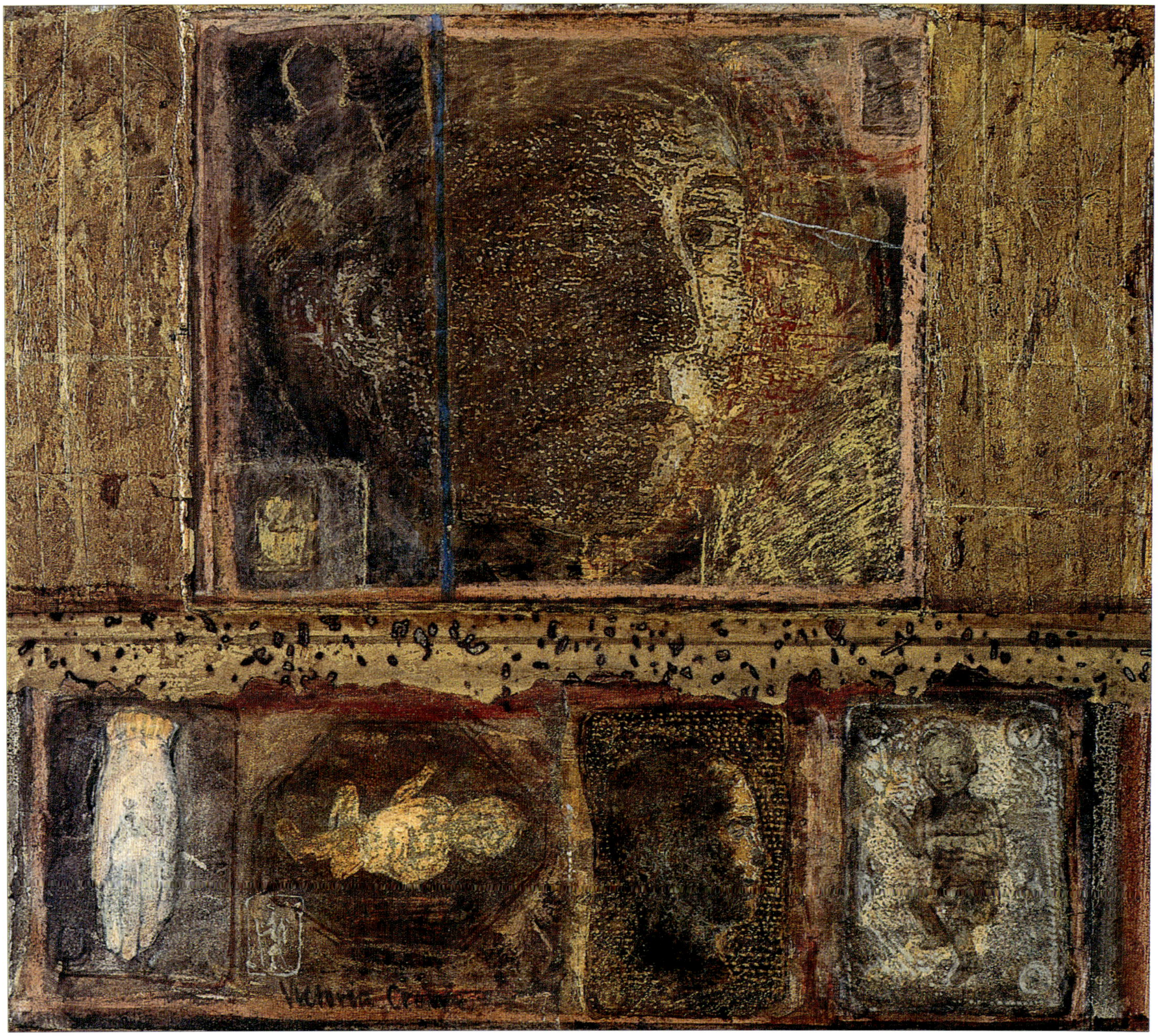

**BRONZED ALTARPIECE** 1997. Mixed media on paper. 11½in. x 13in. Private Collection

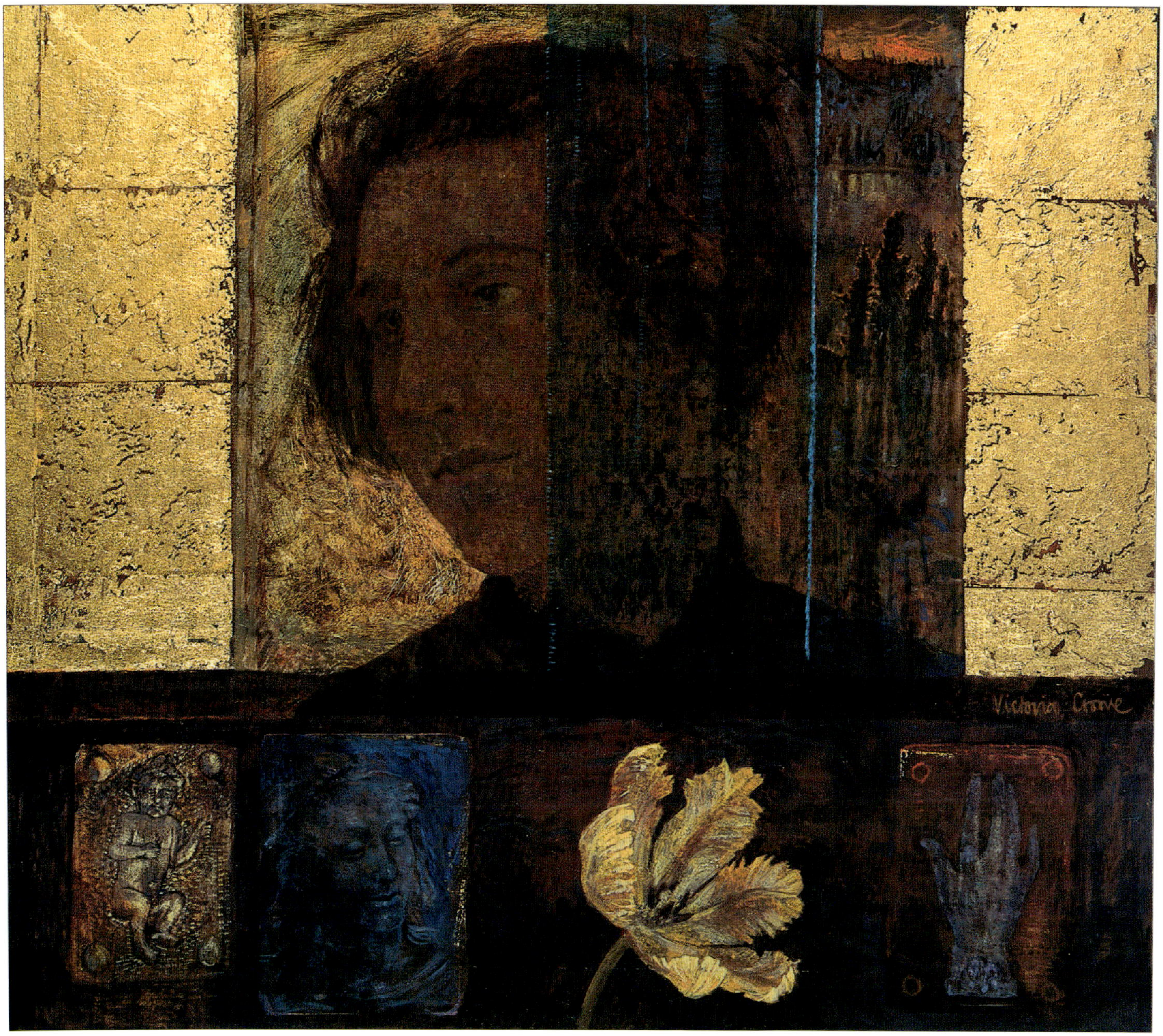


**REFLECTIONS ON GOLD** 1996. Oil and gold leaf on board. 17¼in. x 18½in. Private Collection

dreams, as in meditation, we tap into unconscious and archetypal imagery. In *Night of the Dragonfly* the conjunction of a haloed moon, a wide open tulip, the sea and a desiccated dragonfly set immutable events against ephemeral moments …

… The content of a painting by Victoria Crowe is multi-dimensional but the space in her paintings is non-illusionistic being intentionally shallow, like a film projected on to a screen. This brings us very close to the 'scene' as well as underlining the autonomy of the work of art. Despite her lucid and exquisite skill with paint she does not wish us to forget that the picture is a vehicle for its content, not a simulacrum.

We 'read' *Echoes of Italy* from left to right; from the eternally beautiful sculpted young man via an archaeology of distressed red and gold 'wall' to the menacingly fleshy stalks and leaves and rapacious flowers which explode and fill more than half the picture. Permanence and impermanence we think – but the youth died and is permanent only in art or memory whilst in nature the process is speeded up, almost over even as we watch the petals open. Grassy seed heads arching behind the strong leaves remind us of the enduring cycles of nature of which we are a part, and that 'To everything there is a season'.

## Drawing the dragonfly

I'm drawing the dead dragonfly. With a cold eye and a sharp point I discern and analyse the unfamiliar structure. I understand through drawing the strong pivot of the wing-joints, the axis of the flat head, the angular construction of the thorax.

But look again at the dragonfly; see wings of delicate net-like structure, the transparent substance glinting, catching the light, refracting gold in the summer dusk. Remember in life how swiftly it moved, the strong compact thorax and elegantly jointed abdomen painted fiercely black, yellow, black, yellow. Now above the water the dragonfly clasps the female in ecstatic mating, a winged salute, one above the other in strange harmony.

I remember the other winged insects caught in the syrupy light of that summer evening, weaving and dipping above dark peaty water. An unceasing process of creation and annihilation – a process of such purpose.

Your death still seems to have no purpose. I cannot understand when clear-sighted and wiser friends tell me that however short a life is, it is whole and complete. I cannot comfort myself with thoughts of an integrated dance of life, a flowing of forces, where each and every existence is inter-related into a meaningful whole.

I return in memory to that riverbank. Azure wings, insects spiralling downwards like dust motes in sunshine, water's splash. They weave the patterns of their brief life span, caught in the joyful flow of movement and tight above the darkness of the water.

When eventually I paint about the dragonfly, he's there against a summer's night sky, moonlight shining through the veined wings – tiny flecks of colour on the painting's surface. Below the insect, water gleams, reflecting the moonlight on wave and crest, and a tulip opens its petals wide on to the black night.

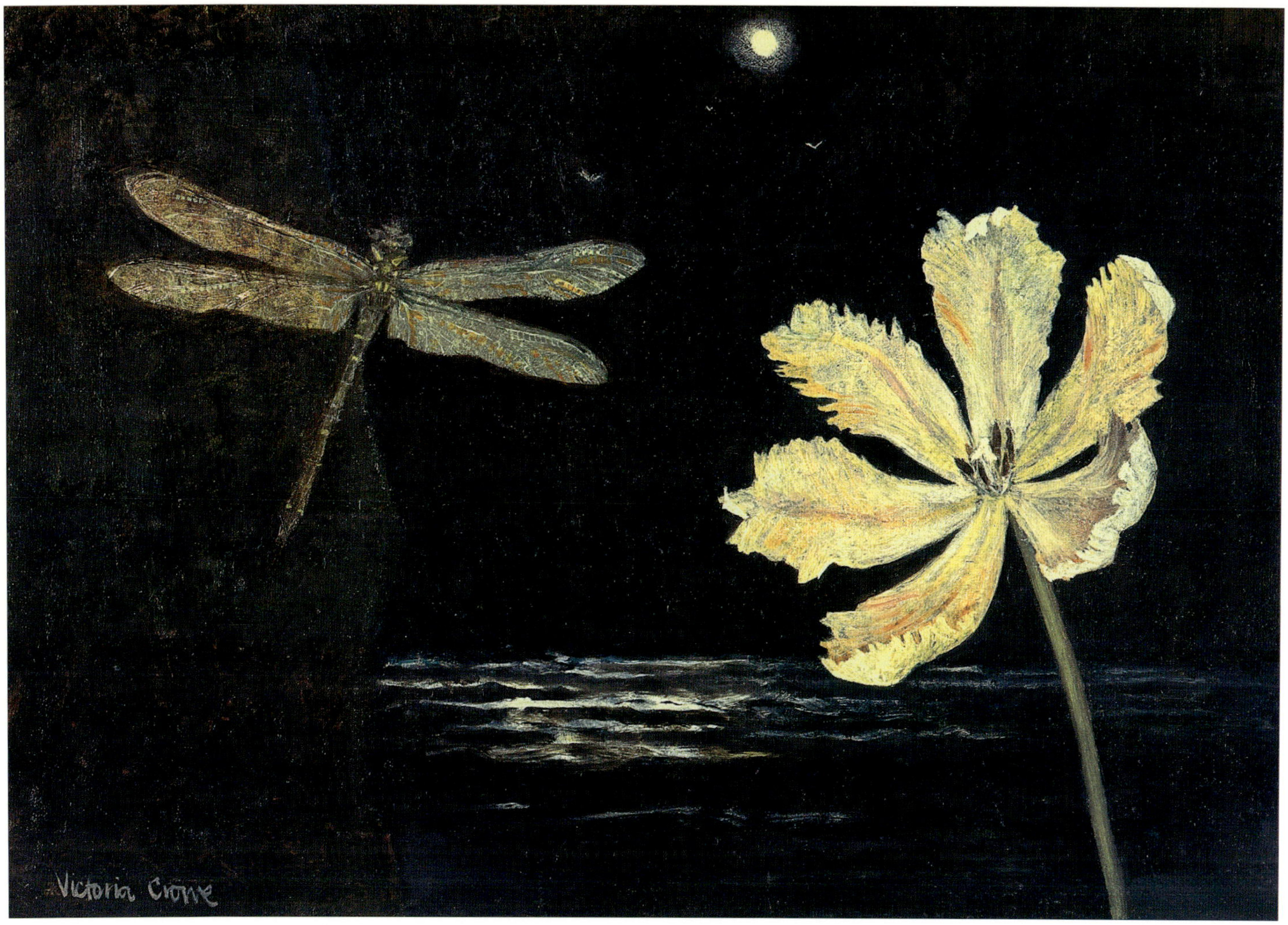

**NIGHT OF THE DRAGONFLY** 1996. Oil on board. 12in. x 16in. Private Collection

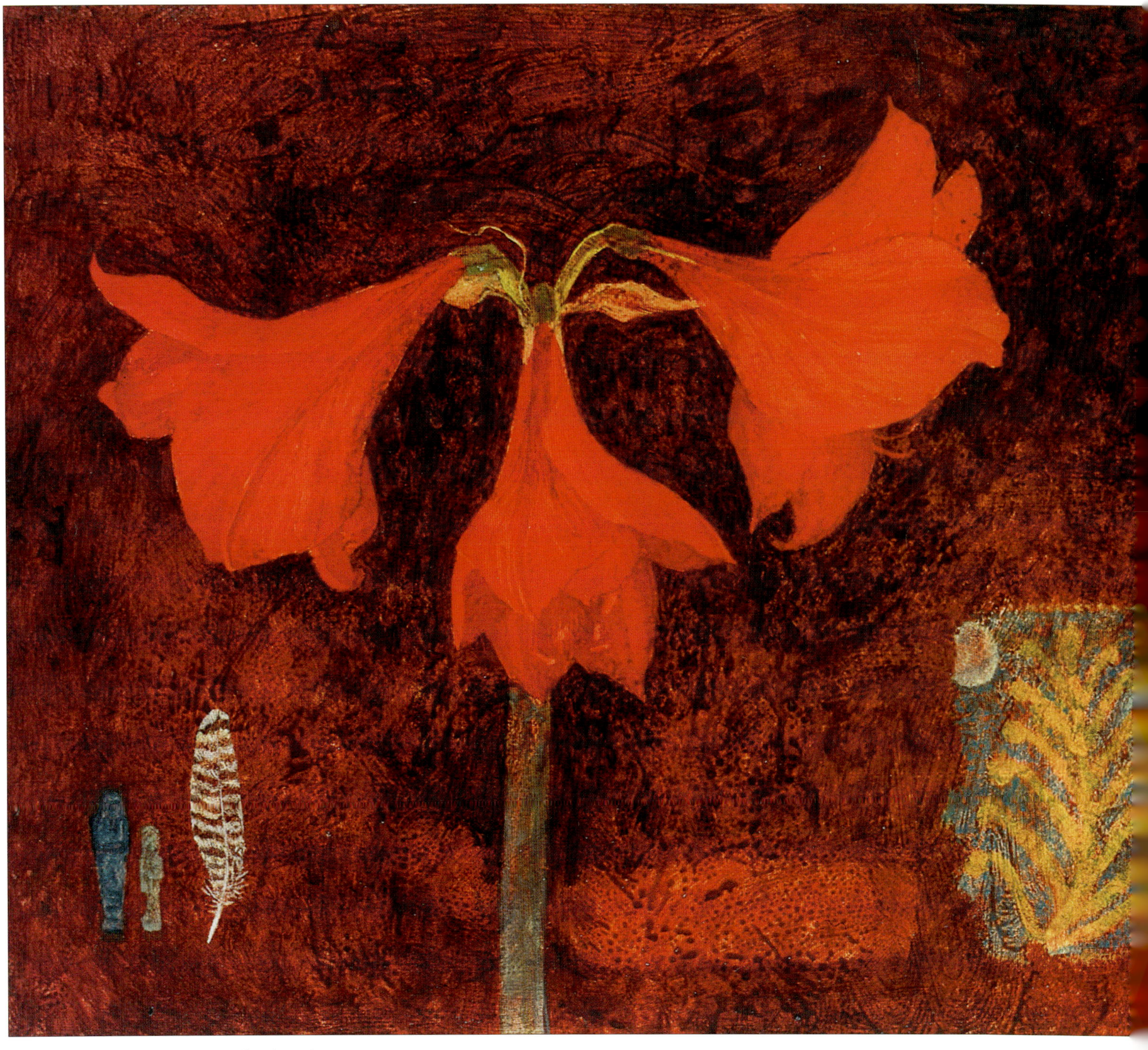

WEIGHING THE GOOD 1997. Oil on board. 16in. x 36in. Private Collection

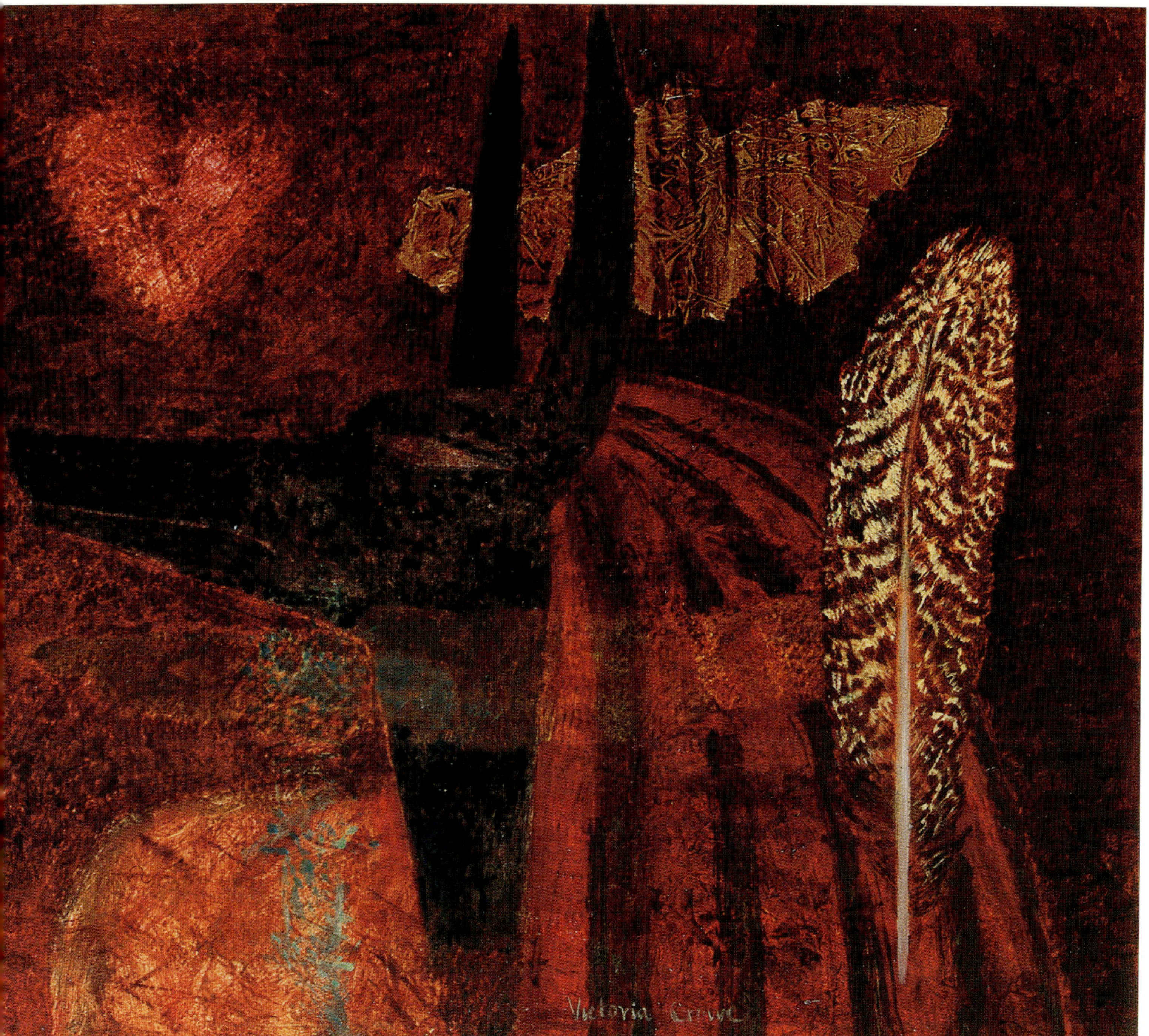
Victoria Crowe

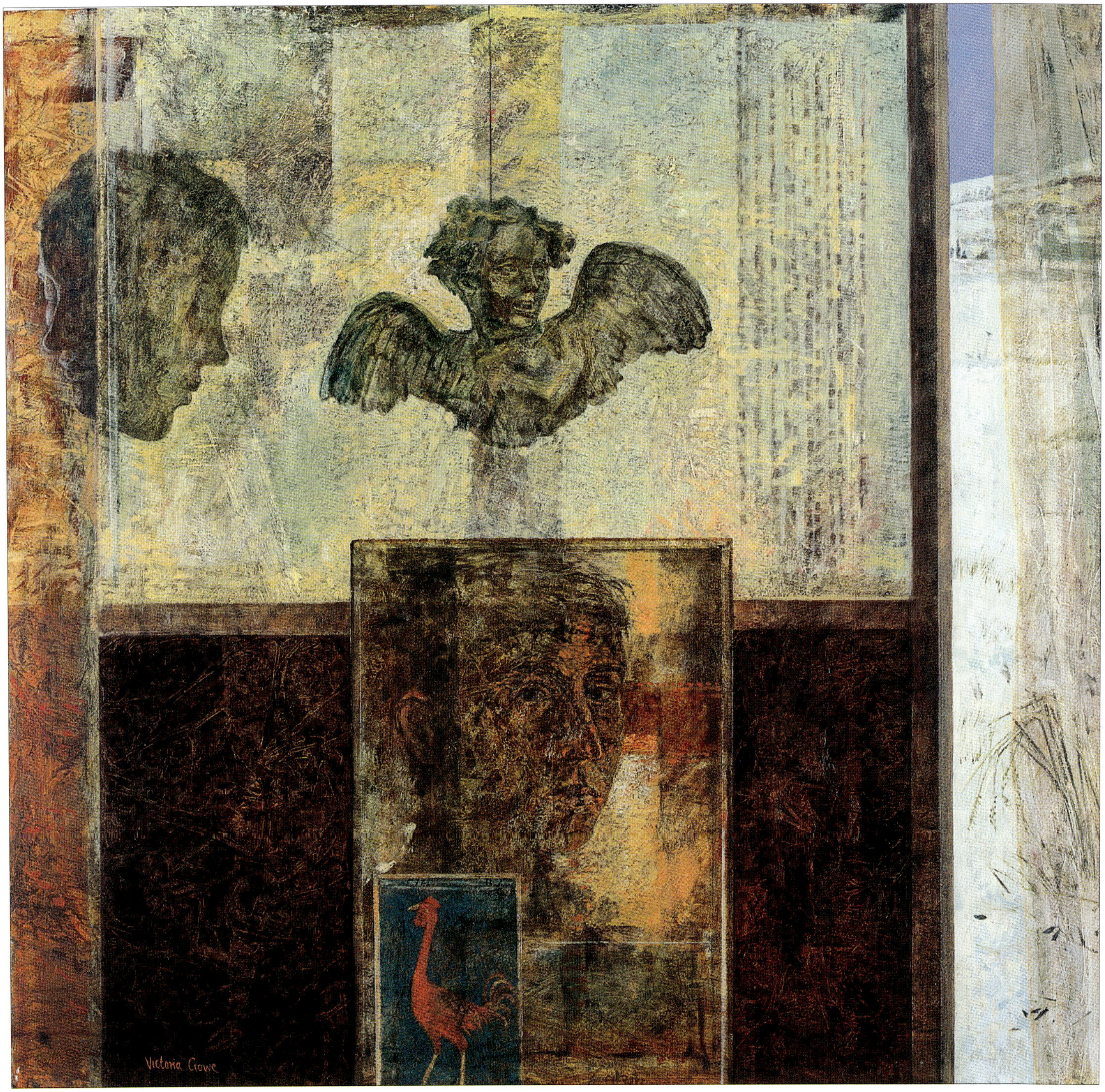


LOOKING OUT, DISTANT LANDSCAPE 1997. Oil on board. 30in. x 30in. Private Collection

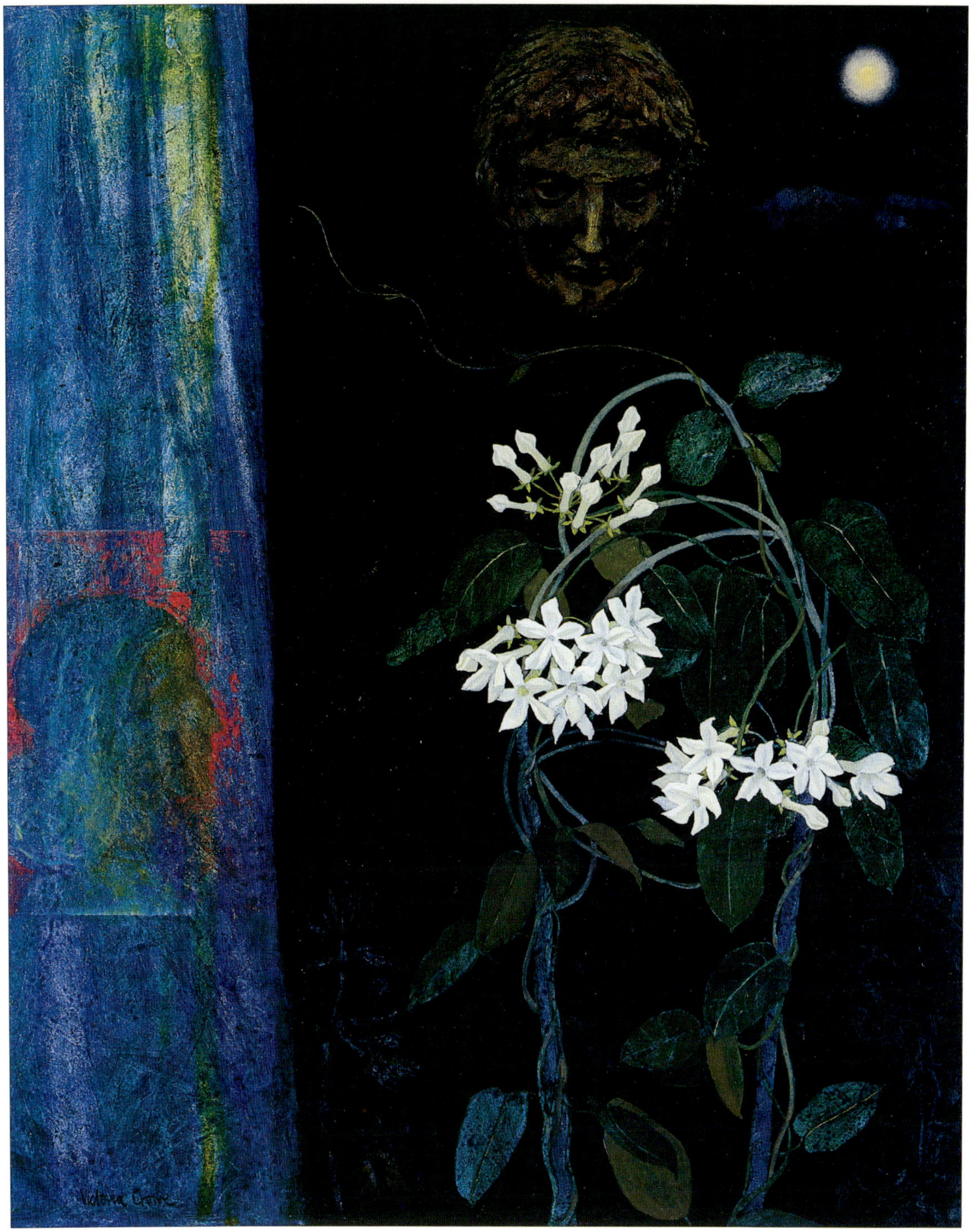

**MIDNIGHT STEPHANOTIS** 1997. Oil on board. 36in. x 28in. Private Collection

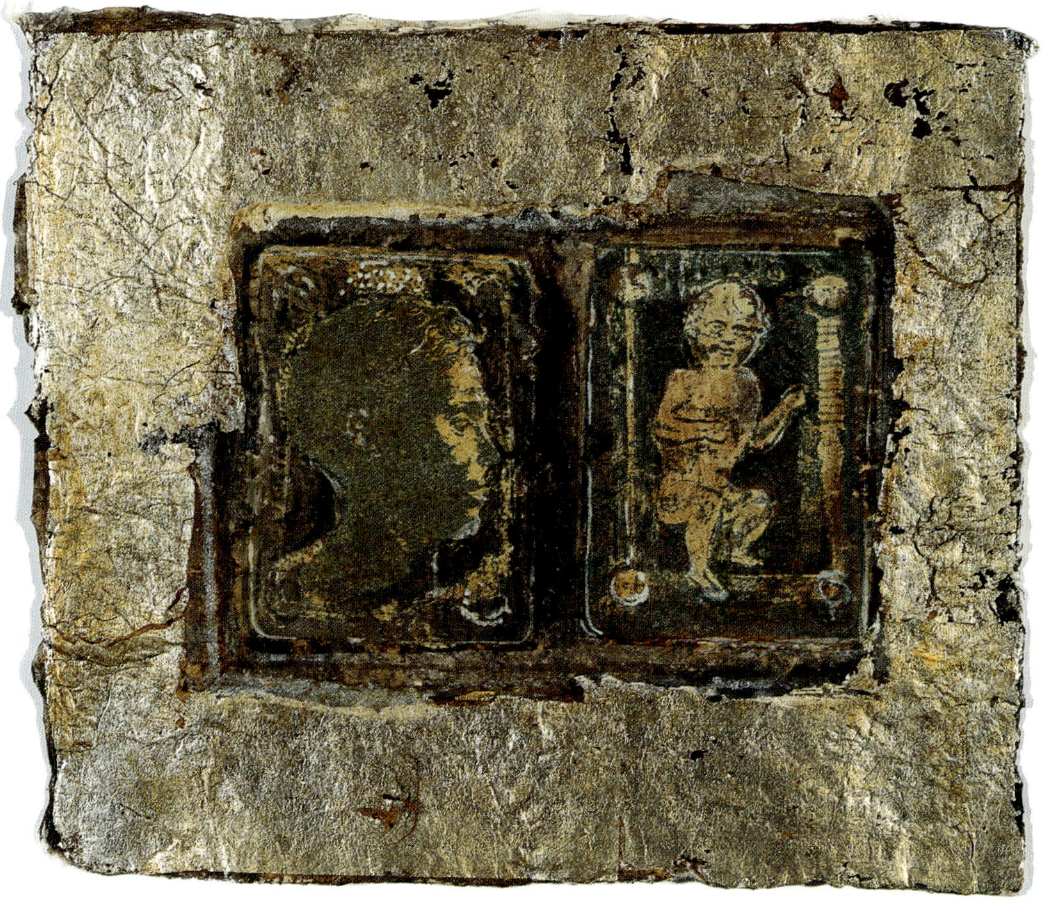

SILVER VOTIVE 1997. Mixed media on paper. 7½in. x 8½in. Private Collection

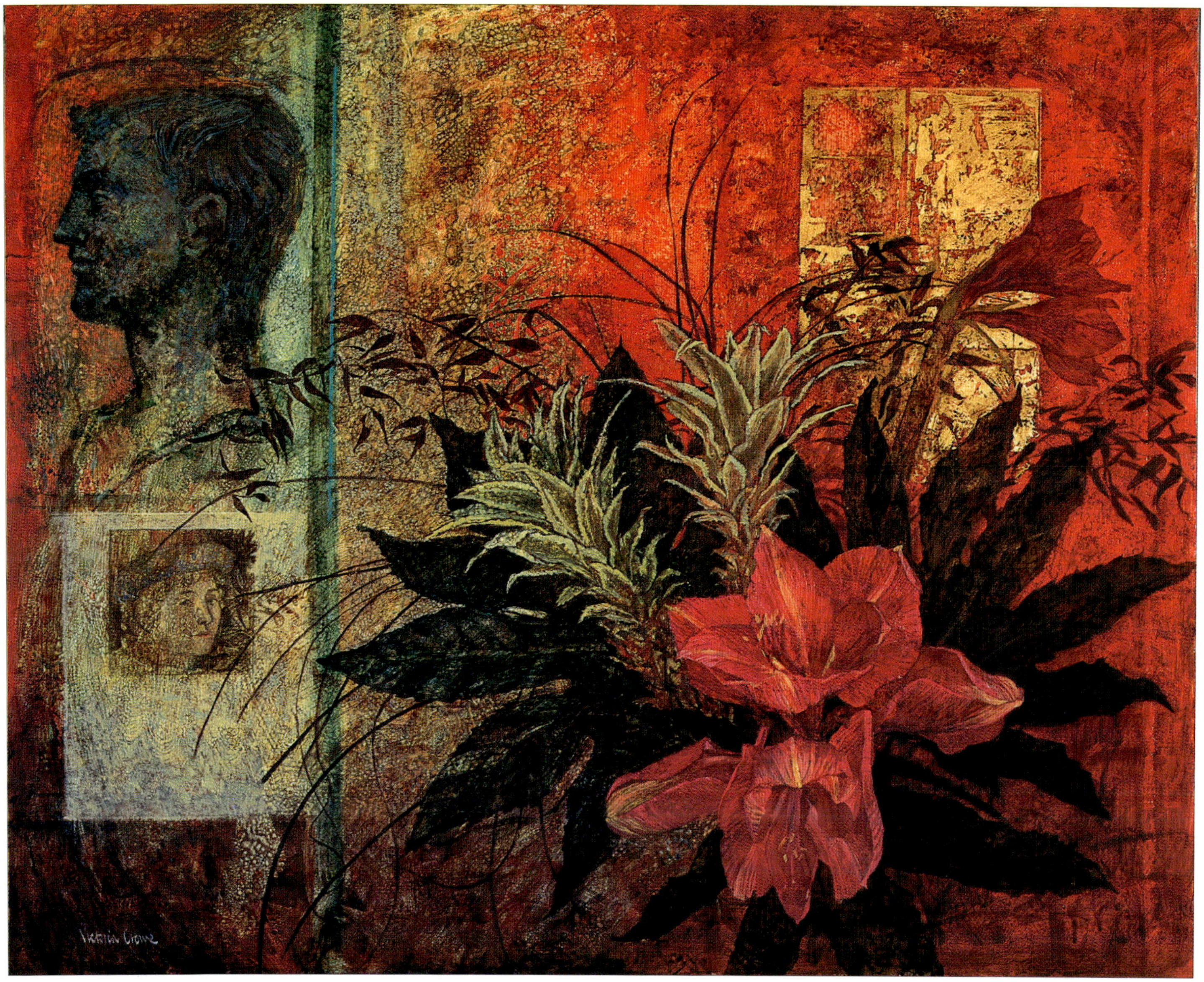

ECHOES OF ITALY 1996. Oil on board. 30in. x 36in. Private Collection

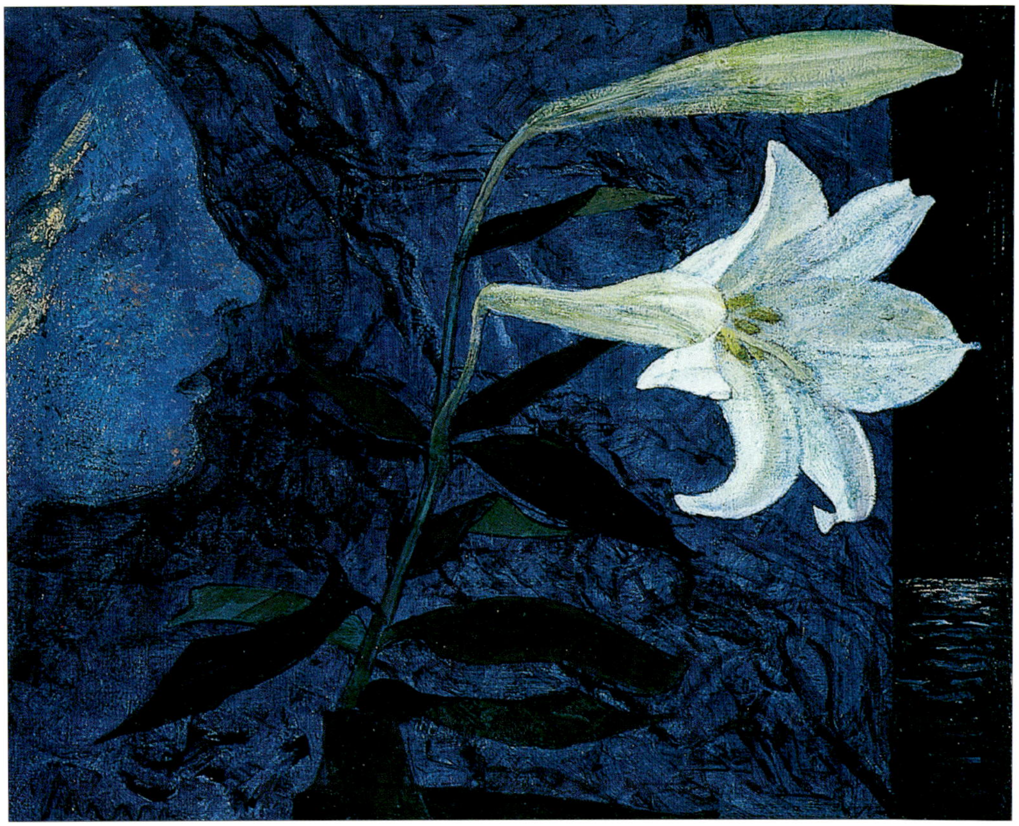

# VENICE

**ENTRANCED GAZE**
1998. Oil on board. 10in. x 12in.
Private Collection

I first went to Venice in the spring of 1998 – and was instantly spellbound by the city. To me, not a great fan of baroque painting or interiors, there was no single heart-stopping image such as I had found in Florence, but a slower response to a changing interwoven relationship, the mystery of the total city, water, mist, colour, light and the past. More than anything else the insistent feeling of fragility was uppermost in my mind. I had the sense of distant tracts of time traced in the surfaces before me, and an imagined memory of buildings, once shining with gold leaf, now dusty, pale and almost crumbling before my eyes.

How to express all of that while avoiding the visual clichés that Venice's canals throw up without mercy! How to get beyond seductive reflections and glints of water beneath pink-ochre palazzi? I wanted to find images which evoked time and timelessness and which questioned our present reality and acknowledged myth and a past certainty.

I saw much of the city and its artefacts, drawing in churches, antique shops and in the squares. I found many evocative images in the Accademia – a fiery wing, a field of gold leaf reduced to fragments on gesso and red earth, a lily against marble graining, an indecipherable script ... and the unknown, to me, Giovanni Bellini

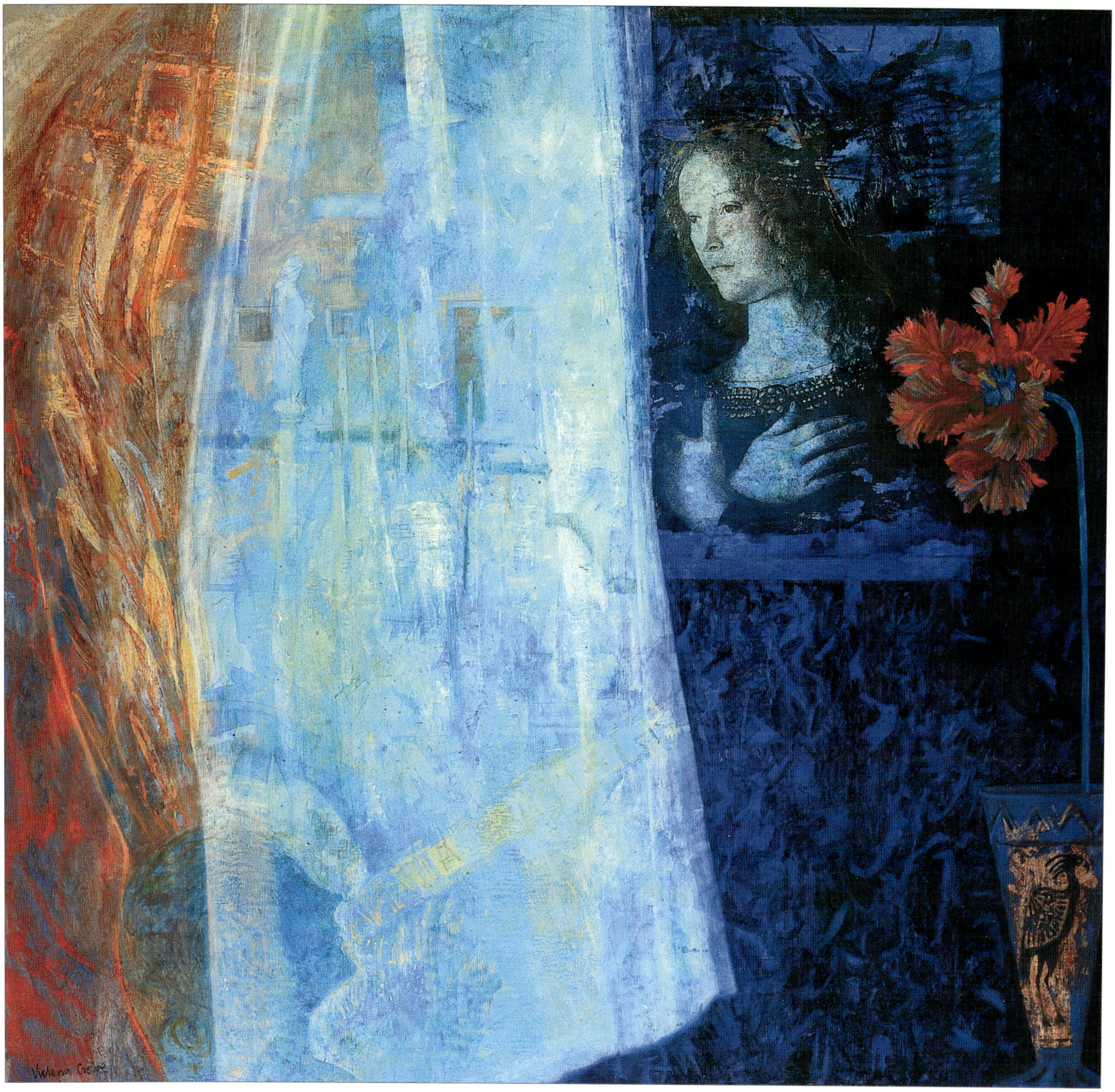

FIRST DAY, VENEZIA: ARCHANGEL WITH WINGS OF FIRE 1998. Oil on linen. 39½in. x 39½in. Private Collection

painting 'Virgin with the Child, the Magdalene and St. Catherine'. I found the mysterious quality of that painting, where none of the protagonists' eyes meets the viewer and the Pietà is prefigured and sensed, by the surely virginal Magdalene, echoed much of the feeling I had of Venice – there was a sense of masque, of destiny being played out and the inevitability of decay.

The group of paintings I made in response to this first visit to Venice contain references to the Magdalene head, gold-leafed grounds and fragments of script. These elements became as much part of the reality of the city as the time-distressed surfaces and the reflected light from the water of the canal glinting through the translucent, blowing curtains of my room.

CATALOGUE, ACCOMPLISHED JOURNEYS, BRUTON GALLERY, LEEDS

## Visiting the archangel with wings of Fire

I have watched Victoria Crowe's paintings grow in intensity and authority over many years. Her art has gradually moved from keen observation of her local surroundings into a powerful vision of the world. The personal and private has become fused with the universal. She is widely travelled yet she has remained true to her roots and convictions. She plunders other cultures to find equivalents for her own experiences. Her ambition is to reinvent mythology, to refashion feelings we may too easily lose in the electronic world of the future.

In childhood we experience the world intensely through all our senses. We quickly learn that the pale soft rose with the beautiful scent has dark sharp thorns that prick and hurt us. This double edge to the world is poignantly made visible in Victoria Crowe's poetic juxtapositions.

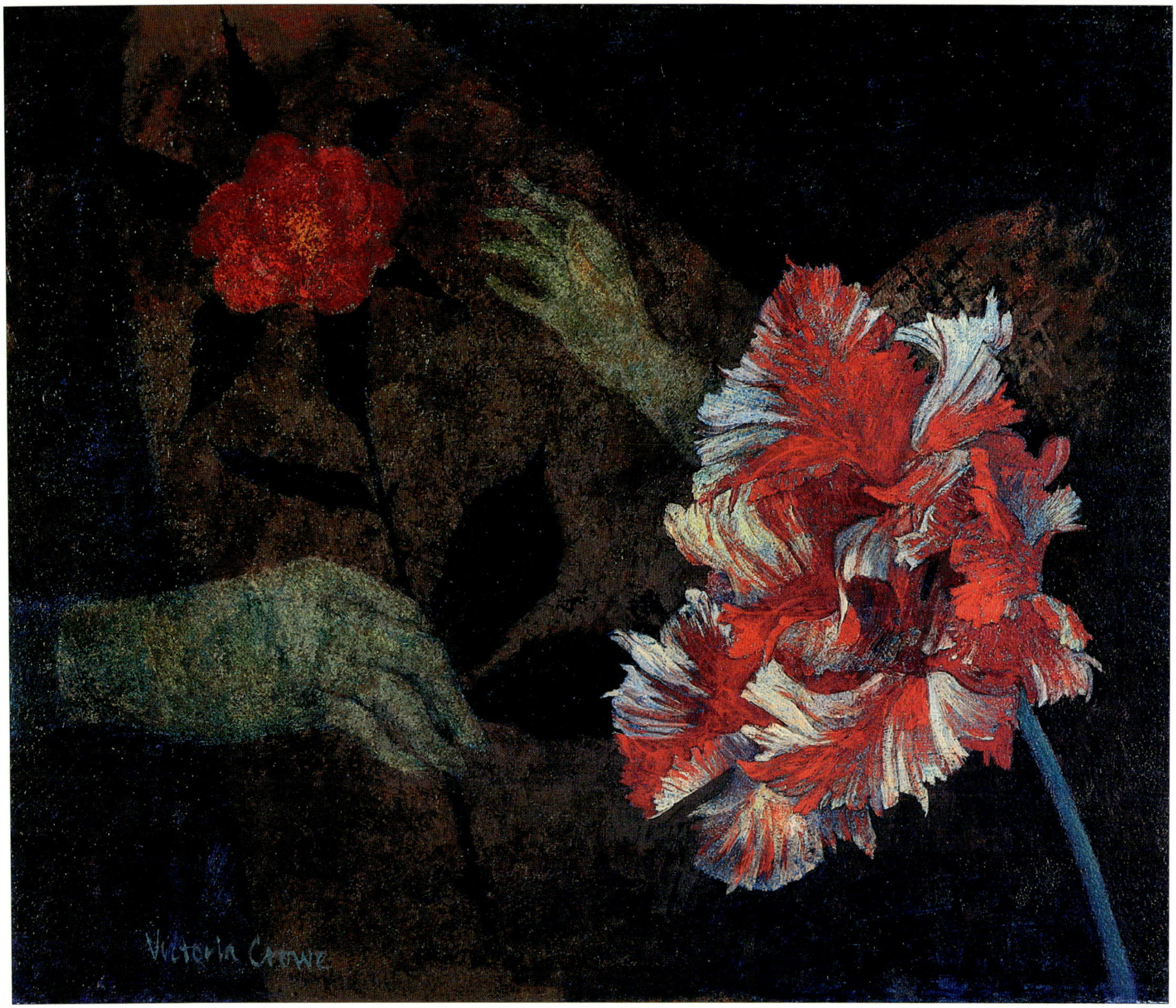


**THE GIFT** 1998. Oil on board. 12in. x 14in. Private Collection

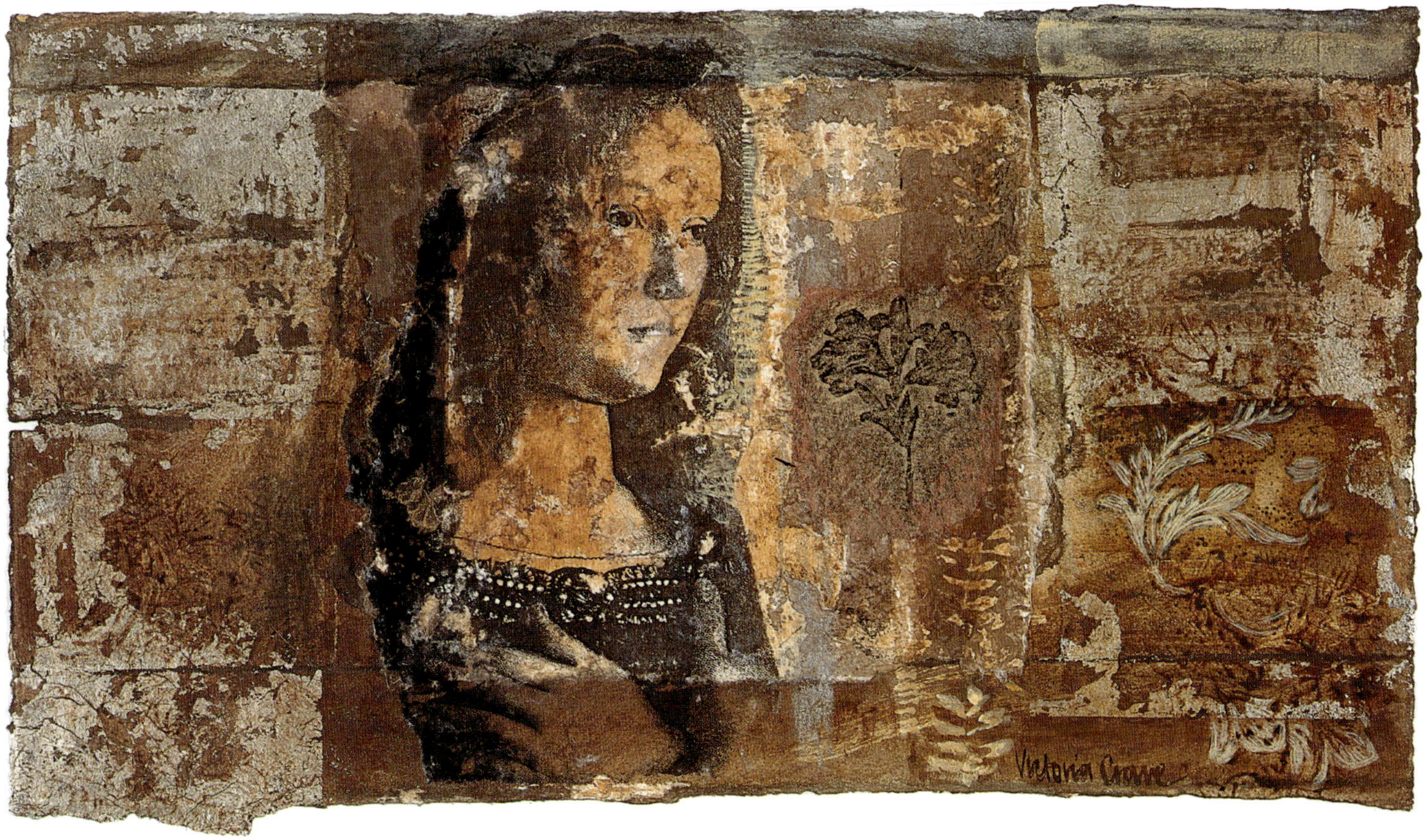


**FRAGILE TRACES, VENICE**
1999. Mixed media. 9½in. x 16in.
Private Collection

MOON. DRAGONFLY. WAVE ANGEL. CURTAIN. FLOWER

Few artists working today use association of ideas, visual metaphors, poetic connections and comparisons as tellingly as Victoria Crowe. She has discovered, or rediscovered by trial and error, a most eloquent and direct visual language. This arises from asking how one can make an emotionally charged painting release its meaning slowly?

Victoria Crowe's most recently completed paintings distil her memories of a visit to Venice. In The Accademia she said of Bellini's painting Archangel Gabriel and Virgin Annunciate 'the red-haired angel rushes from a black void into a panelled room', and of the Lorenzo Veneziano Annunciation 'its gessoed and red rubbed ground clearly visible behind the margins of gold leaf clinging to wing and profile'.

Such paintings must have confirmed her own delight in startling juxtapositions and ritualistic colour. Venice as dying flower, sinking ship, decaying palaces and winged lions!

Under the ravishing textures and celebrations of colour, vividly apparent in these paintings, there is a seriousness about life. Life is wonderful, rich, intoxicating and short. These paintings are about time, and how fleeting are moments of heightened awareness. We all experience such moments. It takes an exceptional artist to give them convincing shape and colour.

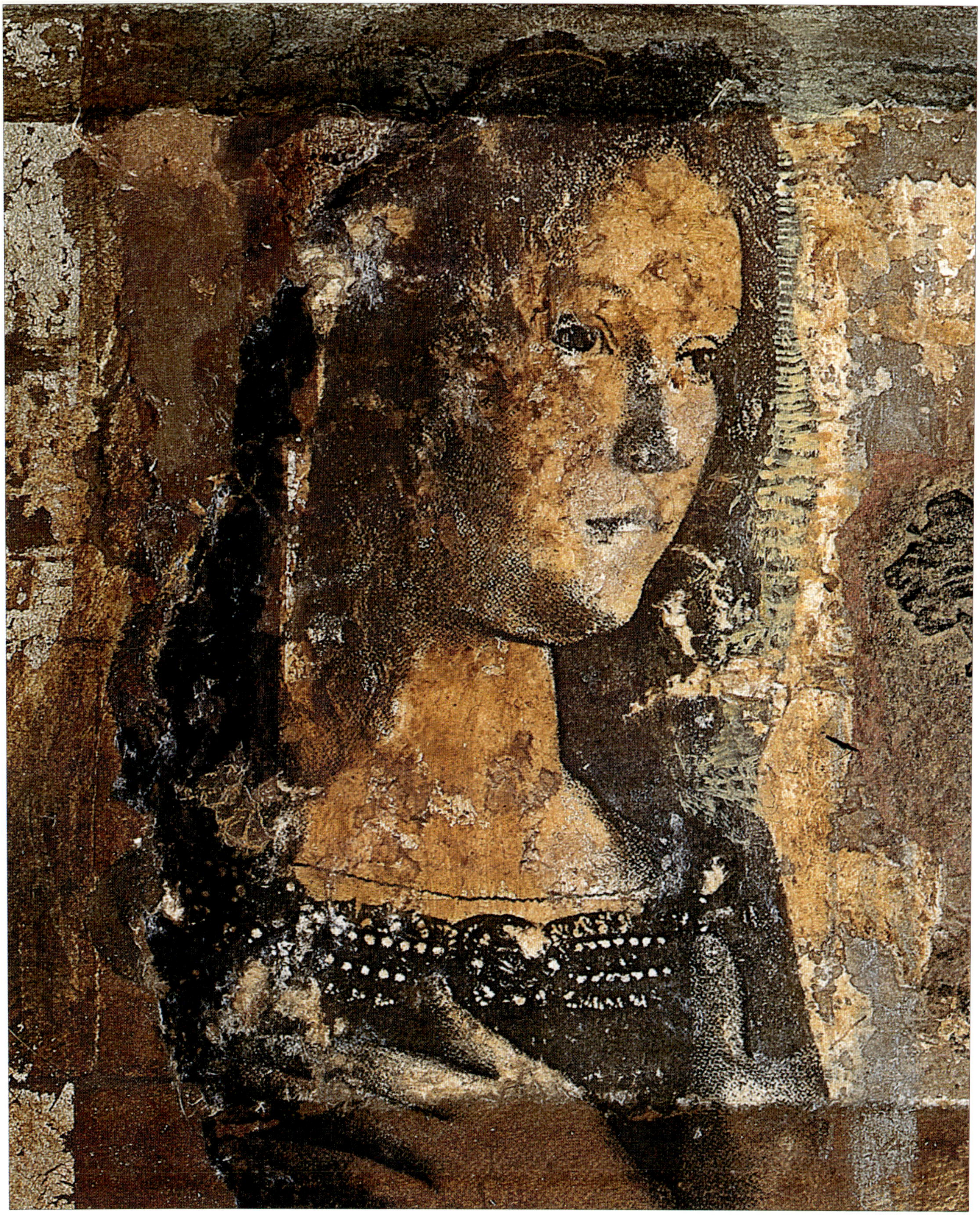

SEE I AM A MAGICIAN.
I TAKE ORDINARY OBJECTS AND BY COMBINING THEM I CREATE MYSTERY.
IF YOU ENTER MY COLOURS YOU ENTER DREAM
THEN RETURN TO THE WORLD REFRESHED.

These are beautiful, thoughtful paintings by an artist at the height of her powers. They generate respect for the alternating contradictions of the world, the joy and sadness, the light and dark.

We are all travellers through time. The lily in the hand of the angel is both a celebration and a warning. Under the moon the young girl looks at the old woman. The old woman bows her head. You can't put it more simply than that.

Derek Hyatt, July 1998

---

Discoveries I made in Venice continue to delight and inspire. There's so much to respond to visually that it's difficult to select what's personally relevant.

It's not a static place – there's a constant movement – of the water, the tourists, the light, the vaporetti; the creep of lichen, the flaking of paint, the fading of colour, the rubbing away of gold … graffiti adds its message to all this too; an emerald green acute angled letter on the bars and Perspex shielding a supplicating stone Madonna – the carving now losing its sharpness, a layer of stone, fine as skin, detaching from the curve of cheekbone. Electric light in a red glass candle holder shines through the nights in front of this crumbling figure, casting the shadow of a plastic flower across the walls of the Sotoportego. The process of change made visible.

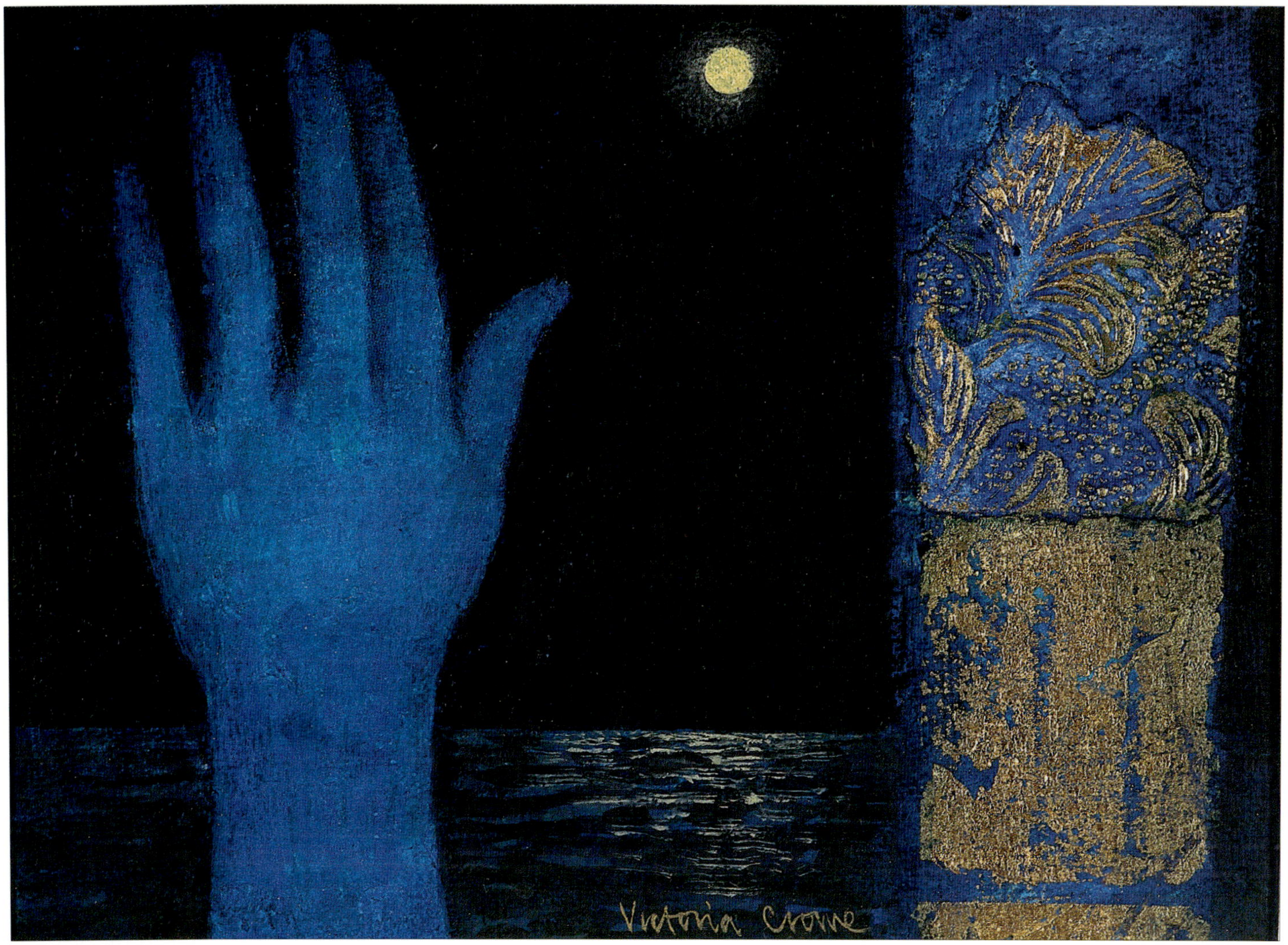


**VENICE NIGHT, II** 1999. Mixed media. 5½in. x 7in. Private Collection

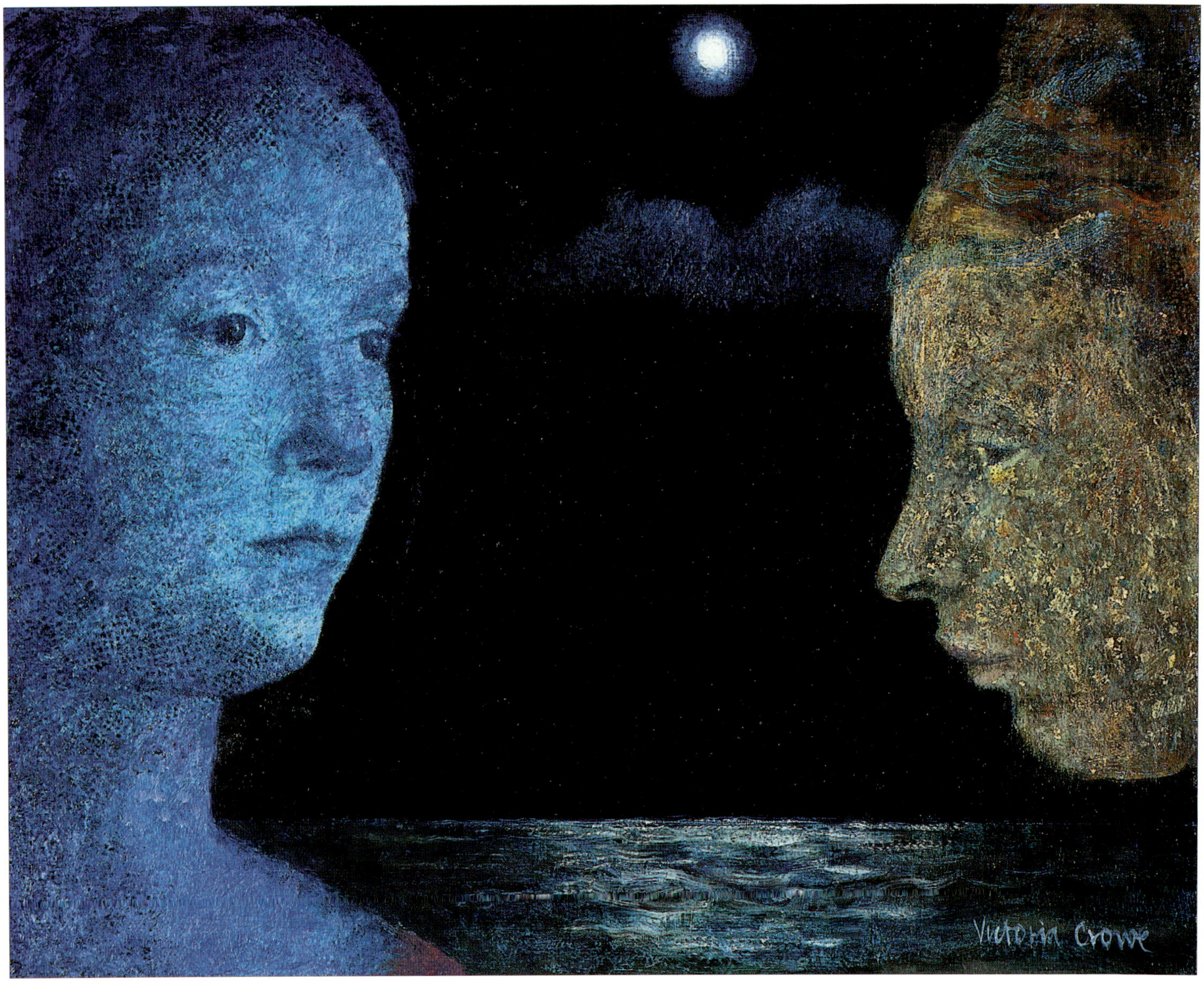


TRAVELLERS IN A SINGLE DREAM 1998. Oil on board. 10in. x 12in. Private Collection

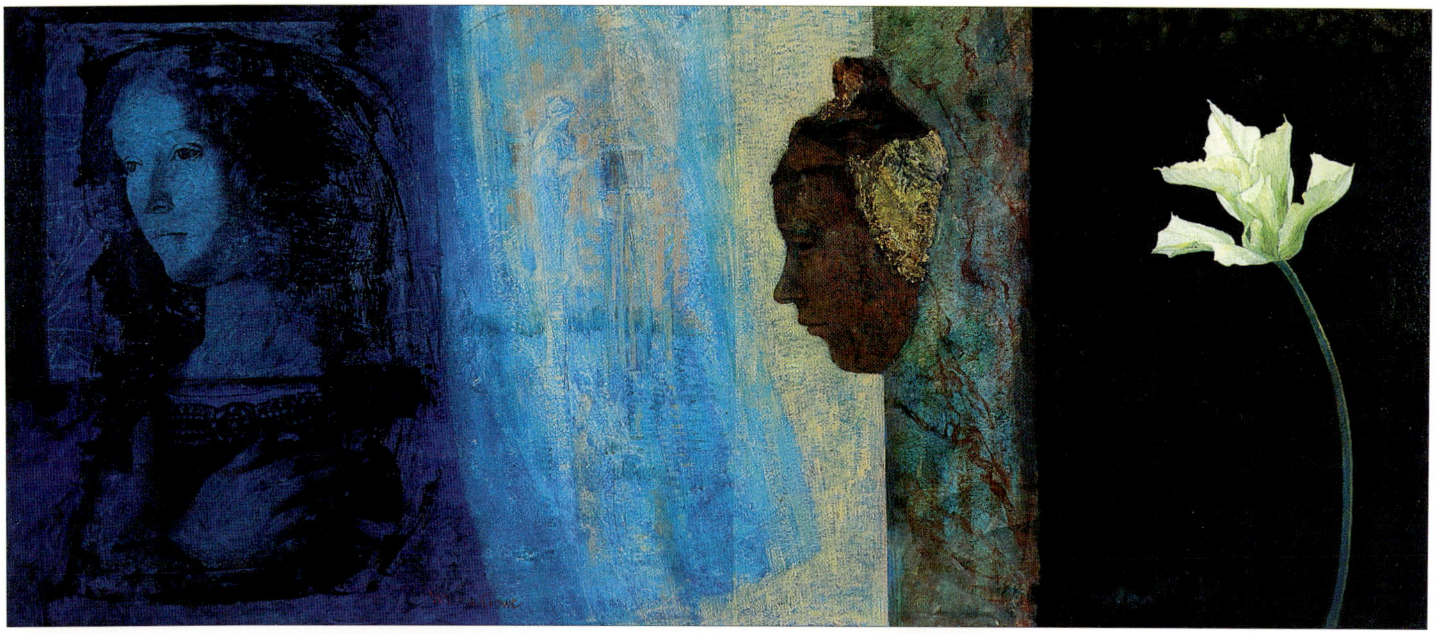

RETURN FROM VENICE
1998. Oil on board. 16in. x 36in.
Private Collection

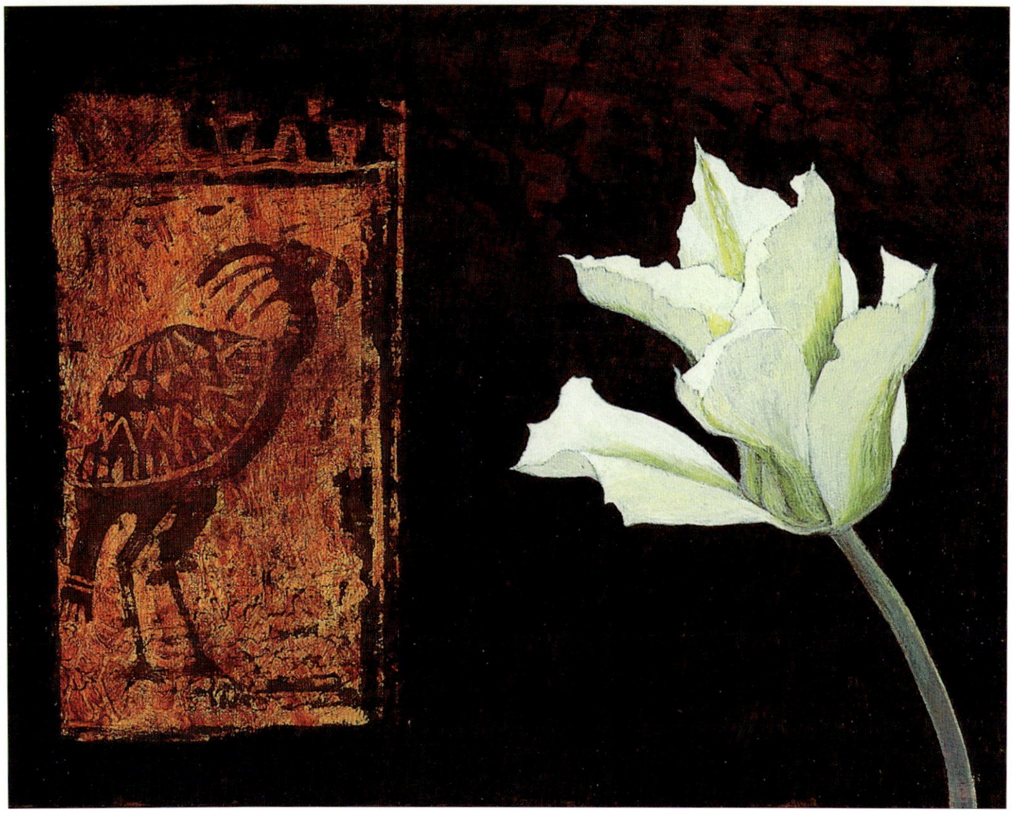

HOT BIRD, COOL BLOOM
1998. Oil on board. 8½in. x 10½in.
Private Collection

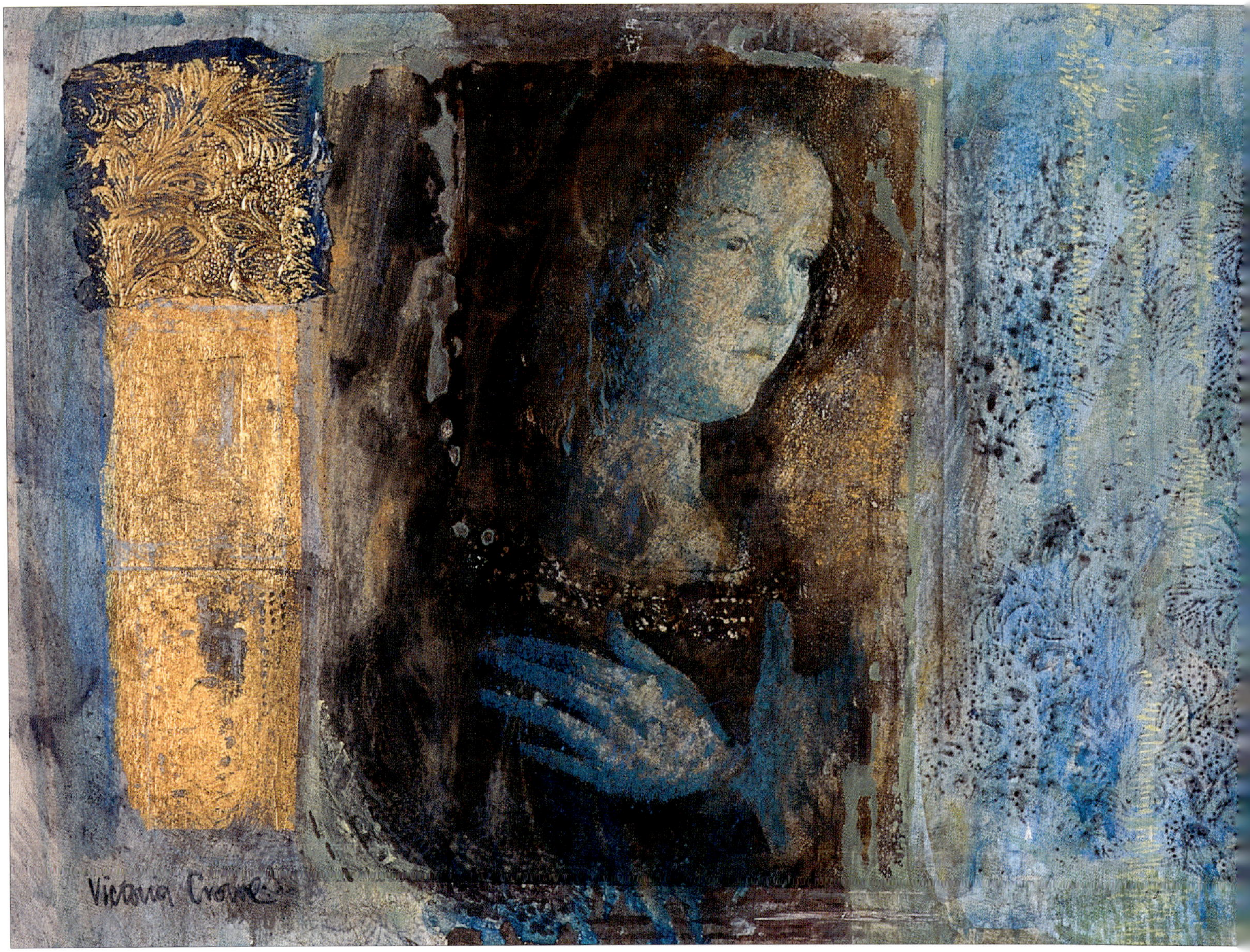


**VENICE: FRAGILE SECRET** 1999. Mixed media. 11¾in. x 30in. Private Collection

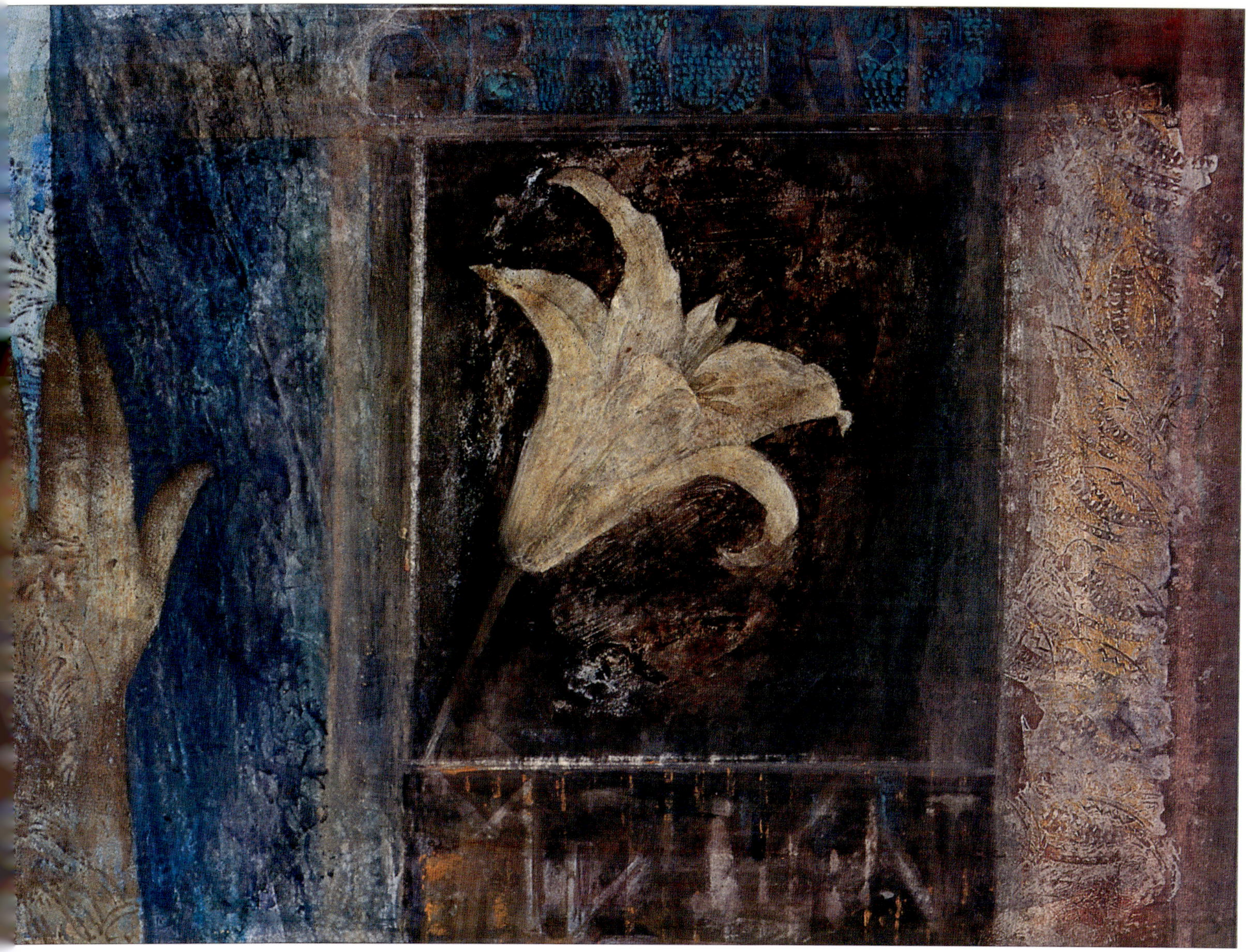

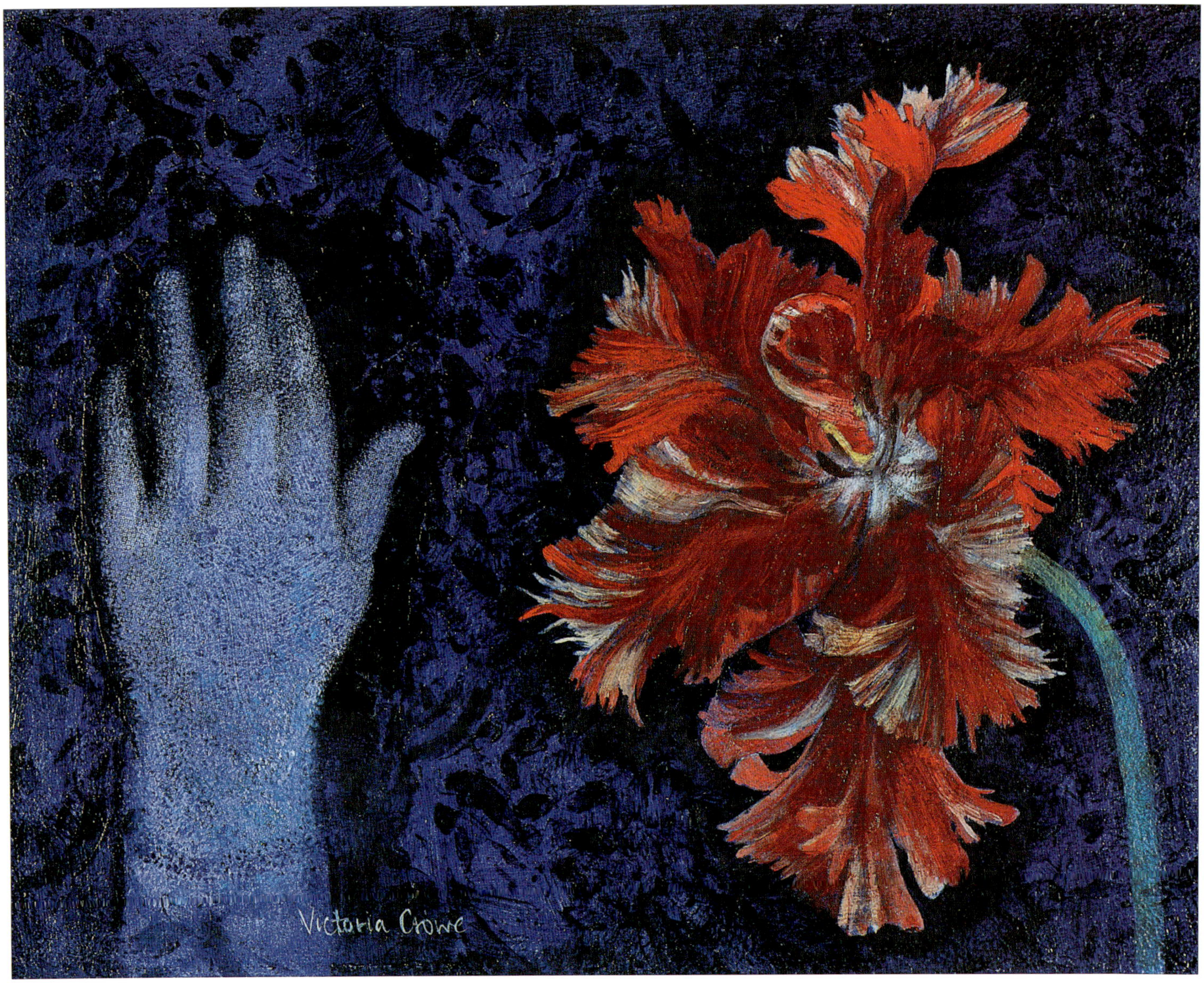


**TENDER, SECRET JOY** 1998. Oil on board. 10in. x 12in. Private Collection

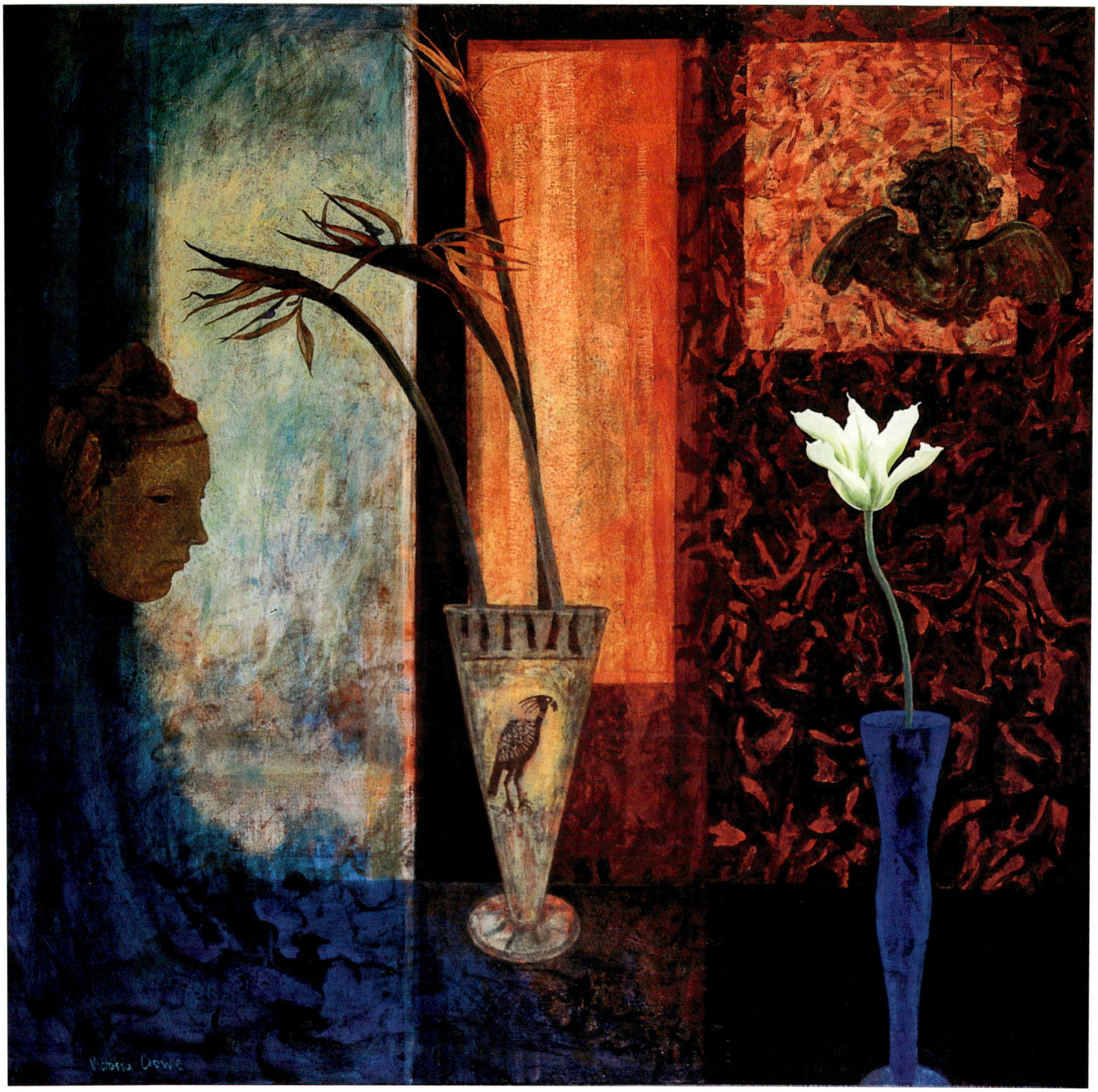

**EACH IN ITS OWN TIME AND PLACE** 1998. Oil on linen. 39½in. x 39½in. Private Collection

# IF THE SUN AND MOON SHOULD DOUBT, THEY WOULD GO OUT

*This section deals with new concerns and working processes in Victoria Crowe's recent paintings. They are introduced by passages from Clare Henry's catalogue essay for the 1999 Thackeray Gallery solo exhibition.*

Sometimes it helps to address life's events obliquely rather than head-on – especially when tremendous forces or emotions are at work. My most recent visit to Victoria Crowe's studio coincided with the morning of the August 1999 solar eclipse. As we drove to her Scottish home in West Linton she remembered a tip from her primary teacher long ago. 'Look at it reflected in a bucket of water. It's easier, safer and clearer.' So we did. And, true enough, it was! I tell this story, not just because Crowe's latest oil is called *Eclipse,* but because it suggests one take on various complexities in her work. It is as if her passionate scrutiny of objects, of nature, and of her own deeply felt emotions, is too fierce to be directly transmitted to us; too keen to bear the searching light of day. As with the solar eclipse, a tangential view is needed.

So Crowe works with exquisite fragments and fractions – adding, subtracting, compounding, reducing – in an effort to clarify her overflow of feelings and search for the truth. Fragments of being combined with fragile memories make up each individual, each day, each life. It takes a lifetime to understand our loved ones. Impossible to comprehend the workings of the world. How to distil its essence? Understand its multi-layered complexity? How do we make sense of it all? Her gift for redirecting and focusing our vision begins with her selection and juxtaposition of disparate, favourite images gleaned from near and far. Crowe's beautiful sketch-books attest to her keen draughtsmanship and tremendous linear gifts. She draws like an angel – and sometimes draws actual angels too! In Venice a crammed antique shop interior caught her eye: carved polychrome figures, a huge array of silver ex-votos as well as 'gratzia recevuto' hearts, next to tin lilies, primitive paintings, old engravings and gilded angels. These odd concoctions are rendered on the sketch-book page with painstaking detail before being absorbed into the bigger picture. She draws because 'you can't get the information I need any other way'.

Although not overtly religious, there is a timeless spiritual dimension to much of Crowe's work that transcends mere brush-on-canvas activity. Many of her mysterious, glittering oils are reminiscent of secular icons.

Her recent travels include a trip to India relating to an artists' project on the *Year of the Tiger.* Here again she took a tangential approach.

'My remit was to examine the jungle and its landscape and I soon became enthralled by the Hindu temples and local villages with their rituals and processions. The whole Indian visit evoked for me a sense of the mystery of the unfamiliar. But I

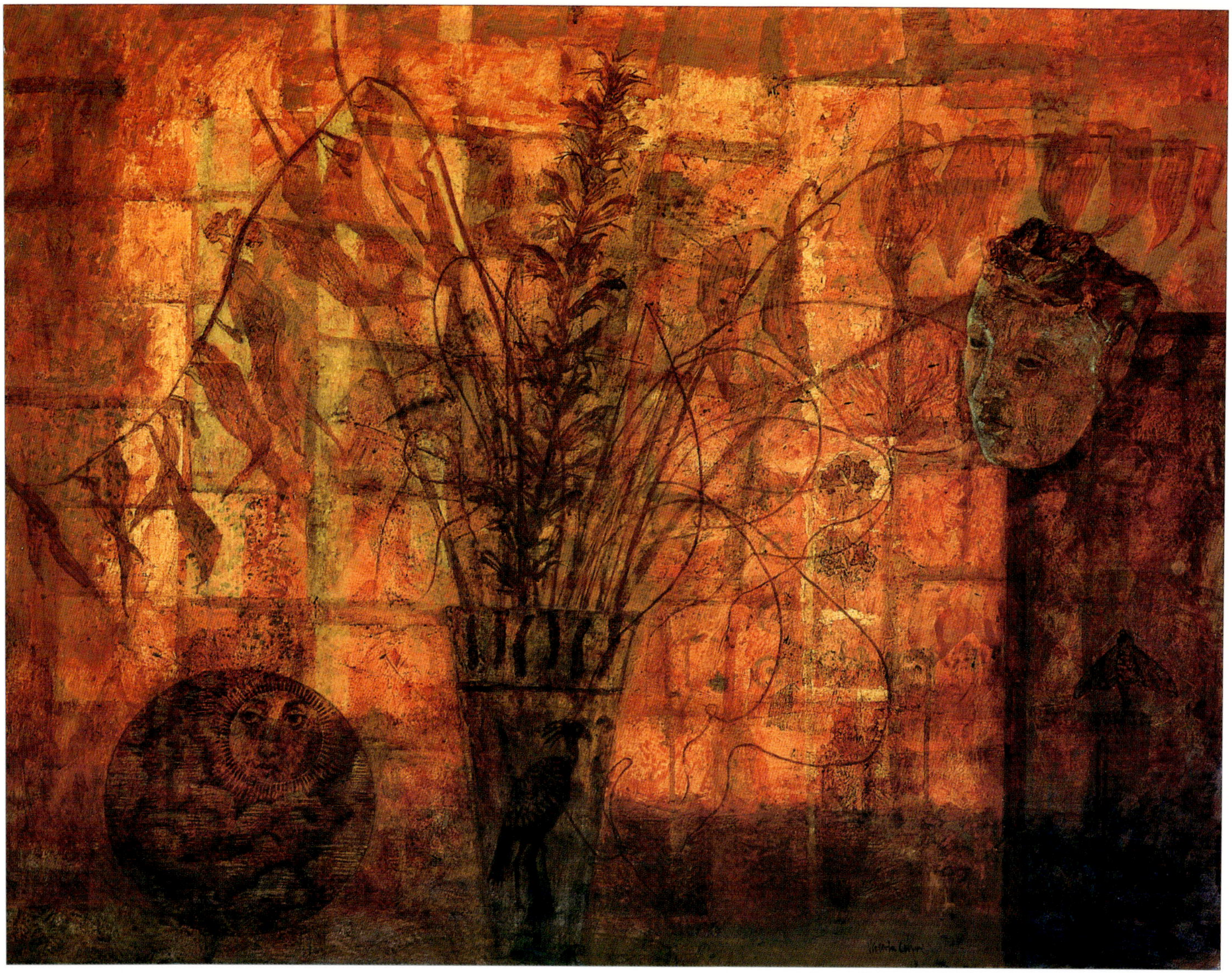

**ECLIPSE** 1999. Oil on linen. 32in. x 40in. Private Collection

was less impressed by my elephant safari to see real tigers than by the imagined and magical sense of the hidden tiger's presence.'

The results are memorable. Her search may be serious, but it also includes a rare vitality, deep appreciation of nature's glories and the occasional riotous and offbeat incident.

Clare Henry, New York 1999

Clare Henry's essay introduces the themes that I am currently working on. It's odd how diverse and unrelated things move us on. I've recently experienced an increasing pull to look again at the landscape. The spectacular comet, the solar eclipse, the full moon distorted by earth's atmosphere, all stir our primitive responses. For me, experiences in India, and again seeing my work from the '70s and '80s in *A Shepherd's Life,* nurtured ideas of using landscape elements once more. In India, after a day working in the landscape, I became lost, separated for about an hour from the other artists. We were in the jungle, on steep terrain, a deserted temple and fort above, the safety of jeeps waiting by a reclining Vishnu statue below. I had foolishly set off alone, missing the track down and taking another, which led me deeper into the wooded valleys. It was about five o'clock when I started out. My head was full of images of the temple where I had been working all day – the deserted lake, the huge ancient figures of tortoise, fish and wild boar carved out of living rock. I had little water in my bottle, I was tired and I realised I was lost. The sun was beginning to go down which can happen so quickly in India and the landscape rose up as shadowy masses on all sides. I felt the power and enormity of the land then – the rock beneath my feet, the total absence of any other human being, the fading light, a group of Langur monkeys, too close for comfort, and the evening noises of the jungle. Of course I was soon missed. I yelled, my friends yelled back, distant voices in the dusk. It was probably over in less than an hour, but what an experience of the power of the natural world.

A different perspective on landscape was opened up by *A Shepherd's Life*. Some of these paintings I hadn't seen for twenty-five years and I had never seen all the work together before. I was surprised that my objective renditions of landscape, now overlaid with memory and time, became almost symbolic, allegorical paintings, images at one remove from reality. I felt again the transforming power of landscape taken out of context – the reflection of a hillside in a worn mirror's surface is seen not for itself, as a *view,* but is changed and set apart by its isolation. Some recent paintings combine landscape imagery with 'interior' elements. These compositional devices are saying 'look again at the meaning of that landscape – its mood, its significance'. As if curtains have been drawn back on a stage or doors slid apart to reveal, for an instant, a landscape in all its intensity.

As with some of my work from Venice I've continued to use text, introducing small areas which are difficult to read: Latin, Greek (and joyfully, after India, some Hindi) with perhaps graffiti, rubbed or semi-erased. The impulse is still to try and decipher it, looking for a greater meaning, whether in painting, life or both – I'm not sure. Many of my sketchbook entries have recently been drawings of fragments and distressed surfaces. One, which I haven't been able to use yet, is of a small parchment or papyrus fragment in the Fitzwilliam Museum in Cambridge. This second century AD scrap contains, according to the museum label, reference to ' … the cosmic power of twenty-six old testament angels …'. Amazing – what a resonant little image.

Questions I get asked, which give me twinges of panic as I formulate an answer – 'What do you paint, then?', or 'What are you painting next?'. Seemingly simple

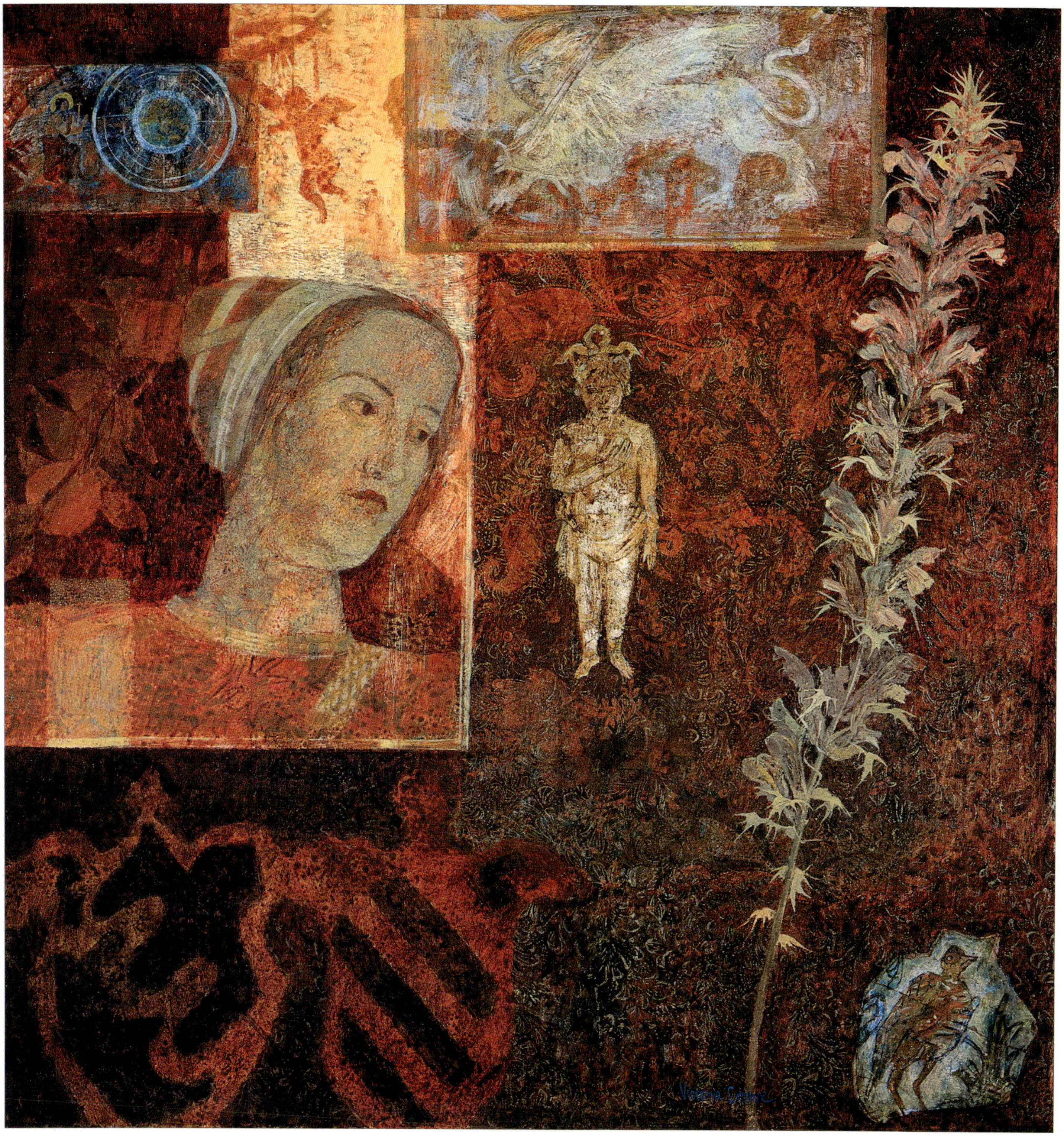

ITALIAN INTERIOR, OBLIQUE REFERENCES 1999. Oil on board. 28in. x 26in. Private Collection

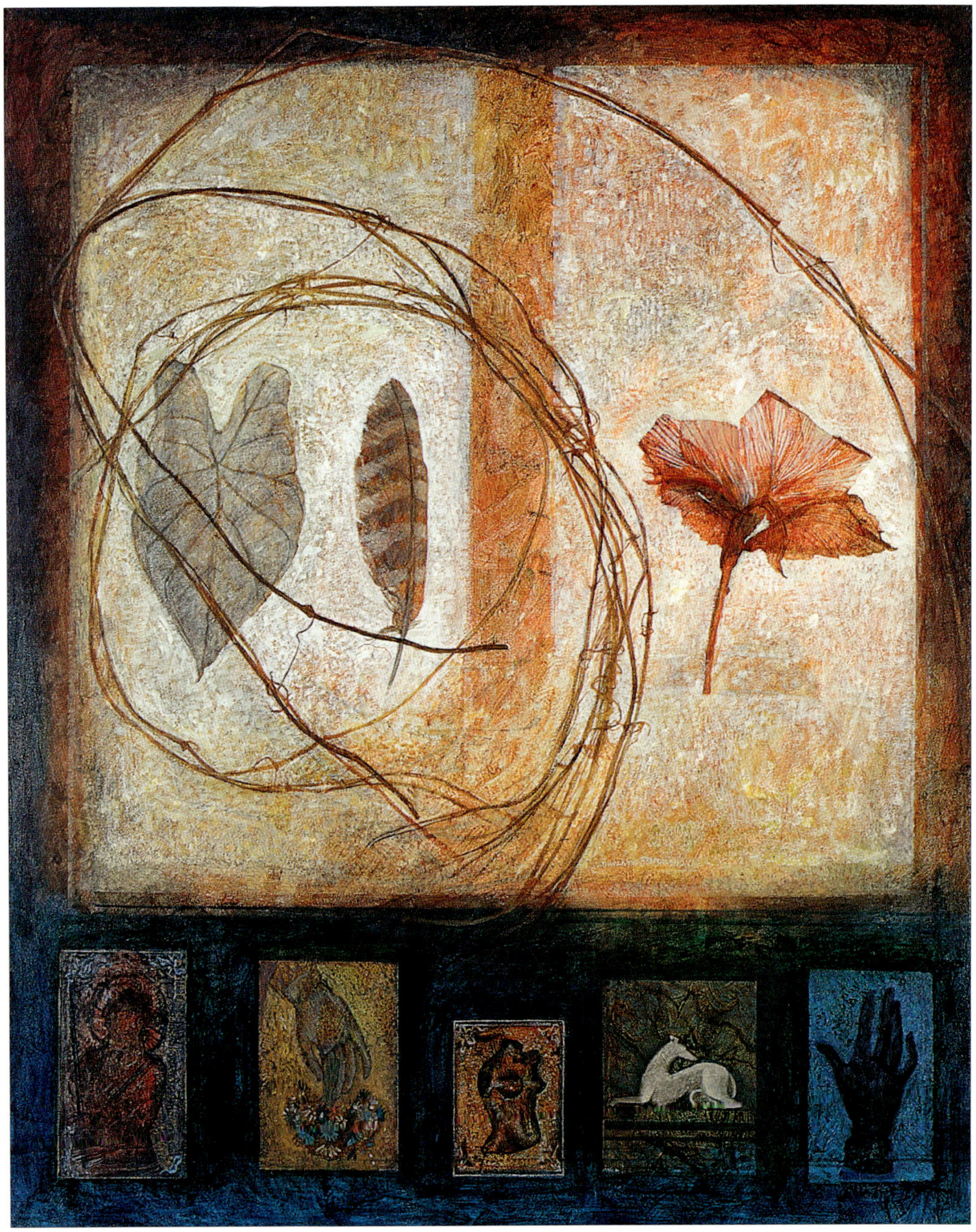

**CONSIDER THE LILY** 1998. Oil on board. 36in. x 28in. Private Collection

(Opposite) **FROM EVENING TO SUNSET** 1999. Oil on canvas. 36in. x 28in. Private Collection

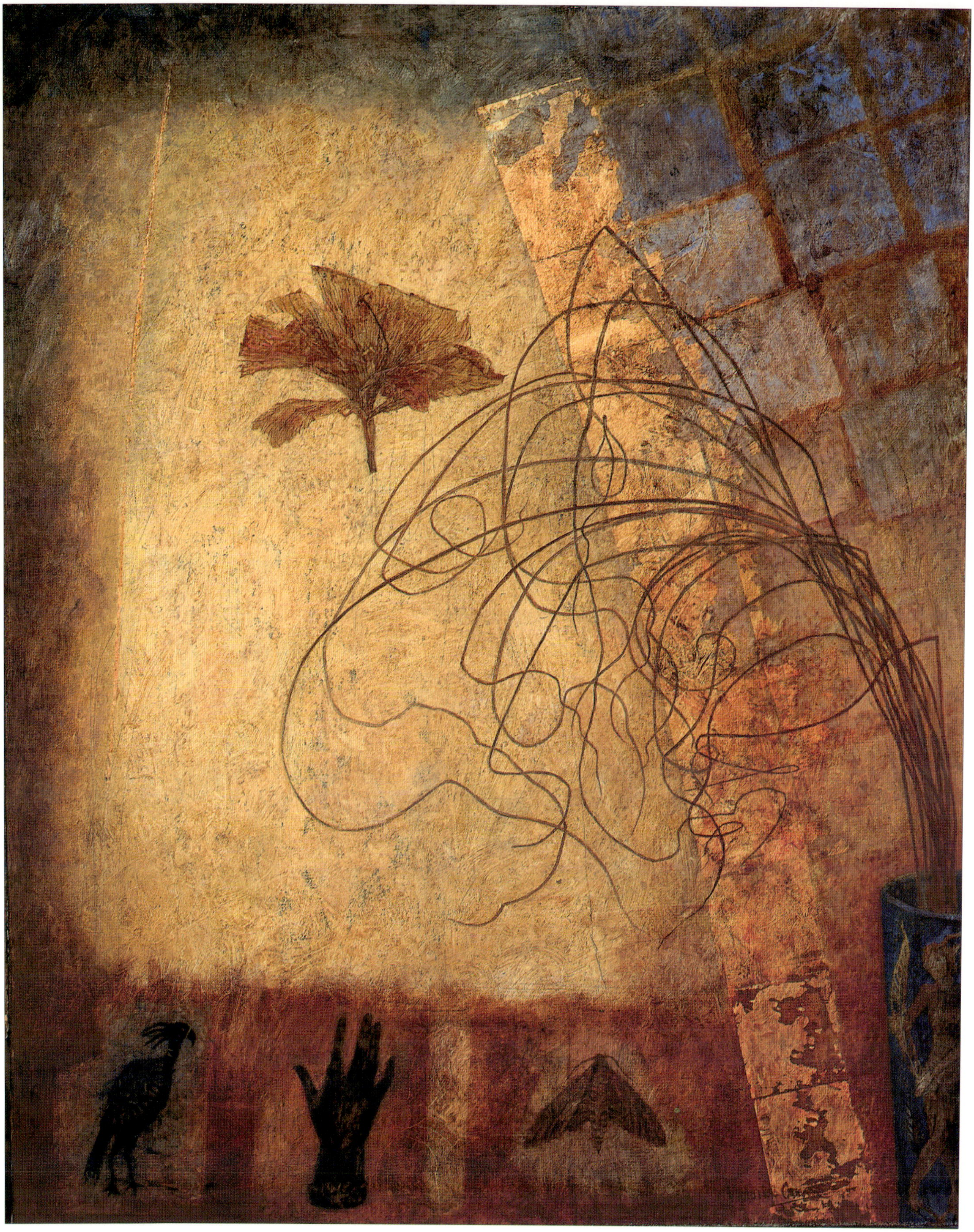

questions, but ones with considerable implications. In order to begin to answer, one has to have insight into one's own concerns and the processes by which they are addressed. Well, I think my life's *concerns* have emerged and become defined over the last few years. I'm beginning to understand how to transform complex thought and feeling into images which are meaningful to me. An understanding of the natural world through observation and drawing is vital to me. The act of drawing underpins so much; drawing is a way of thinking, a visual diary, a page of poetry, a question with no answers and a link with the function of consciousness – our attempt at understanding. So, although I cannot give those deceptively simple questions a specific answer, I know rather more where I'm coming from. I look at today's work and get an inkling of tomorrow's. Each painting is a creative leap taking us to unknown resolutions – a chance to balance chaos and order, the intuitive and the intellectual. The debate on the canvas evolves into a dialogue attempting to resolve the physicality of paint with the intention of content. I work with paint – flecks, marks, spots of colour so the surface has a resonance, I eliminate 'descriptive' brush marks whenever I can. I'm interested in the passages of fresco restoration one sees in Italy, which set out deliberately to say 'this is an illusion, come and look more closely'. Even the most complex of illusionistic images, carrying subtle messages, are simply paint marks, pigments, fractions of colour – just as we are, on one level, tiny vibrations of physical particles. My work does contain passing reference to ideas of philosophy, genetics, visual sensation, consciousness of the self, memory echoes and resonances of a physical order we do not fully understand. I'm beginning to see my own journey and the work that reflects it as having a link to the continuing tradition of human questioning. I find some parallel explorations in music, writing, poetry and film – a meditative, deeply personal response to existence which is both accessible and universal.

From my studio I can see across the street the house where Ronald Stevenson the musician lives. It's deeply reassuring to see the light on in his music room and to know he's battling with his creative impulses, just as I am. We occasionally meet in that other world, the village, our arms full of shopping or lists or letters, and ask how the work is going. Sometimes an ecstatic response – 'just great, really flowing', sometimes a grimace – ''God knows why I do this, it's so difficult.'

Last autumn in one such encounter, feeling reasonably pleased by progress yet still carrying some misgivings, I said 'I wish I was one of those artists, always so sure, so certain of what they're doing. I question myself frequently.' Ronald replied 'Vicky, think what William Blake said, 'If the sun and moon should doubt, they would go out'. I thought that was a wonderful response, as underlying the understanding and humour there is an issue about trust in oneself and the process of living. Now, when I see a solar or lunar eclipse or get asked 'What are you painting next?' I keep William Blake's phrase firmly in mind – 'If the sun and moon should doubt, they would go out'.

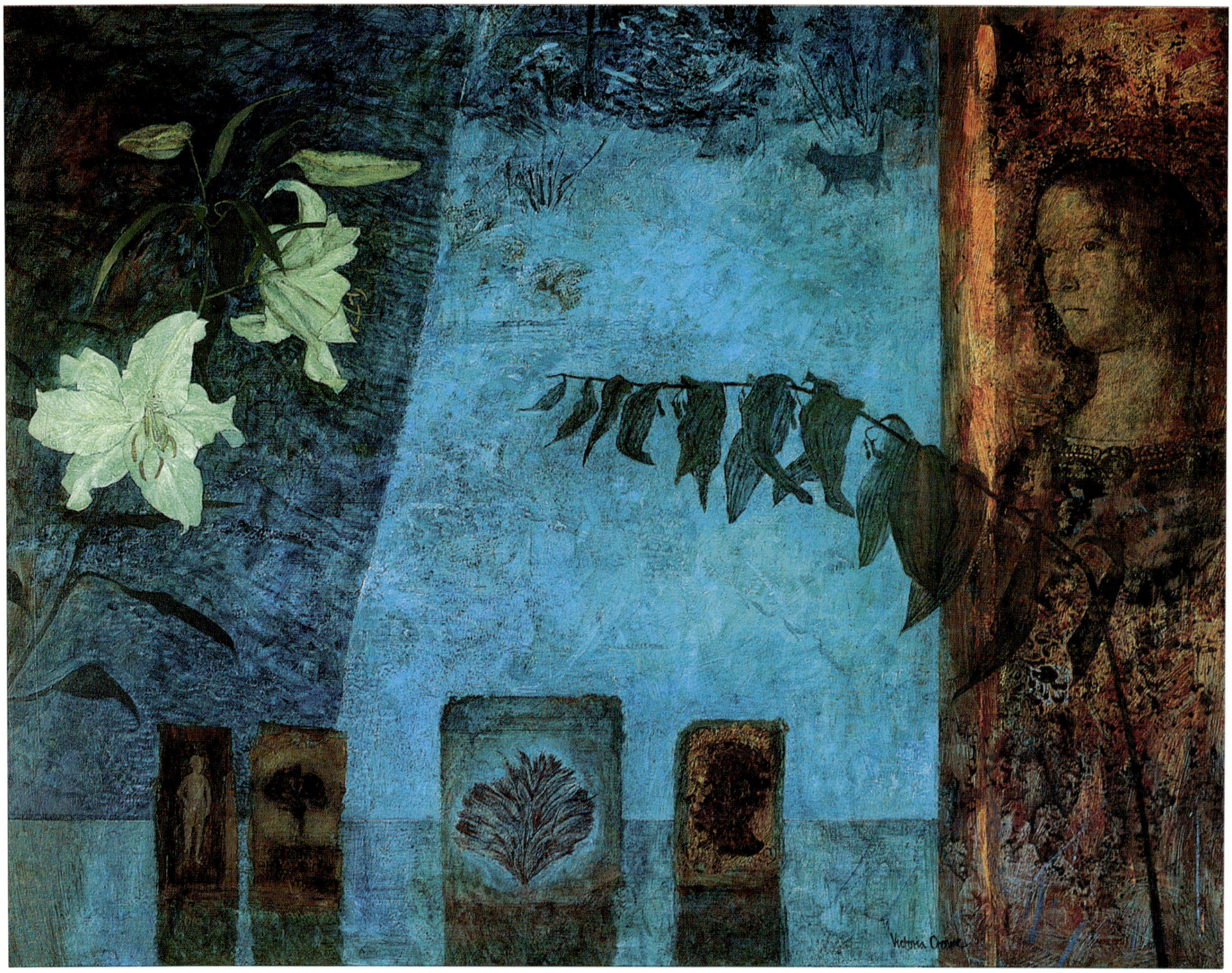

**SNOWLIGHT** 1999. Oil on linen. 31½in. x 39½in. Private Collection

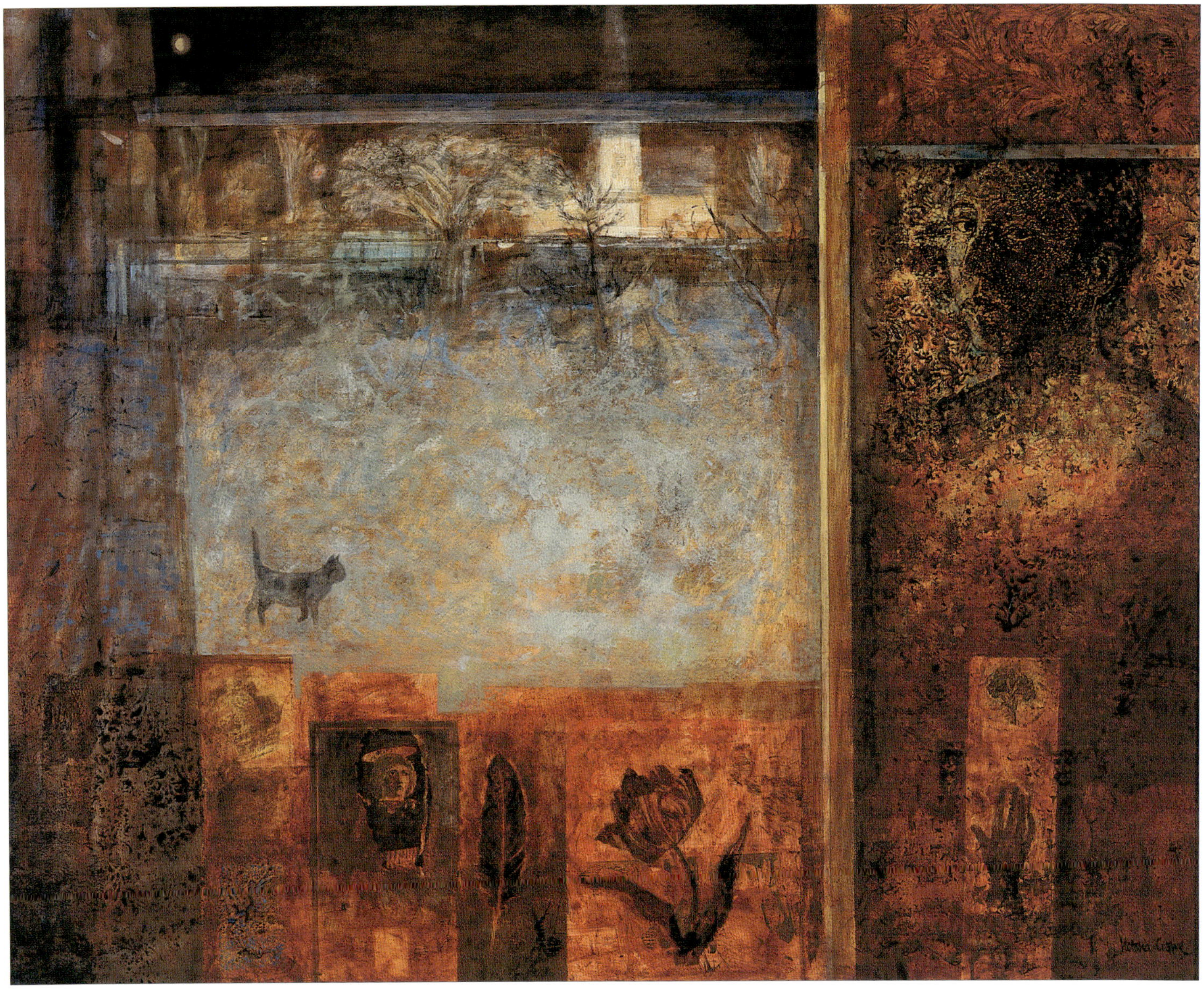

INTERIOR WITH MANY REFLECTIONS 1999. Oil on linen. 40in. x 47in. Private Collection

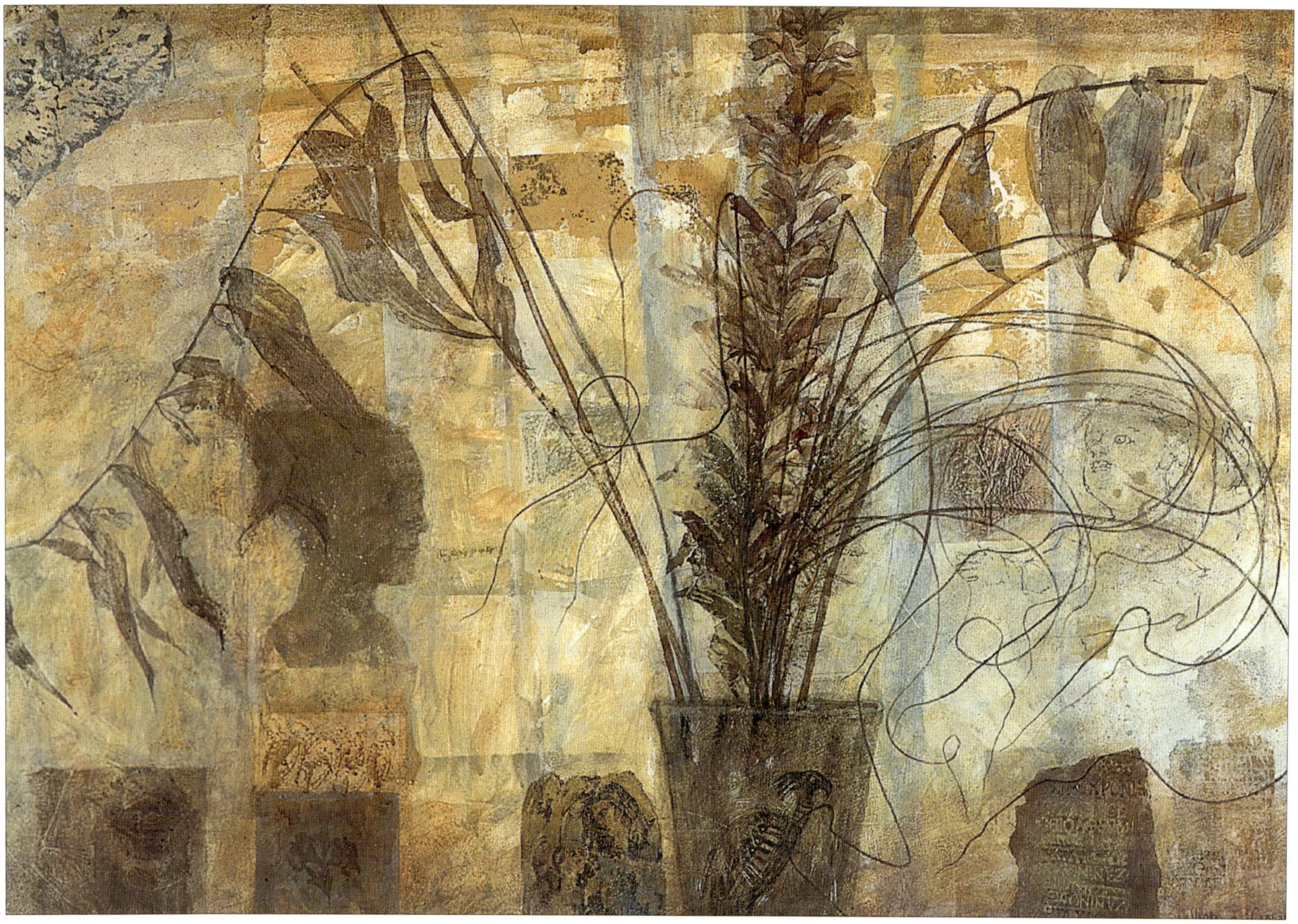

**REDISCOVERED FRAGMENTS** 2000. Watercolour and mixed media. 23¼in. x 32¼in.

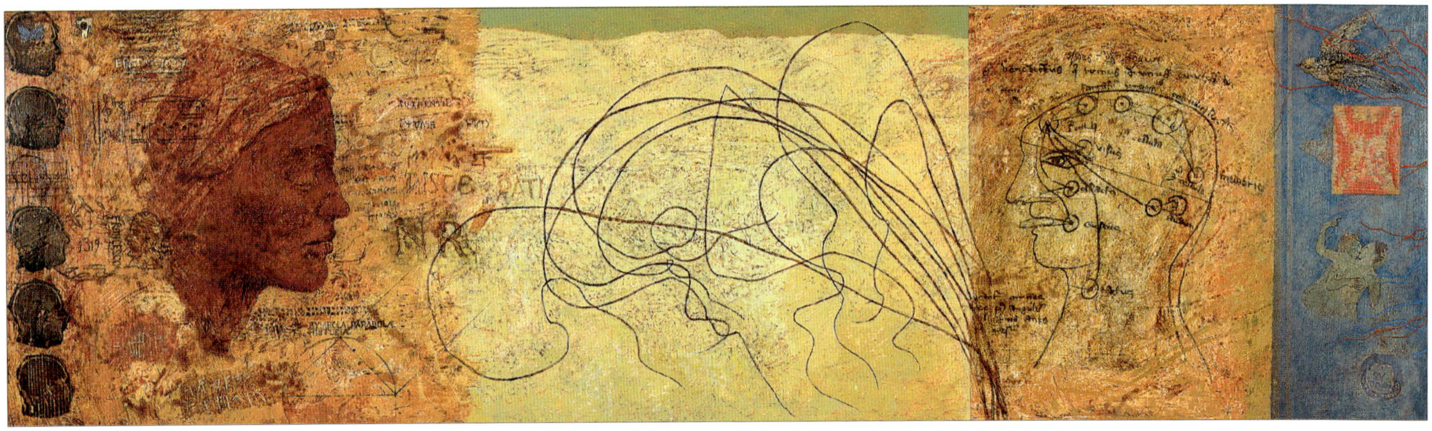

MEMORY, MESSAGES AND CONNECTIONS (left panel) 2001. Oil on board. 16in. x 48in. Commisioned by Department of Neuroscience, University of Edinburugh

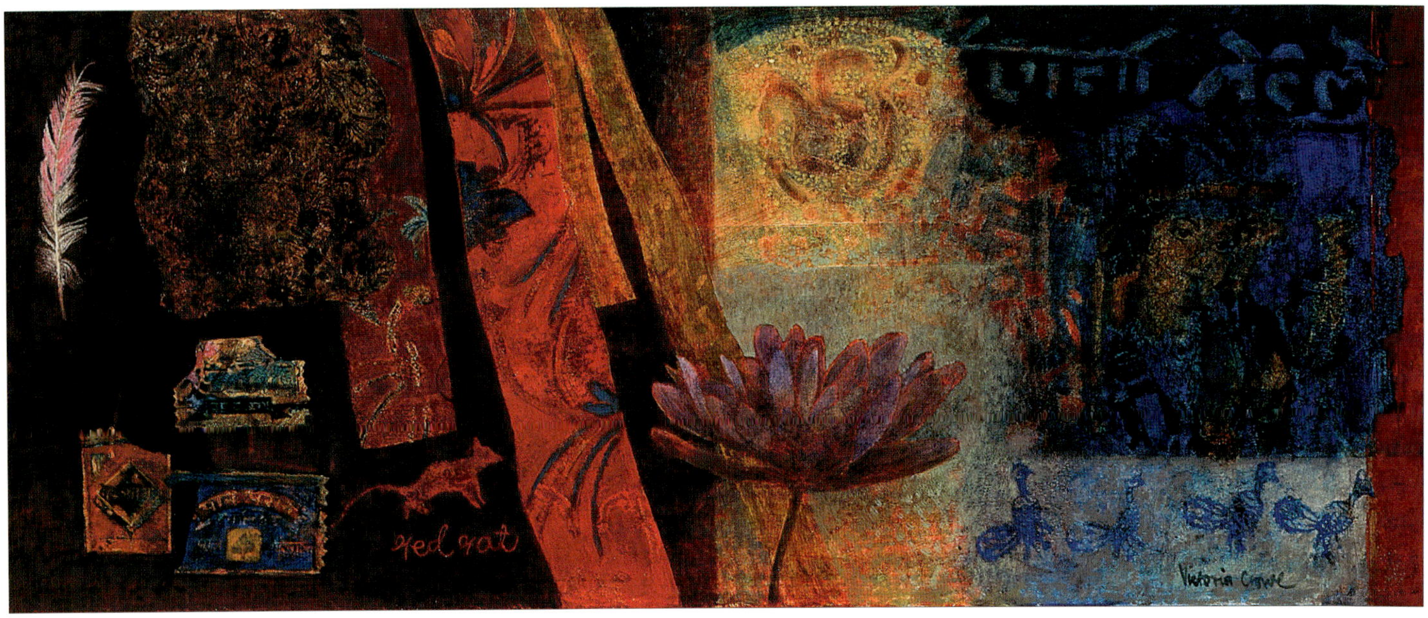


INDIAN STILL LIFE WITH RED RAT 1999. Oil on board. 12in. x 28in.

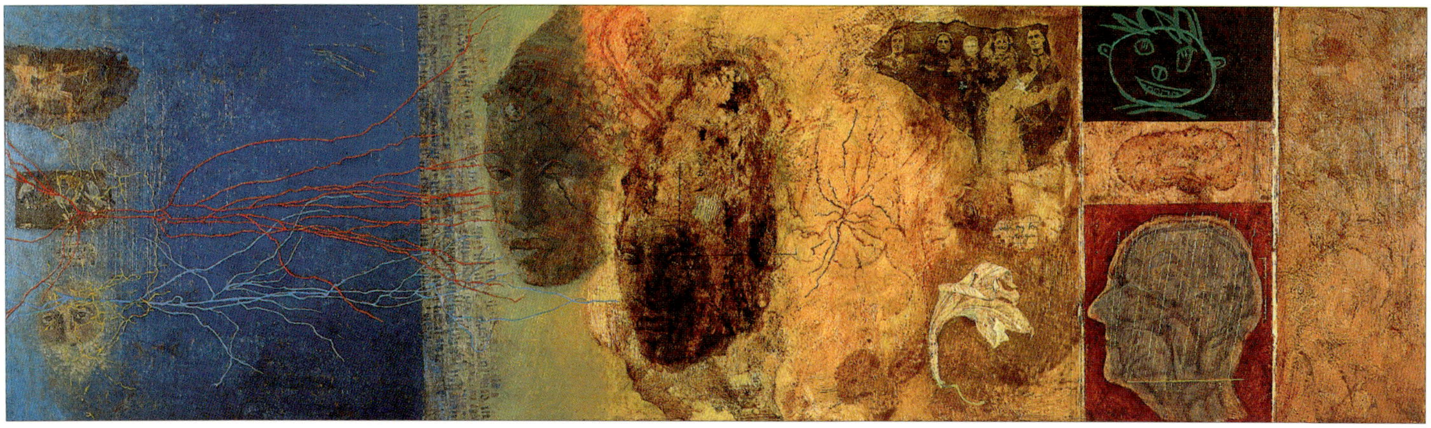

MEMORY, MESSAGES AND CONNECTIONS (right panel) 2001. 16in. x 48in. Oil on board. 16in. x 48in. Department of Neuroscience, University of Edinburugh

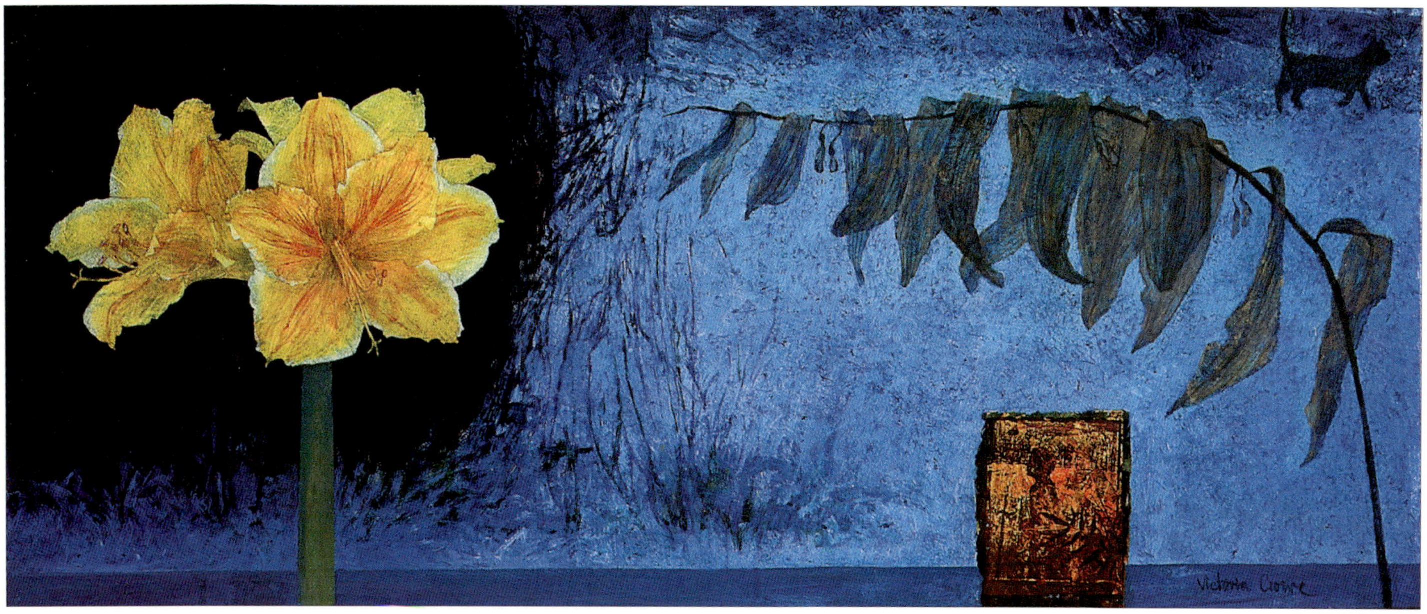

GOLDEN AMARYLLIS, SNOWBOUND GARDEN 1999. Oil on board. 13½in. x 31in. Private Collection

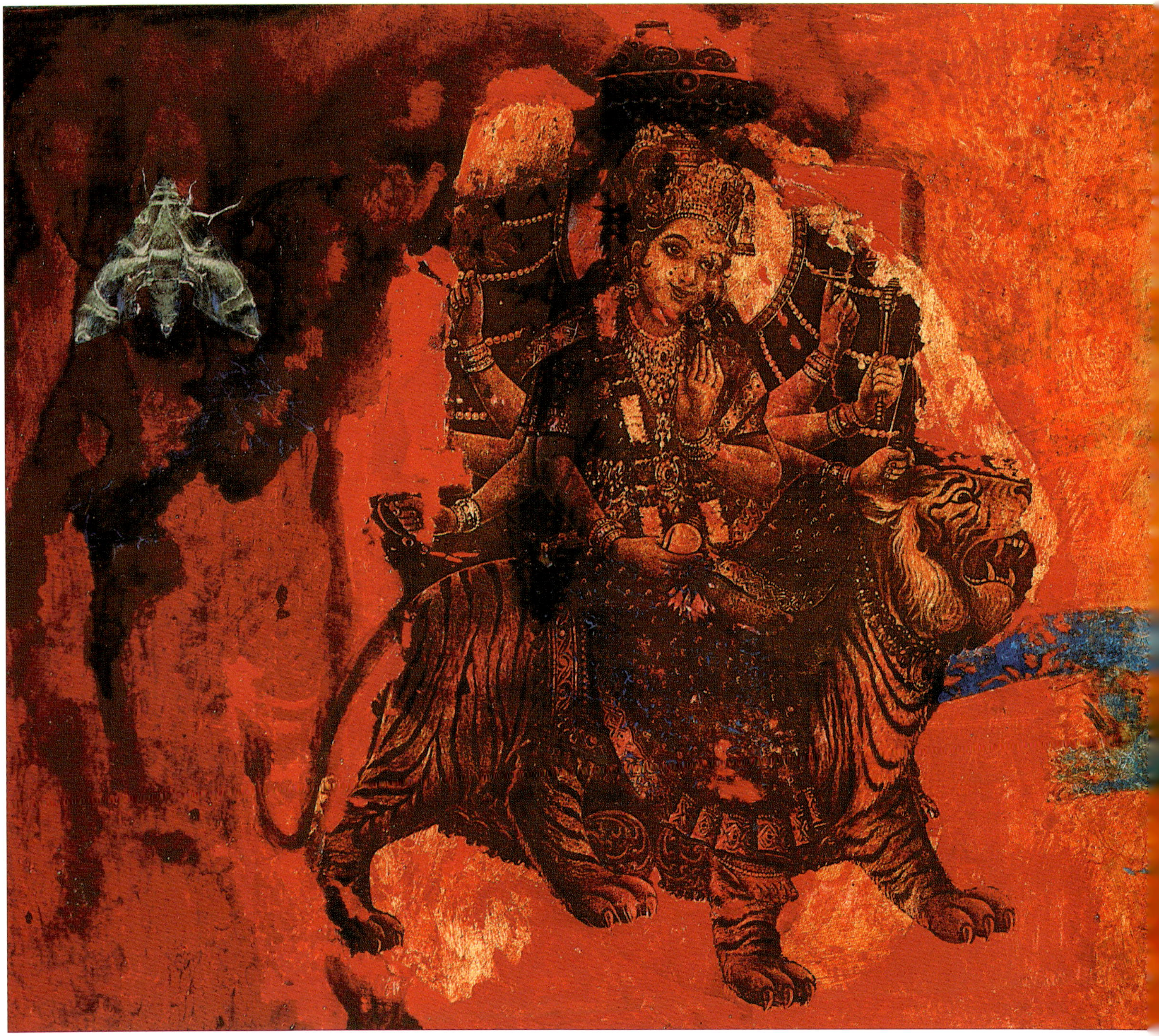

**A LITTLE PIECE OF INDIA** 1999. Oil with gold leaf and print on board. 15½in. x 35in. Private Collection

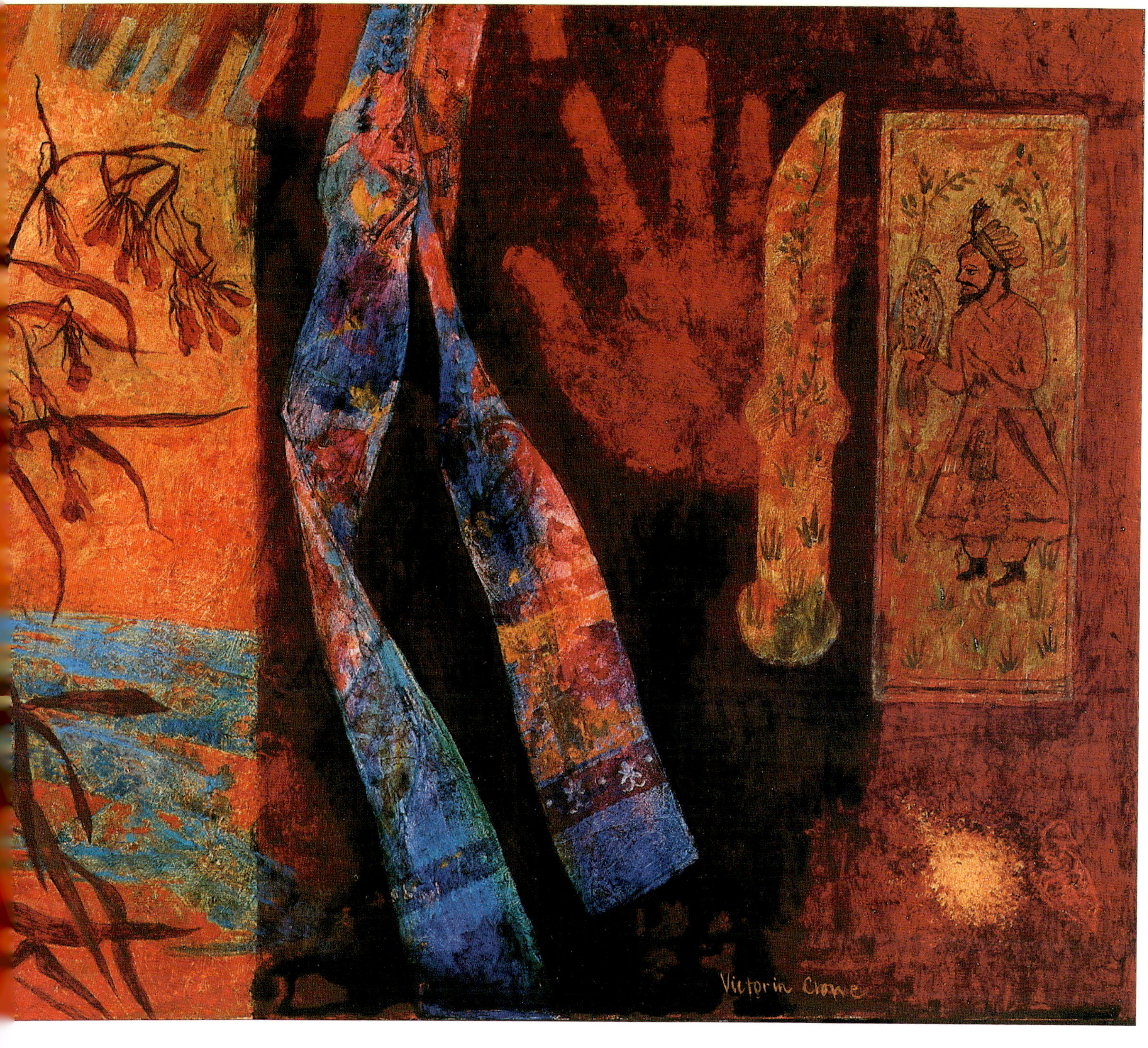
Victoria Crowe

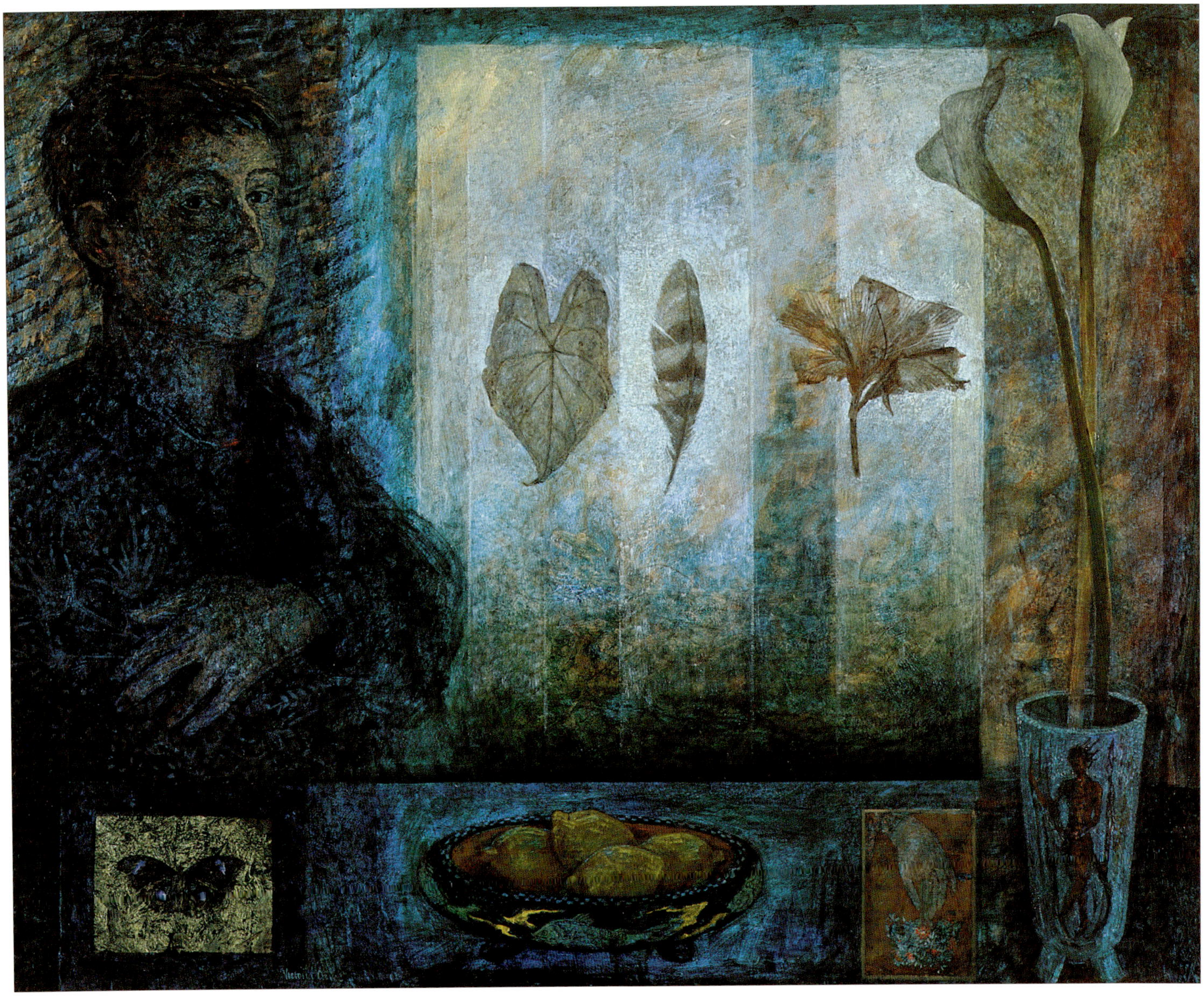

WATCHING BY MOONLIGHT 1998. Oil on board. 40in. x 48in. Private Collection

# CHRONOLOGY

| | |
|---|---|
| 1945 | Born Kingston-on-Thames, Surrey |
| 1961-65 | Kingston School of Art |
| 1965-68 | Royal College of Art, London |
| 1968-98 | Lecturer in Drawing & Painting, Edinburgh College of Art |
| 1982 | Elected member of The Royal Scottish Society of Painters in Watercolour |
| 1987 | Elected Associate of the Royal Scottish Academy |
| 1991 | Elected Associate of the Royal Watercolour Society |
| 1992 | Invited by Artists for Nature Foundation, funded by World Wildlife Fund, to join a group of international artists working on a conservation project in the Biebsra and Narew Valleys, Poland |
| 1994 | Invited by ANF to work on a conservation project in the Extremadura, Spain |
| | Collaborated on two co-productions with Edinburgh Printmakers Workshop |
| 1997 | Commissioned by Danish National Portrait Gallery to paint the Danish Resistance leader, Ole Lippmann, for the 20th Century Collection of Portraits at Frederiksborg Castle |
| | Invited by Glasgow Museums and Art Galleries to take part in the 'Tiger, Tiger' project at Bandhavgarh National Park, India |
| 1998-2001 | Printmaking co-productions with Graal Press |
| 2000 | Invited artist for short list of Jesus 2000 commission, Glasgow |

# SELECTED SOLO EXHIBITIONS

| | |
|---|---|
| 1969, 71 | Waterhouse Gallery, London |
| 1970, 73, 77, 82, 95, 98 | The Scottish Gallery, Aitken Dott, EdInburgh |
| 1975 | Lantern Gallery, Manchester |
| 1975 | Loomshop Gallery, Lower Largo |
| 1983, 85, 87, 89, 91,94, 99 | Thackeray Gallery, London |
| 1986 | Mercury Gallery, Edinburgh |
| 1988 | Abbott Hall Gallery, Kendal |
| | The Fine Art Society, Glasgow and Edinburgh |
| 1989 | The Bruton Gallery, Somerset |
| 1993 | The Bruton Gallery, Bath |
| | Ancrum Gallery, Borders Festival |
| 1997 | Corrymella Scott Gallery, Newcastle upon Tyne |
| 1998 | Bruton Gallery, Leeds |
| 2000 | Cambridge Contemporary Art |
| | Scottish National Portrait Gallery, Edinburgh, Exhibition curatored by the SNPG, *A Shepherd's Life* |
| | The Scottish Gallery, Edinburgh, *A Shepherd's Life,* related works |
| 2001 | Festival Exhibition, The Scottish Gallery, Edinburgh |
| | Thackeray Gallery, London |
| 2001/2002 | *A Shepherd's Life,* TourIng: Mercer Art Gallery, Harrogate<br>Duff House, Aberdeenshire;<br>Hatton Art Gallery, Newcastle University |

# AWARDS

| | |
|---|---|
| 1968 | David Murray Landscape Scholarship |
| 1973 | Anne Redpath Award |
| 1969/75 | Scottish Arts Council Bursaries |
| 1981 | Glasgow Herald Competition Prize wInner |
| | Scottish Arts Council Printmaking Bursary |
| 1987 | Winner of the Daler/Rowney Prize for Watercolour, Royal Academy, London |
| 1988 | Hunting Group Major Award Winner |
| 1991 | Royal Watercolour Society London Major Award Winner (Chris Beetles Prize) |
| 1992 | Sir William Gillies Bequest Royal Scottish Academy for travel and study in Italy |

## SELECTED GROUP EXHIBITIONS

| | |
|---|---|
| 1969 | Richard Demarco Gallery, Edinburgh |
| 1979 | *The Plant*, Scottish Arts Council Touring Exhibition |
| | *Interiors*, Touring Exhibition, Lincolnshire, Humberside |
| | *Artist and Teacher*, The Fine Art Society, Edinburgh and Glasgow |
| 1980 | Scottish Festival Week, Ridderkerk, Holland with The Scottish Gallery |
| 1981 | *Contemporary Art from Scotland*, Touring Exhibition |
| | Basle International Art Fair with The Scottish Gallery |
| | *The Stormy Blast*, MacRobert Art Centre, Stirling |
| 1983 | *Etching and Other Intaglio Techniques*, Scottish Arts Council |
| 1984 | *Different Kinds of Good Weather*, Scottish Arts Council Touring Exhibition |
| | *Portrait 84*, National Portrait Gallery, London |
| | *Contemporary Scottish Drawing*, The Fine Art Society |
| | *Light from the Window*, National Galleries of Scotland |
| 1984/85 | *Portraits on Paper*, Scottish Arts Council Touring Exhibition |
| 1985 | *Dublin/Edinburgh*, Festival, Exhibition, Edinburgh College of Art |
| 1988 | *The Chosen Few*, The Open Eye Gallery, Edinburgh |
| 1988, 90, 93 | Sunday Times/Singer Friedlander Watercolour Exhibition |
| 1988 | Hunting Group Exhibition, Winners' Selection |
| 1989, 91 | *Scottish Painters*, Fosse Gallery, Stow on the Wold |
| 1989 , 91, 93, 97 | The Morrison Scottish Portrait Award Exhibition, RSA |
| 1997, 98, 99, 00, 01 | Bohun Gallery, Henley-on-Thames |
| 1998 | Galerie Susanne Hojriis, Copenhagen |
| | *500 Years of Scottish Portraiture*, Frederiksborg, Denmark |
| 1999 | Scotland's Art, City Art Centre, Edinburgh Festival Exhibition |
| | The Flower Show: Flowers in Art in the 20th Century, Harewood House |
| 1999, 2000 | *Connections*, RSA Festival Exhibition, Edinburgh |
| 2000 | *Wild Tigers of Bandhavgarh*, Burrell Collection, Glasgow |
| | *Jesus 2000*, Glasgow Museum of Modern Art |
| | *Northern Highlights*, Bruton Gallery in Cork Street, London |
| 2001 | *Narcissus*, 20th Century Self Portraits, SNPG |
| | *Mirror, Mirror*, Women's Self Portraits, NPG, London |

## PORTRAITS (include)

| | |
|---|---|
| 1982 | *Dr Winifred Rushforth*, in the collection of the Scottish National Portrait Gallery |
| | *Dr Winifred Rushforth*, in the collection of City Art Centre,Edinburgh |
| | *Ronald Stevenson*, in the collection of the Scottish National Portrait Gallery |
| 1985 | *R.D. Laing*, commissioned by the Scottish National Portrait Gallery Edinburgh |
| 1986 | *The Very Reverend Professor John McIntyre*, commissioned by New College, Edinburgh |
| | *Kathleen Raine*, in the collection of the National Portrait Gallery London |
| | *Dame Janet Vaughan*, in the collection of the National Portrait Gallery, London |
| 1987 | *Tam Dalyell, MP*, commissioned by West Lothian Council |
| 1988 | *Lord Provost, Tom Morgan*, commissioned by Edinburgh District Council |
| | *Mr and Mrs Tam Dalyell MP*, commissioned for "The Binns" |
| 1988/89 | *Principal Tom Johnston*, commissioned by Heriot Watt University |
| 1989 | *The Earl of Wemyss and March, Kt.*, commissioned by the National Trust for Scotland |
| 1990 | *Professor Michael Oliver*, Royal College of Physicians of Edinburgh |
| | *Dr Jean Keeling*, commissioned by colleagues |
| 1990/91 | *Principal George McNicol*, commissioned by Aberdeen University |
| 1991 | *Professor Bill Hayes*, The President, St. John's College, Oxford |
| 1992 | *Professor Geoff Chisholm*, commissioned by the Royal College of Surgeons, Edinburgh |
| 1994 | *Professor Piers Mackesy*, Historian, commissioned for the family |
| 1996 | *Lady Emma Tennant*, commissioned by the Marquis of Hartington |
| | *Harry Tatton*, the Worshipful Company of Goldsmiths, Assay Office, Edinburgh |
| | *Callum Macdonald*, Scottish Literary Publisher, commissioned by the SNPG, Edinburgh |
| | *Piers Ben-Gough*, Her Majesty's Representative at Ascot, commissioned by the racecourse authority |

| | |
|---|---|
| | *Graham Crowden,* Actor, gifted to the Scottish National Portrait Gallery |
| 1997 | Exchange Commission between Scottish National Portrait Gallery, Edinburgh and Danish National Portrait Gallery, Frederiksborg, Copenhagen. Selected Scottish artist to paint Ole Lippmann, head of S.O.E., Denmark |
| 1998 | *Sir Peter Main,* commissioned by Boots |
| 2000 | *Mary James,* commissioned by the Governors of St. Leonard's School |
| | *James Wright,* Vice-Chancellor, University of Newcastle, commissioned by the University |
| | *Sir Iain Noble Bt., OBE,* commissioned for the family |

## SELECTED PUBLIC COLLECTIONS

Aberdeen University; Bank of Scotland; Calderdale Museum and Art Gallery; Carnegie Dunfermline Trust; Contemporary Arts Society; Danish 20th Century Portrait Collection, Frederiksborg Castle, Copenhagen; Edinburgh City Art Centre; Edinburgh District Council; Edinburgh Education Authority, Edinburgh University; Edinburgh University, Department of Neuroscience; Glasgow Museums and Art Galleries; Harlow New Town Council; Heriot-Watt University; Inner London Education Authority; Mercantile and General Reinsurance Company; National Portrait Gallery, London; National Trust for Scotland; Newcastle University; Nuffield Foundation Pictures in Hospitals (Scotland); Oxford University; Readers Digest; Fleming-Wyfold Art Fouondation; Royal Academy, London; Royal Bank of Scotland; Royal College of Art, London; Royal College of Physicians, Edinburgh; Royal College of Surgeons of Edinburgh; St. Leonard's School, St. Andrews; Scottish Arts Council; Scottish National Gallery of Modern Art; Scottish National Portrait Gallery; Smith Art Gallery, Stirling; Scottish Life Insurance Company; Scottish Media Group; Trustees Savings Bank; West Lothian District Council; William Bowmore Collection, Australia

## TV AND RADIO

| | |
|---|---|
| 1991 | *Portrait of the Wild* – Grampian and STV, half-hour programme on Victoria Crowe working in the Landscape. Transmitted 1991 and 1998 |
| 1998 | *The Usual Suspect,* BBC Radio Scotland |
| | *Look North,* BBC Television – Review of the opening of Bruton Gallery Show |
| 2000 | *Johnnie Walker Show,* BBC Radio 2, February 2000 |
| | *A Scottish Connection,* BBC Radio Scotland, February 2000 |
| | *Brian Morton,* BBC Radio Scotland, February 2000 |
| | *Landward,* Arthur Anderson, BBC2, March 2000 |

## MAIN PUBLISHED WORK ON VICTORIA CROWE

| | |
|---|---|
| 1994 | *Victoria Crowe* (catalogue) Mary Taubman, Thackeray |
| 1995 | *Victoria Crowe* (catalogue) Duncan Thomson, Scottish Gallery |
| 1997 | *Victoria Crowe* (catalogue) Mary Sara, Corrymella Scott |
| 1999 | *Victoria Crowe* (catalogue) Clare Henry, Thackeray |
| 2000 | *A Shepherd's Life,* National Galleries of Scotland |

## SELECTED PUBLICATIONS

| | |
|---|---|
| 1981 | *Contemporary Art from Scotland,* The Scottish Gallery |
| 1984 | *Portraits on Paper,* James Holloway, S.A.C. |
| 1986 | *A Picture of Flemings,* Robert Fleming Holdings Ltd. |
| 1987 | *Royal Academy,* Illustrated 1987 |
| 1990 | *A Patron of Art,* Royal Bank of Scotland |
| | *Doubletake,* National Portrait Gallery |
| | 'A Sunlit Room, Victoria Crowe', *The Artist,* May, pp.26-28 |
| | 'A Painter's Inspiration, Victoria Crowe', *The Artist,* August, pp.32-35 |
| 1991 | *Society of Scottish Artists – First 100 Years* |
| | *Scottish Art in the 20th Century,* R.W.E.A. |

1992 *The Portrait Award 1980-89,* National Portrait Gallery
1993 *Portrait of a Living Marsh,* W.W.F., Inmerc. BV
1995 *Artists for Nature in Extremadura,* Inmerc. BV
*Royal Academy, Illustrated,* 1995
1996 Scottish Print Open1996, Glasgow Print Studio
1997 *Five Hundrede Ars Skotske Portraetter,* National Galleries of Scotland
*In the Eye of the Beholder,* Oxford University Press
1998 'Artists Diary' by Victoria Crowe, *Art Review,* Dec./Jan. 98, pp.30-33
*Victoria Crowe,* Derek Hyatt, Bruton Gallery, Leeds (catalogue)
*Royal Academy, illustrated* 1998
1999 *The Flower Show,* Harewood House, Jane Sellars
'Artist's Diary' by Victoria Crowe, *Art Review,* October
*Scotland's Art,* City of Edinburgh Museums and Galleries
2000 *Tigers,* Artists for Nature in India, ed. Nicholas Hammond, The Wild Life Art Gallery

## SELECTED BIBLIOGRAPHY. ARTICLES AND REVIEWS

1969 'Review of Richard Demarco Exhibition', Edward Gage, *The Scotsman,* 23 June
1970 'A Talent of Many Disguises', Edward Gage, The Scotsman, May
1971 'Scottish Artists Free of Current Mannerisms', Terence Mullaly, *Daily Telegraph,* 16 April
1973 'Review of Scottish Gallery Exhibition', Edward Gage, *The Scotsman,* 2 July
1977 'Avoiding the Pitfalls of Representation', Edward Gage, *The Scotsman,* 28 March
1981 'Glasgow Herald Competition Winners', Andrew Young, *Herald,* 24 March
1982 'Prophets, Poems and Pale Profiles', Edward Gage, *The Scotsman,* 17 May
1983 'Review of Thackeray Exhibition', Clare Henry, *The Glasgow Herald,* 27 April
1984 'Profile of a Portrait Painter', Jean Smith, *The Scotsman,* 21 August
'Recent Acquisitions', National Galleries of Scotland Annual Review
1986 'Timely Reminder of Traditional Values', Edward Gage, *The Scotsman,* 24 March
1987 'Portraits and Possibilities', *Scottish Field,* November
1989 'Review of Thackeray Exhibition', Robin Stemp, *Arts Review* 7 April
'Victoria Crowe at Bruton Gallery', Mary Taubman, Arts Review, 20 October
'A Fine Likeness', *The Scotsman,* 25 January
1990 'A Portrait of the President', *Heritage Scotland,* Spring, p.21
1993 'Victoria Crowe', Mary Taubman, *Galleries Magazine,* October, p.23
'Views from the Interior', Edward Gage, *The Scotsman,* 14 October
1995 'Sitting Pretty', W. Gordon Smith, *Scotland on Sunday,* 23 April
1996 'Brown Studies Beckon', W. Gordon Smith, *Scotland on Sunday* 12 November
'Golden Glow Defies Despair', Clare Henry. *The Glasgow Herald,* 13 November
*R.D. Laing, A Divided Self,* John Clay, Hodder & Stoughton, p.226
1998 'Victoria Crowe', Clare Henry, *The Herald,* 15 January
'In the Frame, Victoria Crowe', *Scotland on Sunday,* 25 January
'Victoria Crowe at the Scottish Gallery', Iain Gale, *The Week,* 24 January
'A Rare Beauty, Redolent of Life's Wonder,' Clare Henry, *Homes & Interiors* Scotland Issue 7
1999 'Contemporary British Artists', Anthony Lester, *Antique Collecting,* February
Victoria Crowe, Thackeray Gallery, *Galleries Magazine,* 'Nicholas Usherwood, October
2000 'One Woman and her Flock', Margaret Morrison, *Scotland on Sunday,* 23 January
Andrew Walker, *The Scotsman,* 28 January
'Pick of the Week's Entertainment', Rachel Devine, *The Sunday Times Scotland,* 13 February
'Art, A Shepherd's Life', Gabe Stewart, *Metro,* 16 February
'Art, Private View', Richard Ingleby, *The Independent,* 19 February
"Gallery Review', Duncan Macmillan, *The Scotsman,* 22 February
'A Flock of Dreams', Brian Swanson, *The Express,* 12 February
'Keeping a Dream Alive', Graeme Virtue, *Sunday Herald,* 13 February
'Through a Shepherd's Eyes', Clare Henry, *The Herald,* 21 February
'Around the Scottish Galleries', Giles Sutherland, *The Times,* 22 March
'Art in Scotland', Mary McGlynn, *Wall Street Journal,* 28 April
'Recording a Life', Nicola Wood, *Hi Ya Magazine,* Summer
2001 'A Shepherd's Life', Angus Urquhart, *Scots,* February
'Victoria Crowe', Nicky du Preez, *Atlanta,* March

# INDEX OF ILLUSTRATIONS

## PAINTINGS



## PORTRAITS



## PHOTOGRAPHS

Anche nell' ombra è il sole
Quando l'anima cante

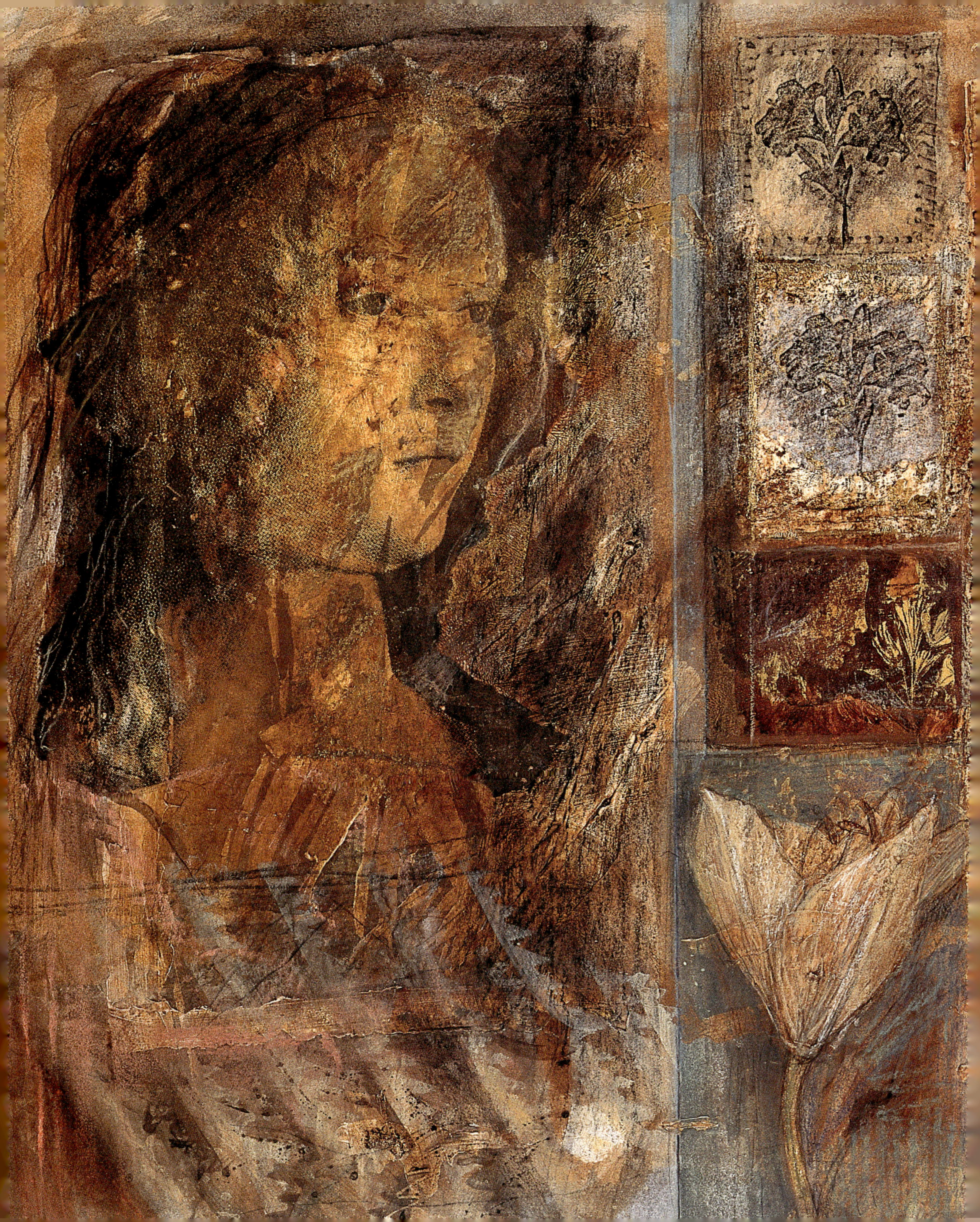